# Diary of a
# City Priest

*John P. McNamee*

**Sheed & Ward**

Sheed & Ward™ is a service of The National Catholic Reporter Publishing Company.

_____

**Library of Congress Cataloguing in Publication Data**
McNamee, John P., 1933-
    Diary of a city priest / John P. McNamee.
        p.    cm.
    ISBN 1-55612-662-X (alk. paper)
    1. McNamee, John P., 1933-    . 2. Catholic Church--
Pennsylvania--Philadelphia--Clergy--Biography. 3. City clergy--
Pennsylvania--Philadelphia--Biography. 4. Catholic Church.
Diocese of Philadelphia (Pa.) 5. Philadelphia (Pa.)--Social
conditions. 6. Pennsylvania--Social conditions. 7. Church work
with the poor--Catholic Church.  I. Title.
BX4705.M47655A3    1993
282'.092--dc20
[B]                                                              93-11924
                                                                    CIP

_____

Published by:    Sheed & Ward
                 115 E. Armour Blvd.
                 P.O. Box 419492
                 Kansas City, MO 64141

To order, call: (800) 333-7373

*Cover photograph by Ed Simmons*

# Contents

# Diary of a City Priest

# 1.

## *Spiritual Progress: Very Poor At It All*

# 1

After the hectic weeks of Christmas, we arrive exhausted into the New Year. Around here Christmas is a blur of food and gifts arriving from the suburbs and going out into the projects of the neighborhood. The church was mostly empty on New Year's Day. A large suburban family did attend: parents of 15 children, the children themselves with wives and husbands, even unto grandchildren. Despite their deep and serious Catholic family life, not one of these many children has chosen the priesthood or the religious life. Thirty years ago several of them would have made that choice. What does that say to fellows like myself who did make that choice? That early choice of celibacy is especially painful at Christmas. Driving along the cold winter streets at night, returning to an empty rectory, one notices the warmth of family life framed in lighted windows. If that choice of celibacy does not have the immense spiritual meaning communicated to us who chose it 40 years ago, no wonder the younger folk who were at Mass here this morning are not making that choice.

And as Dave Hagan insists, the family scene has a mythology all its own. If I did have a family, I could hardly be driving back to that empty rectory. In a sense, poor myself and able to live among the poor because I have that freedom.

# 2

I come from a nearby cloister chapel where I have sat or prayed for some hours, where a nun knelt motionless behind the cloister grill before the Blessed Sacrament exposed. Just before noon the other nuns came out for midday psalms.

I came here to get some quiet and space almost completely unavailable in a rectory where I both live and work. I came here because I am so exhausted from Christmas and need something or other to step from the holidays into the New Year. I even came here because last night I noticed that today is the birthday of St. Thérèse of the Child Jesus, a Victorian Carmelite nun whom some might call hysterical. Thérèse promised that from heaven she would look after us priests, so here I am looking for her care.

How is that for living off the past? Even when I do pray, I fear that the Church and her traditions are at least obsolete. This is what those young people sense when they do not even consider the Church vocation that their kind would have easily chosen those 30 years ago.

I shall tentatively and fearfully hold on to the possibility that such moderns as Pascal and Simone Weil knew pessimism also. In my own confusion I shall try to hold onto John of the Cross, the medieval mystic who seemed also to understand this kind of darkness.

## 3

The Christmas food rush continues. Needy families and the fellows who stand around the neighborhood liquor stores discover us for the first time. The fellows are looking for more than a few cans of soup. They come after hours with a story about needing carfare to get to work the next day or a few dollars to feed their children. Everything about their appearance says that they have neither worked nor worried about their children for years. When they come in the dark after everyone here who usually takes care of them has gone home, I am beside myself with annoyance—an annoyance which is usually communicated to the often intoxicated fellow ringing the doorbell.

One fellow rang tonight. I answered the door expecting the arrival of a priest friend from California and his sister whom he is visiting after the holidays. I had just given the begging fellow three dollars because that is the easier way to deal with him, easier than the guilt of sending him empty-handed back out into the cold, easier than trying to assemble a balance of canned foods which he has no place to prepare, easier than being worn down by the endless plea that this is again a unique situation, an emergency or he would never have come at this late hour.

As the caller was walking down the front path with the three dollars, my friends arrive to treat me to dinner in a moderately-priced restaurant downtown which is a luxury, an indulgence which the fellow leaving has never known for one hour of his wretched life. Here I am among the poor. Hardly poor myself. I have never for one moment of my life had to knock on the door of a complete stranger and ask for a dollar.

And the manner in which I give him the few dollars! Simone Weil says that the charitable exchange that is real charity or love is more rare, more a miracle than walking on water. Usually the meeting of benefactor and beggar reinforces their mutual positions of someone humiliated and someone humiliating. I am afraid that is often the case with me, despite my many years in these neighborhoods. I am very poor at it all.

# 4

The architect doing the modest appraisal of the physical condition of this lovely 140-year-old church came around with an artisan-restorer who can repair the altar rail broken three years ago when we leaned a huge Christmas tree against it. I have no idea what the longtime destiny of this old place is or how much that destiny is tied up with my tenure here. I do know that I should allow and even want myself to be "stuck" here the way the people are. I want to surrender the ease and facility of moving on sometimes when the whole place is coming down on me, or I feel that the place survives only because of my fundraising or ego or whatever. I want to be a thousand miles away— as in Donegal looking out on the water. Anyhow the architect and artisan want to know the long-range prospects for the place, and here I am worried about getting a lay school principal for next year or exasperated with a temporary employee who tells me that I, rather than he, should pay the taxes and Social Security on his generous wages here. One of the most difficult matters for me in this work is the presumption on the part of some: that I or the Catholic Church has money, and the way to get at it is to pressure and demand and insist and beg. Of course the opinion is relatively true. The dollars are there if I dig deep enough or look far enough. My 20-year friend just left. Earlier he had called, as he often does, for carfare for the week. He will not be paid until next Thursday, and he is completely out of funds. For 10 years he has worked at an office job, but his life is so confused by support for his children, elsewhere now with his former common-law wife, or the cost of his weekly methadon therapy that he is always out of money.

Someone coming to church slipped an envelope with $20 into my hands earlier, and out went the $20, together with another ten from my wallet. I hope this is the Gospel exchange of "left hand not knowing what right hand is doing" and "you have received freely, freely give." You can be sure no one is slipping $20 into his hands.

When I think of him alone in that walkup room he rents, the isolation and uncertainty of his life and his shattered dreams, I do not mind that some of those dollars of mine wind up buying him a drink or two on the way home. I do not deny myself that drink. I do not begrudge him that drink.

## 5

The architect was complaining about a nearby Catholic church which last Sunday was on an architectural tour of the area. He said the priest who welcomed them just presumed the group was all Catholic and spoke to them about Catholic devotional life, rather than the architectural interest which brought them there. The architect is of Scottish Presbyterian origins and can handle a Catholicism that is ecumenical and courteous. He is offended by that Catholicism which presents itself without accommodation.

His mild complaint reminded me of a recent funeral: a young Irish-Catholic woman lawyer married to a fellow from this parish died of cancer, and the widower seemed to want me to attend the Mass of Christian Burial in a downtown Catholic church.

With a church full of lawyer colleagues, many of whom must be Jewish or Protestant or nothing, an intelligent-enough young priest went on and on about the Immaculate Conception, because that feast was the day the woman died.

And there I am up in the sanctuary, squirming and uncomfortable, certain that the congregation does not know the Immaculate Conception different from the Virgin Birth. What is going on? Does the priest feel that he has to "put it to" these people . . . the truth undiluted and undiminished? Or is the reality more innocent and mindless? Priests so out of touch with the secular landscape, living in such a pious ghetto that they are disconnected from human communication? I thought to myself: poor old Jesus would not himself do this. Present himself in a way that raises the hair on the back of strangers' necks or puts their teeth on edge rather than attract them.

Another funeral yesterday in a suburban church. Again a priest teaching nonsense in a church so cheaply and vulgarly decorated for Christmas that I was uncomfortable just being there. This time the priest was talking nonsense to a Catholic congregation. He went on about how the moment of death is the most important moment of life. I know what he means or what he is trying to say, but my experience is that life is so often so diminished, exhausted and spent that any mental focus or attention is gone. We are saved by grace, not by the mental clarity with which we die. That priest has been around longer than I have. We should know better than to talk such nonsense.

Maybe the problem is myself. Surely the God who was born in a stable and suffered those Apostles is more patient with this than I manage.

# 6

A letter from the fellow of this parish serving a life sentence in the state correctional institute about 30 miles distant. He is a graduate of the local Jesuit high school. About 15 years ago, he was involved in an armed robbery or something where a victim was shot and killed. In the contingencies of plea bargaining, the "shooter," as the State Pardons Board member called him, did only 18 months, and our parishioner is doing life for the same crime.

I met him during the illness of his mother several years ago. He came to see her when she was dying at home. Again in shackles, he came to church for a brief visit just before her Mass of Christian Burial.

Gently enough, his mother entrusted me with the work of getting him free. She recognized clearly what the authorities recognize so rarely—that an earlier mistake does not mean that this young life must be forever wasted in prison.

Only once have I been to visit him in the prison. The distance, the preliminary requirements, together with everything else make prisons and prisoners a forgotten world by everybody, including myself, who by location here have good reason not to forget them.

Last fall, Sister Catherine and I did travel to the state capitol for the Pardons Board hearing where Steven received a unanimous recommendation from the Board members for release. His character, his prison work with the Lifers' Association and the Prison Literacy Project were most persuasive, despite the fact that pardon and release for someone so young as his 40 years who has served only 15 years of a life sentence is quite rare, almost nonexistent.

The recent letter was acknowledgement and thank you for a small Christmas gift and card. The gift was a few dollars someone had given me at Christmas for some needy family or person. His letter is extraordinary.

Imagine sitting in that prison crowded to twice capacity by riots and ruin at another state prison and describing the last weeks as "a great holiday season"! Especially when you are waiting daily for the newly-reelected governor who with his two-term limit and no political liability now can act on the unanimous recommendation of his Pardons Board.

Talk about "spiritual progress": Steven at 40 and a Muslim makes me at 57 and a Catholic priest look like a beginner. Imagine finding anything good to say about that place. Imagine being anything but bitter about life and confinement during one's best years in that awful place.

On my visit I did notice how serious and meditative a presence Islam seemed to be. How both Protestant and Catholic Christianity seemed to suffer by comparison. The latter seem routine, uninspired, formal. The Muslims, by contrast, created their own mosque in the prison basement. They seem more serious about prayer and fasting and go about the ritual of removing shoes and ceremonial bows and reverences with care that manifests something deeper.

# 7

To come from the desolate grim winter streets to the Academy of Music, to Riccardo Muti, to the Philadelphia Orchestra, to Vivaldi and Prokofiev is certainly a lift. Especially the "Four Seasons" of Vivaldi. The music is like a human echo of the beauty of the world or nature or flowers somewhere out there sounding the beauty of a Creator. At least my nervous system or whatever rests more in the assurance of belief or a sense that the world and life have meaning and significance. As I listen to this beauty, I can rest, let down the guard I consciously or unconsciously maintain against the next minor or major difficulty or crisis.

How strange life is. Each of us lives in a small world of his or her own story and responsibilities and arrangements and entertainments. The larger picture does not really impinge upon us.

And how strange I seem to myself. Why can I not simply be here, enjoy the music, allow it to refresh me, to help me believe more easily for this while if I can? Or why do I need to believe anything at all? I sense people are not so distracted. Perhaps life makes sense, perhaps not. In either case, the music is able to be enjoyed, and we have to live on meaning or no meaning.

Perhaps being a priest is the problem. Tomorrow is Sunday, and people will come to church, and I shall have to say something to them that makes sense to myself as well as them. Perhaps being a priest is so connected with life having some meaning that the modern world threatens me. I suspect a conspiracy of silence out there: people are courteous to us priests, not telling us that they cannot and need not and do not believe anymore everything or anything that we stand for.

What do I do with my doubt? Spend more time listening to Vivaldi? Let the doubt paralyze? Exercise faith like some muscle that improves with workouts?

Perhaps this holding on with fragile grasps is the human condition. Something I should endure more patiently and calmly. Even Paul said we only see "dimly as in a dark mirror." And Simone Weil and also John of the Cross, I suspect, say that God is more like nothing than any of our images.

One response that I do not want in myself is to run with some excess, proclaiming the social relevance of faith. I fear that is what happens in Catholic colleges, where often enough any traditional doctrinal courses are simply not available and theology or whatever becomes exposure to the teacher's agenda of social concerns. I think that Dorothy Day would have believed everything she did, even if the world did not need her spiritual or corporal works of mercy.

# 8

Dreadful normalcy continues at the door. Again the stream of people to the front door wanting food or dollars continues. Here at Saturday noon I am alone in the huge old rectory, waiting to admit the AA group who uses our facilities and who will arrive any moment. This afternoon, a visit to a neighboring Baptist church where a gentle, friendly pastor is celebrating his 25 years as pastor there.

I am distracted by two opportunities between phone and door interruptions: the prayer I missed this morning by not rising early enough or some writing (as this journal) or reading. I choose the prayer, and since the church is far too cold to endure, I occupy the chair beside my bed and try to neglect the compulsion to make the bed first. Sometimes I remember the seminary years by proclaiming ceremoniously to others around: all spiritual wisdom begins with making your bed! A hint of our spiritual training: good housekeeping, not unimportant yet hardly enough.

Yesterday a 20-year-old from the streets called for $20 dollars. The request was so soon after his last request that I was suspicious. I asked whether he was using drugs again—along with the methadon treatment he has been receiving for several years.

He admitted he was using and reminded me of his request last week that I work on his admission to detox and the residential treatment at the nearby hospital where I know some administrators. He does have some kind of medical insurance which may or may not cover treatment. He will need two weeks' notice to arrange vacation from his job.

Later he came around with his little daughter and I did give him $20 dollars, which he knows that I know will go for drugs. What can I say? He does need a fix. When he married some months ago, his bride wanted the whole package, honeymoon and all. I protested I could not afford to pay for his honeymoon. He explained that his methadon clinic does not have "take home," and my few dollars would buy street methadon to cover the days on honeymoon away from daily clinic dose.

I shall have to work on his hospital admission before this relapse becomes too expensive for him and, of course, for me.

The parish council meeting went well enough this morning. I was somewhat apologetic about the letter to their friends from those young lawyers who help us. They want to raise funds for us by calling the neighborhood "abjectly poor." Understandably the parish council members are uneasy with that label. A neighborhood where they live immediately around the church is pleasant and quite middle-class.

Since the letter is already printed—400 copies here—I asked their indulgence by describing the procession of 18 to 20 callers a day to the rectory door for food as evidence of "abject poverty" by people who are in some extended sense our parishioners. Then the project women whom Sister Catherine has gathered for regular meetings are "abjectly poor" by any honest measure. I shall be sure to offer the same explanation tomorrow at Sunday Mass. Other parishioners not on parish council might also take offense. Even as I make this entry, I have been interrupted four times by people looking for food. No items in the pantry for the poor. I have been taking pasta and pasta sauce from our own kitchen shelves. That makes up for the times I have taken some unusual item—usually a can of soup from the poor people's pantry. Some of the callers this last hour are the familiar fellows who probably sell the food for the few coins they can obtain for drink. Well, Saturday early afternoon has me here alone, and I cannot get into all that.

# 9

A friend from the streets calls in the early morning because he needs dollars to travel to work. His common-law wife from years ago and the mother of his youngest child calls last week from another state to say that she and several children were without food or clothes or warmth or whatever, and he should send still more money than the usual support for his child.

Last week I told him that he cannot simply respond with dollars. She has a job; her new husband also works, and the ability of my friend to assist is severely limited by his own resources of salary and living expenses. Besides, why are they in need if both are working?

Of course, the emergency call came the day of his biweekly pay envelope, which day she knows. The story is that the new husband and she are temporarily separated.

Last week my impatience was fierce; he can support this hustle if he chooses. Yet when he has impoverished himself for the next two weeks by sending her 50 of his remaining $60, I have no intention of picking up his living costs for the next two weeks.

Despite my strong advice, he did send her the $50 and is now unable to pay busfare to work. What can I do except give him the dollars he needs for a transit pass that will last for one of the two weeks until payday? I know his desolate life is pushing him in the direction of drugs again. I also know him long enough and well enough to know that the main problem and expense is that the former wife still has some powerful hold on him. I've known her over the years. She is as tough as they come—able to chew him up and spit him out.

# 10

The weekly run through the hospital full of poor people. Because the place is located within the geography of the parish, I am responsible for Catholic sacramental ministry there. Two religious Sisters tend the sick regularly now, and after eight years of inadequately trying to cover the place, I need go now only weekly and have one of the Sisters take me when someone in desperation only needs the Anointing of the Sick.

Lots of disease there particular to poor people: tuberculosis, AIDS, of course, liver disease, all the illnesses associated with substance abuse, including emphysema and asthma and other respiratory illnesses which comes from smoking. Poor people still smoke. More, I think, than others anymore. Their bodies already beat up from other troubles, they decide almost unconsciously: what the hell, what difference a cigarette or two.

Perhaps the smoking and other addictions are in some deep sense a self-destructive urge and suicidal. Sometimes I notice in the whole manner of street friends with multiple, impossible troubles an obscure death wish, the sense that there really is nothing out there for them beyond this impossible web of addiction and women with children dependent on them and these grim streets and demanding jobs. So the sense that the sooner it is all over, the better.

Over at the hospital, I have discovered another refuge or hideout. Now with the Pink Sisters' chapel and the shrine of St. John Neumann at the neighboring church, I have this linen closet of a chapel at the hospital.

The chapel was obviously an afterthought. The room has no windows and is no larger than a walk-in closet. Fluorescent lighting behind simulated stained glass panels with Protestant, Jewish and

Catholic symbols for interfaith effect. Two small church pews face a pedestal where a statue of Madonna and child are encased in a plastic cylinder to prevent theft.

Not an attractive or generous space, but the place is dark and quiet. As I enter, I recall that psalm antiphon which so puzzles me: "The Lord hears the cry of the poor." I have not the slightest idea what that means. What seems true is the awful silence of God in the face of the human suffering and poverty.

Simone Weil says that religious truth is more to be embraced with the heart than understood with the head.

Finishing my hospital run, I leave the Sister and enter the dark closet-chapel. I talk to God and/or myself. Well, if you hear the cry of the poor, then this is as likely a place to address you or find you as any. I reach for my beads, conscious that I am surrounded by little Puerto Ricans curled up in fetal positions in beds, often enough so entwined in their bedsheets that a nurse or aide needs to unwind them. Just outside the door, the intensive care unit where two prison guards sit all day alongside the bed of an emaciated young black fellow about to "expire," as health care people say, with the complications of AIDS.

So if the Lord hears the cry of the poor, then I can join my distracted, doubting prayer to the tears and cries and moans going up from there. Besides, when I get back to the house a whole other world waiting. Best that I slip in here, sit a while in the darkness, run the beads through my fingers, see if I can hold it together for the rest of this day. Feeling so fragile, so undone, I am.

# 11

A call this morning from one of my friends from the streets. This label not accurate for him since he works 10 years now at a suburban business center which is both expensive and almost impossible to reach by public transportation. His job really white-collar work.

The call is usually about money. Today the call is not just about money. He is sick at work and has no carfare home. I offer to pick him up. During the ride home, I discover that since Christmas he is using drugs again and that is why he is both sick and broke and leaning on me more often than usual.

I ask his game plan going home. He says that he will take a nap, iron some shirts and call a fellow later. The call later means a drug dealer and the plan is to get a bag and relieve the withdrawal symptoms which have him ill. On the initial phone call his voice was hoarse, and I thought he had a heavy cold. Only when we stopped for lunch in a delicatessen and he was unable to eat did our conversation come around to his renewed drug use.

Back in the car he talked another game plan: perhaps he would go back into methadon treatment if one of his two former methadon centers would take him back, despite his unpaid bills there.

So here we are with two very different plans: trying to detox by getting the heroin habit down to one bag a day and eventually none or back on methadon.

After protesting—more gently than usual—that I certainly could not afford his drug habit and neither could he, I offered to drive him immediately to the methadon center. My offer was accepted.

The methadon center is part of the hospital I tend, and I am very aware of this service. My identity gives me immediate access to director, physician in charge and everybody else. Otherwise my friend would sit there all afternoon and the session would probably get little past his delinquent bill.

The clinic director took us off to see the medical director through a labyrinth of basement passages and elevators and offices and tunnels connecting the several buildings. I had no idea this underground network was so vast.

Finally we surfaced in a clinic of doctors and technicians and patients coming and going, AIDS patients with their children, people being tested for admission to some outpatient and inpatient program, wasted-looking women and men showing the ravages of their addiction.

We passed a Spanish couple. He seated with his elbows on his knees and his face in his hands. She had a miniature Bible and was murmuring some passage into his ear as he waited in this clinic queue to see a doctor or whomever. She no doubt trying to share with him the comfort of her Pentecostal faith—such a *purgatorio* of human misery, like something Dante walked through indeed. What a strange creation this is. I was reminded of that time after Christmas when the social worker and I visited the high-rise project looking for a woman on drugs about to be evicted for rent delinquency. Children everywhere, many of whom should have been back in school after the holidays, the dangerous, unprotected elevator where a child had fallen to death a week earlier filled with plastic bags from the residents who took their trash no farther. "What did He have in mind?" I said to the sister and myself. "I don't know," she replied, "but He should go back to the drawing board."

# 12

Family court again. New security routines require a person-by-person search through a machine called *FRISKEM*, and the inevitable delay has the line forming outside on the cold street.

At first interesting to be downtown. The brisk vitality of professional people walking toward their offices, the expensive clothes, attractive women, fur coats, and early shoppers. Hard to do anything else than watch the parade and wait in line until I move into the crowded, overheated foyer where four or five sheriff's officers direct this procession of the poor to the elevators which ascend to courtrooms and offices called on the lobby building directory: child support, or writ servers or social services.

Beside me a 17-year-old Hispanic girl holds her sister's baby of six months while the mother is somewhere upstairs seeking support from the father who is not her husband. This sprite of a girl talks to the baby in Spanish, telling the child that I, the object of the infant's stare, am "a giant." When the little woman learns that I understand her Spanish, she apologizes to me for the label of giant.

She is still at school, but not attending today to accompany her sister to court. A long wait in this lobby where there are no benches or chairs and a baby in your arms. We have both been here an hour and a half with no means or idea concerning how things are going upstairs. She waits better than I. The poor are accustomed to the waiting. They spend their lives waiting.

I am less patient. I think of all that needs doing back home. I try to pray. Perhaps moving the beads in my pocket can be my holy hour today. The noise of crying children and casual conversation among the others waiting is meaningless enough to be a kind of silence. And the Mystery whom I approach in prayer is here. His promise is that he lives in us, in one another, especially the poor.

The sense of wasting time persists. Of course it is. Often enough, prayer seems like wasting time anyhow.

The clerical collar not much help getting me any consideration though. I must admit the sheriff's officers are quite courteous to us all. The collar seems to appear odd to the other people here; what is a priest doing in family court? One would' think that priests would be here often enough through mediating or assisting family troubles. I am here because the two private attorneys whom I asked to assist the quarrelling couple need me for an informal legal agreement. She will deliver the children to church on Sunday morning, and he can meet them there without the couple having the direct contact which was the occasion of recent trouble.

# 2.

## Belonging Nowhere

# 1

I do not really belong anywhere. In a sense no more at the chicken dinner last week honoring a local Baptist pastor than in a suburban parish where I sense I would not be comfortable at all after these years in the poorer neighborhoods.

Not belonging anywhere seems true also from these journeys downtown for family court. Not belonging anywhere made me think of the early Irish monks and their vow of exile to leave Ireland and never return, as expression of the truth of exile as theological expression of the human condition. That wandering sounds like "belonging nowhere."

# 2

News from upstate that a seminary classmate died: a priest of a neighboring diocese and a monsignor. We were fairly good friends years ago, but I only saw him recently every few years at the infrequent class reunions. I knew he was ill but did not know the illness was cancer. His close friend and another upstate classmate of mine said he was heroic these last months: lots of pains and lots of patience.

The monsignor always seemed to carry a heavy Irish burden. The family priest carrying the religious role which sustains all the family in their own stories and lives. Many of us came to the priesthood from that cultural origin. As good as any, I guess. No doubt many physicians and lawyers from more secular cultures carrying family pennants, also.

My departed classmate always said to me on meeting: "Where's all the promised joy, Mac?" The later seminary years were focused mightily on the ecstasy of the ordination. I recall fellows one-week-ordained coming back to say Mass for us and give us their new priestly blessing saying: "Stick it out, it's worth it!" The other upstate friend says that more recently they have been saying, "It's not fun anymore." I shall travel upstate to the funeral.

The fourth classmate to die from among 24 of us. Three as priests and one who had left the priesthood angrily, throwing his white plastic Roman collar on the sidewalk after a painful meeting with the then archbishop. All the way back in early seminary he was restless, more ambivalent than the rest of us. His father was a labor radical, a non-practicing Catholic, and his father's perspective influenced his own view of the Church.

This death surfaces painfully my own aging, fragile and vulnerable self. I do wish I were younger, had the opportunity to do some things over differently. Age also makes my situation here more precarious. Three years ago I was having chest pain and the original stress test suggested some scary problems. I remember thinking: my whole being here—staying here depends so on my health holding up. Not only because of the one-man stand but also the sheer stress of the place and being among the poor where everything is often chaotic and so many emergencies and so many times you must answer the door yourself and find food for the caller in our own kitchen pantry because the food in the other pantry is exhausted.

I am not afraid of dying in any dramatic sense. Recently the Gospel readings for the Feast of the Presentation remembered old Simeon, the old man around the Jewish temple. Somehow he had a sense that he would not die until he had seen the Christ.

I hope it is not presumptuous to think that I will live until some particular things are accomplished: the priest-worker play, a few good poems, some spiritual progress beyond this detoured, fixed, retarded self I painfully am. As Hopkins says, "My taste is me." I would like to finish off more transformed living so close to the sacraments and daily Mass and daily tasks that should give me a keener sense of the important, the *unum necessarium.* You would think I would be further along.

Simone Weil says we do not go out that way: reading all those unread books, bringing together all those loose strands of life like the final chapter of a cheap novel. Death comes, and we are simply interrupted. Such an outcome is intolerable for us even to think about, so we push the thought as far away as possible.

Well anyhow, I am getting older: the funeral of a classmate tomorrow, I can expect some health problems, can hope nothing serious or debilitating happens.

# *3*

Up earlier than usual for the weekly convent Mass. Back in my room I read the epilogue of a biography of St. Margaret Mary which I finally finish.

I first read this biographical novel about 35 years ago in the seminary and the religious sensibility has changed immensely since then. The style of the book is almost Victorian in the deliberate evoking of sentimentality.

I wanted to read the book again because when I slip into the church joined here to the house, I find myself sitting in the sanctuary facing a huge stained-glass window on the south with the traditional rendering of Christ revealing his Sacred Heart to the lowly nun, Margaret Mary.

Gradually, I feel drawn back into an earlier piety. I began praying the litany of the Sacred Heart again and trying to absorb the truth that no matter what else is happening within or without, we abide in love like fish in water.

Especially I have a difficult time sensing the divine love for my own ragged self. My memory of the Margaret story is that she was indeed a ragged self—so ragged that William James uses her as an example of religious hysteria or pseudo-mysticism in his *Varieties of Religious Experience*. The great Abbé Bremond, the immense scholar of spirituality, said, however:

*Sainte Marguerite Marie, si fragile and si haute, si*
*douloureuse et si exquise.*

Saint Margaret Mary, so fragile and so lofty, so dolorous
and so exquisite.

Hard to hold onto that sense that we live in love like fish in water. Especially when I feel so ragged inside so often. Most often the terrible sonnets of Gerard Manley Hopkins' last years are an appropriate expression of how I feel inside.

# 4

Ash Wednesday. Ash enough the reality of this neighborhood. Already enough abandoned cars, trash-strewn lots, uncollected trash to remind people of the somber realities.

But we still do it. Someone should study the excitement around ashes and palm on Palm Sunday and the blessing of the throats on the feast of Saint Blaise.

Even the school children come over for their Lenten ashes. 180 of our 200 are not Catholic, and ashes do not work on black children as well as on the pale skin of us white folk. Some materials make white ashes, though not palm from last Palm Sunday.

Last night we had the other six or seven neighboring parishes for Mass and anointing with ashes. On the following Wednesdays of Lent, we shall attend in turn those other churches. A large crowd. Uplifting for our people to see a full church now and then. Again I mention the shadows from our broken spotlights, and also the shadow of the great rough Lenten cross draped in purple which looms out over the whole church.

# 5

St. Valentine's Day. Some thoughtful cards from gracious friends. Lonely life, this priesting. Amazing how a few kind words comfort. How needy I am! I wonder whether others are so needy or this business of not being married increases the need?

The day did not begin well. Before dawn a call from the daughter of a lovely woman who works here at cleaning and laundry. I am embarrassed to confess such amenities, and I know myself well enough to know that I would neglect those areas. Even in this age of feminism, the woman's touch.

However, the matter at hand not my embarrassment but the woman's tragedy. Her son was murdered last night coming home from the movies with his girlfriend.

As early as possible I was down at her tiny house in the projects. Inside her place is a modest palace: furniture chosen with care, tasteful art reproductions and everything as neat and clean as she keeps things here.

Hard to disentangle the story. The victim was mistaken for someone else. His girlfriend was wounded in the struggle, not clear whether the fatal weapon was a gun or knife, and the young assailant was himself shot or stabbed by still another party.

Gradually the tiny kitchen filled up with women: our cleaning woman, her sisters, her daughter, the young woman who was wounded, later her mother—and myself.

What suffering and strength in these women. They experience constantly in their children the brutal wounds of these neighborhoods. Sitting around the kitchen, expressions of religious faith are expressed: "God will just have to see me through this" or "My only strength is in God now" or "I guess his (the victim's) time had come; we can't question." And here I am questioning every twist and turn in my own petty melodrama, to say nothing of tragedy like this. I say little, nothing. I am with stronger, more believing people here. I would not know what to say. I have no children. I cannot even imagine her pain.

Earlier this month, the slaying of a young policeman in the neighborhood. A manhunt for the slayer leads the police to a nearby home. The alleged slayer flees across the rooftops of the row homes, crashes through the skylight into the bathroom of another house, douses himself in nail polish remover and ignites himself, crying and shouting that he did not mean to kill the police officer. Later, I hear that this crazed unfortunate has two children in our parish school.

# 6

Perhaps because of the quiet and the day and time of late Friday afternoon, I find myself considering the fragility and difficulty and elusive nature of friendship. Somehow when I see working people going home on Friday to the warmth of family weekend, I feel my aloneness very much.

With few illusions concerning the difficulty and demands of marriage, I have decided that only marriage seals relationships or friendship so that people are "no longer two." I notice how even out among friends, a married couple still sit together at table. Most often, how life is just understood as doing almost everything with this other person and the doing confirms and seals the union.

And the vows are important. Without the vows people do not need to endure the difficulty of one another. They wander apart or look for less difficult relationships.

I recall a friend, whose marriage is less than satisfying, threatened by someone leaving an unhappy marriage because "you only go around once." My friend responded that she was going to stay and work at hers also because "you only go around once."

So here I am alone, back in this large and now empty house on Friday evening. I lament that absence in my life of something that would seal and hold someone close to my heart. The Church is almost cruel asking this loneliness of so many ordinary men and women. Life is difficult enough; we do not have to create further difficulty. Simone Weil says there will always be enough affliction to make us saints. More than enough, she says. Our task is even to diminish the affliction so that holiness is not so difficult. Peter Maurin of *Catholic Worker* origins says we need to make a world where it is easier for people to be good.

I know I am spelling out only one side of the picture; many find marriage and family so difficult that they would welcome the luxury and personal space I have at home. I know also that I could not live among the poor and serve them so freely if I had a companion or a family. I recall someone years ago responding to news that a young friend was leaving the religious life to marry: "Some of you fellows should belong to everybody rather than somebody. My experience is that once people marry that can no longer be true."

I know also that this dream or fantasy of mine remains untested. Perhaps like so many others I am so limited or wounded that I could not sustain a relationship or succeed in that most basic and most difficult human effort. I shall never know. All I know is that the pleasant healing hours with an old friend today gave me the elusive, fleeting feeling of friendship as something so much less than the possibilities of marriage. Besides, it is early Friday evening and I am feeling my aloneness.

# 7

An almost frivolous surprise arrived by mail on Valentine's Day: my Irish passport.

Because my father was born in Ireland, I am *de facto* an Irish citizen and have claim to the passport. Several years ago I casually filled out the form, but when the Irish Consulate General in New York City required various documents difficult to research, I let the matter go.

Later, my brother expressed interest since his work has him travel in EEC (European Economic Community) countries and the passport has some convenience. Working in NYC most days, he was able to visit the consulate and work things out. I did finally obtain necessary birth and marriage .certificates, and the St.Valentine's Day parcel was a nice surprise.

During this Jesuit year, the observance of 500 years of Ignatius and 450 years of the Society of Jesus, I decided to look more closely into Jesuit spirituality and even try some spiritual direction. Late in life to be looking for direction, but sometime around my age, Thomas Merton said his life was one of frequent darkness and deepening contradictions. My own similar experience has me looking for direction.

Anyhow. Something that came up in the effort at spiritual direction is the experience of desire. "Eliciting Great Desires" is a paper in the Jesuit spirituality series which the Jesuit director gave me. The idea is that the love of God is intrusive into our lives, constantly trying to break through our defenses, and if we can learn to listen and heed our desires and needs and feelings and fantasies, even we can discern our way.

One fantasy I entertain—the Irish passport enhanced it last week—is the idea of retiring and living more or less alone by the ocean. Concretely that desire expresses itself in an image of the wilds of northern Donegal. I imagine steady hours of prayer, long walks along the sea, writing—but especially the praying. The Jesuit father says this means I am being called to a more contemplative way here and now. Somehow find or make time for that more serious prayer in the present.

The details of the fantasy or desire are an early retirement and some modest income beyond my meager savings. No doubt this thought or fantasy is a reaction to my present harassment by door and telephone and people who want me here and there. I feel burnout, over-stimulation, weariness and even a chronic exhaustion. The poems do not get written, the priest-worker play remains raw and unfinished, and I shall be 58 years old in two months. And who says the poems or play will be worthwhile anyhow? Besides, the pen is worthless, as Camus or somebody said.  One of the published poems talks about changing the clay chalice for daily Mass to a silver one in Advent so that the candle flame can reflect off the underside of the silver cup—round as the Virgin's carry in the very first Advent season.

Last Advent, whoever puts out the cup for daily Mass still put out the clay chalice.  So much for poetry.

Again the idea of some luxurious leisure of retirement might offend the reality of being here, privileged to share the life of the poor, however clumsily I do that.  The real poverty is that they are "stuck" here, and they know that.  This is the whole story for them.  Perhaps in the spirit of poverty, I should neither imagine nor even remotely plan getting free of here someday.  Be content just to be here, work, read when I can, write when I can, pray early morning and those hours stolen at the nearby cloister.  Be poor in possession of my own time and life and talents, if any.  As Thomas Merton says, the goal of our spiritual effort is not success in prayer.  The goal is charity or love, and prayer is a crucial means to that goal; but charity, not excellence in prayer, is the purpose.  Simone Weil, by her extolling of necessity, suggests that the *habitus caritatis* comes from what happens to us and afflicts us and hollows us out as well as anything we might choose, like a particular prayer regime.

# 8

*Shalem alicheim.*  The greeting of the prayer leader at my first Muslim funeral, even though I am 20 years in North Philadelphia.  The slain son of our housekeeper apparently joined Islam as a teenager.  His mother and some of his sisters are Christian.  One of his brothers seemed fairly familiar with the Muslim ritual there in the funeral home.

The scene was almost surreal.  The electricity was down in the entire block of that busy main thoroughfare of North Philadelphia—Broad Street.  Charles Dickens apparently noticed or noted Broad Street as the longest straight street anywhere.

No electricity meant a completely-dark entranceway into the funeral parlor.  No one could recognize anyone else until entering the funeral parlor itself, where large windows admitted daylight.  The closed coffin was turned somehow toward Mecca, and the Muslim men lined up three deep for silent prayer after the teaching, which was heavy on the need not to lament because any death is completely and explicitly the will of Allah.

Later at dinner, another priest commented on the grim, uncomforting message so implicitly censorious of Christian belief in the Trinity. I said that the message was hardly more censorious or whatever than things I had often heard at Christian funerals—Catholic or Protestant. Somewhere Islam was an elegant tradition, and criticizing this inelegant expression was hardly fair. I thought of Averrhoes and Avicinna and Thomas Aquinas learning Aristotle from them. I thought too of the fellow from St. Malachy serving life at the state prison, sustained and nourished by Islam in his intolerable fate. Something to be said for fatalism if one can walk the line between stoicism and cynicism. We do have to get around to playing the hand we have been dealt, as the heroic mother manifests at this funeral of her son.

# 9

Fear follows me everywhere. Fear of getting up and facing the day. I hate to see daylight. I try for Hopkins' eagerness for the "brown brink eastward" as promise of light and life. No avail. Hopkins knew that fear also. Something in the terrible sonnets about "I wake and feel the fell of dark, not day . . ."

Fear of being alone and losing my precarious faith. Fear of getting old and fear of the exhaustion I feel. How can I go on? Fear of one more telephone call or one more person wanting something of my time. Fear that I will die before I do the few things that seem worth doing, like the priest-worker play.

Fear that I will lose altogether the ability to pray, so painful now is the effort sometimes. Yesterday I did place myself in the cold church before the great window of the Sacred Heart, and in some obscure way felt drawn into the mystery. The pierced heart an access or doorway into the love in which I want to believe that we live.

Fear of the future: what will happen to me and this lovely old place? Does its present fragile, yet steady existence depend so completely on me? Does the financial support I gather mean that it is little more than some expression of my ego? What good is that?

At times the fear is paralyzing. Difficult to rise from bed or take on something new, or something old, awaiting a surge of courage or energy.

Fear of dying and fear of living. Fear that I am on the wrong path or into a detour, a cul de sac.

I do not know what to do with all this. Somewhere John of the Cross says that eventually all these emotions—like fear or love or hate or anger or whatever—will surface and must be faced. I do not suggest that I am in some advanced mystical state, but Jacques Maritain says that for persons living ordinary lives, people and work and failure and whatever pass through us in ways that purify us similarly to the way in which people leading a more contemplative life are purified by the great interior trials of the active and passive nights of the spirit. Talking about oneself, and almost petty moods or fears or whatever they are, seems so trivial in a world at war where even children are dying and starving and cowling in corners from bombs.

Yet pain does produce that flattening of consciousness. One has a severe toothache say, and worry about war or weather or work or season goes out the window. One does not care whether the sun is shining or it is summer or winter. All one knows is: my mouth hurts. How can I make the hurt go away? Today I hurt. I am afraid, and the fear cripples me and makes me anxious, and the anxiety or worry makes me more afraid.

# *10*

A Lenten Friday. Sometimes Lenten Fridays are full of memories: Stations of the Cross and Holy Hours and the Novena of Grace. Devotions of childhood and seminary years which have more or less disappeared.

The fear of the other day stills haunts me so in late afternoon, I take it into the cold church. The late light will illumine two windows: my Sacred Heart window and the Agony in the Garden window, also on the south side of the church. I had just read something from Henri de Lubac, the great Jesuit theologian who lived so long under a shadow and was made a cardinal in his old age. Something about taking our bruised, hurting selves into the laceration of Christ in Gethsemane and saying what Peter said at the Transfiguration: "Lord, it is good for me to be here." Taking my pain to his, where the promise is that I will not be rejected.

As I make my way into the cold church, our young gym teacher, a lay volunteer from California, is also arriving for his daily after-school session on our piano.

"No privacy," I mutter to no one but myself, noticing how completely difficult to find time alone or quiet, even in a cold church.

So with him there working out some light Bach melody and another Beethoven piece, I try to make the best of it. Without book or rosary or many words, I simply stare alternately at the Sacred Heart window and the Gethsemane window. I imagine my prayer a plucking of my own inner strings or heart, clumsy and always starting over from distraction, like the teacher at the piano further down in the church trying to catch the melody, losing it and beginning over or from where he faltered. Not bad. Some kind of prayer. Trying to make my turbulent heart connect with the heart pictured up there in the window, trying to see my loneliness and fear and craving for human comfort in the light of His; the Gethsemane window is child-like in portraying Him suffering and praying and sweating blood while Peter and James and John are slumped against one another in sleep. Bringing my laceration to His, as de Lubac says. I do not know what that means clearly. I must learn to let go, let this time take more of my heart, not to make the hour stand or fall so on my effort to understand or figure things out. *Cor ad cor loquitur* was the motto or whatever of Cardinal Newman. No one more heady than he. Somehow I must learn and allow myself to enter more fully, more quietly and confidently into the Mystery. A phrase from the deepest consciousness of childhood: "Most Sacred Heart of Jesus, I place my trust in Thee." Over and over like a mantra.

After a half-hour, the teacher leaves. I stay another half-hour perhaps.

# 11

A busy weekend. First the regular Saturday morning Mass at the parish. A few friends come regularly and we have coffee afterwards.

Then off to the northeast part of the city for the Mass of Christian Burial for the Irishman who asked to see me about a week or two before his death. During one visit he was in obvious pain, and not knowing what else to say, I offered: "Well, it's Lent, Harry." He responded: "I think your Lent is going to be longer than mine."

His fellow Derryman who plays the Irish fiddle came and played. It was lovely, and as people were leaving, many had moist eyes. Even I felt something almost stirring in me for a moment during the music. I say almost because the full emotion never quite happens. Up in the head I know when something is beautiful or touching, but nothing much happens otherwise. Dave Hagan and I talk about this and wonder whether the lack is some form of burnout: when something tragic happens, we surely know it, and tragedy happens often enough. But we don't feel it—the joy or the tragedy. Perhaps it is not important, perhaps we are dangerous or pathetic or just burnt-out.

Burnout or no burnout, we both want to stay around these neighborhoods. Nowhere else to go. Nothing else so real. Important to be here for the opportunity to help out now and then, find somebody a free lawyer or a job or a residential detox program. Perhaps someday we shall feel something again. Perhaps not. I guess I cannot allow that to matter, even while I try to be open to the possibility of full human feeling. God, am I caught here in some trendy psychological setup?

# *12*

Instead of returning to the church after the visit to the sister parish, an opportunity to crash at an empty house for a quiet day. Very quiet. Sleep mostly.

The house is empty because someone is away and generously allows me to wander from bed to television to refrigerator to window. Amazing the privacy in the heart of the city. I rented two movies at a video store and "junked out" on spy stories.

The house is near the downtown cloister which I frequent, and I did manage a lengthy visit, just sitting there trying to connect with the prayer of the Sister kneeling motionless behind the grill which separates the enclosed front end of the chapel from the public part where I sit.

I imagine myself sunbathing. The Blessed Sacrament up there in a stylized sunburst and myself here on the human beach soaking Him up. The promise is that if we approach, we will not be rejected. I move the beads through my fingers or pray the hours of the breviary or repeat some phrase. I am so weighed down by my heavy spirit, my aging body, my distracted self. Simone Weil says that perfect attention is prayer, so most of all I just try to be attentive, bring my mind back when it wanders. I must be very visual. The visual contact is an immense help. I do not know how much of this one needs or must do. I sense that the Lord was always at it: in the Garden, at the Transfiguration, all night sometimes when the Apostles were looking for Him and found Him off alone, "having passed the night in prayer."

Anyway. Paschal says I would not be seeking unless I had already found Him. Even the desire to visit and sit in that chapel is itself a great grace. Not many others there. A few elderly folk. Perhaps the desire and pull there is such a wonderful rare gift that I should sense the privilege as much as lament the awful distance and poverty I feel when I am trying to pray.

I leave the chapel just as the sun is setting, and the early evening light is lovely on the downtown towers just over the top of the closer houses. Cold but the late light and clear blue sky hint at spring. Something merciful about winter up in my neighborhood. The raw, sweaty life seems calmed by winter. A blanket or comforter or something. One has ambivalent feelings about the new season a month away and the summer in the city which follows.

# 13

A trip to a travel agent to plan a vacation in Ireland immediately after Easter.

I know what is forcing me to take this month-long break: a chronic sense of exhaustion. I am always tired, always feel that I am running too fast or doing too much or answering too many phone calls or just too available to everything going on around me.

Recently I had a conversation with an older and wiser priest. Right off he noticed signs of overwork, overactivity. Perhaps as one grows older, one has to learn to do less, not more.

I am conscious that these reflections occur in any area where people have little choice concerning how much life they can handle. A teenage daughter becomes pregnant and the new grandmother must begin again the consuming tasks of early motherhood because daughter who is now young mother is unable or irresponsible. No Ireland for them. They do what they have to do, what comes next, what unfolds. The idea of measuring their response or available energy never arises.

Yesterday I was appalled at my behavior with a fellow at the door. He comes whenever he needs a dollar or a sandwich or a can of soup. I ask him not to come after work hours. He has a stutter and tells me that he is in some job training program, and after-hours is the only opportunity he has to come and beg something for an evening meal or carfare for the next day.

Yesterday his arrival was so untimely for me. I was so tired, so weary seeing him again after-hours, so annoyed at his again ignoring my request not to come so late that I lost control and began shouting that he does not care about our mutual agreement or my harassment or that I am alone here with phone and door often going at the same time. My shout was so loud, my exasperation so extreme that even while screaming at him I was becoming afraid for my lack of control and began fumbling in my wallet for some dollars that would end his visit and my frenzy.

He took the five dollars and then began to tell me in a frantic stutter about the job training and why he comes so late so often. Watching him walk down the pathway from the door, I felt the regret of another gracious opportunity lost. Simone Weil says that the begging exchange which is true charity or love, when the encounter does not reinforce the positions of humiliating and being humiliated, is rarer than walking on water.

All I can say for myself is that the outbursts are less frequent in me. Perhaps I should not try to say anything for myself. Let the truth be seen: there he goes wandering the streets, utterly humiliated, with a few dollars which will hardly relieve his situation at all.

Here I am going back to some amenity so unimportant and indulgent that my outburst is shocking. One reason to go to Ireland. Perhaps a good rest will make me less brutal on these poor fellows.

All this by way of saying why I need to get away. I should not analyze it so. Just go. Do whatever I need do for the long haul here.

Some conservation of energy. One does not run long distance with the same intensity as a short sprint.

I also need to acknowledge that life and joy are gifts, too. The Irish trip a Christmas gift which I should gratefully accept. I am better at that, I know. I do not need to do some elaborate reasoning to allow myself this vacation. I knew from the start I would go, was pleased with the opportunity and will enjoy the stay. You just get used to being around here, the routines. Not stuck here; I do, however, have difficulty rousing myself from those routines

Another reason to go is the encouragement I receive everywhere about writing. A great gift if writing is really in me. I notice how difficult and even impossible writing is for most people. They hardly even try—ever. Graham Greene says that the writer must be something of a spectator in life, someone who watches the human parade rather than being fully within the parade. I would not want to consider myself a spectator and this place involves me more than necessary or, I fear, wise. I attend and respond and involve myself in far too much so that prayer and thought and the quality of work suffers. Perhaps some more moments on the sidelines watching the parade are in order. Besides, writing will give whatever I have to say some permanency not otherwise possible. I am surely glad that G.M. Hopkins managed to write those poems despite his spiritual misgivings about the vanity of poetry. And what a help to me in my many desperate moments his terrible sonnets are. I am grateful also that Simone Weil wrote those notebooks to save herself from the moments of her headaches.

No Hopkins or Simone Weil, I should see this lifelong desire only seeping in late middle age through. Ireland can help me to explore that tendency somewhat.

# 14

Yesterday was a 51st birthday for Dave Hagan and I will treat him to dinner tonight. A rough year for him this year after Hank Gathers dropped over and died on a Los Angeles basketball court before 5,000 people. Dave coached Hank in elementary school, guided him through high school and college, and loved him like his own son.

Dave is still trying to make some religious sense of that tragedy. I know him well enough to know that his main grief is for the family—the lost opportunity for this poor woman to escape public housing and the poverty of North Philadelphia. Also and just as important for Dave is the lost joy for Hank himself and all those young fellows who would bask in that success and joy just because one of their own was making it. The death is also a tragedy for them: one more reason not to try against all odds.

Trying to making religious sense of the tragedy is more my impulse than that of Dave Hagan. He does not have the inordinate lust to understand which another wise friend noticed in me.

Dave's effort is not so much understanding as acceptance, and even there he is further along than I am. He lives with a keen sense of the impenetrable reality of this landscape. Hank was his only real success story in 20 years up here, and by success I mean someone making it by our usual standards of achievement. The odds on Hank going down as he did and even dying are so impossible that even now, a year later, the wound hurts Dave as much as that first awful phone call and those days around the funeral.

For all his rough intolerant ways, Dave Hagan is as close to the real thing as anyone I have known. Real because the precious in him is enclosed in such a humanity of contradiction. He is cranky and lethargic. The years have visibly taken their toll. He is careless about invitations and social amenities. He should be more sensitive about cigarette smoke offending others present. He should gear remarks to the capacity and limitations of his listeners and does not. He should place more limits on those young fellows who come and go in his house.

No one has a keener sense of the meaning of the Holy Eucharist, yet unless he were needed as celebrant he would walk past others at Mass and have a smoke while waiting for one of those others like myself.

Once talking to some young seminary students about his life and work, he was asked with concern about his neglect of formal prayer. He dismissed that concern with a remarkably accurate self-measure: one must be a contemplative to work inner city. No one else I know could say something like that without being offensively self-conscious.

And in this matter of Hank Gathers he has again this amazing ability to cut through media hype and friendship and tribal loyalties to the heart of the question: if inappropriate financing of amateur athletes made the mother financially dependent on her athlete son and the same financial arrangements kept Hank in college a year longer than he might otherwise have decided, then all this should in justice be spelled out no matter who is embarrassed. Dave has no desire to injure or even embarrass anyone. Just to say what must be said so that justice may be done even if that means misunderstanding for Dave himself. Dave Hagan's main agenda is not Dave Hagan. A case of real virtue looking like its opposite, Divine Love seeming like indifference since it is so inclusive.

Dave is going to want me to speak at his October anniversary of 25 years as a priest. I shall have to remember and say some of these things more elegantly than I say them this first time here.

# 3.

# *The Long Haul*

# 1

Today is the first anniversary of the death of Hank Gathers on a basketball court in Los Angeles before 5000 people.

I did not need Dave Hagan's notice that he would not be at our school for his drug preventive classes today. I knew the anniversary was going to be a heavy day ending a heavy year for him. He said that he was not going to work again on March 4th ever. He anticipates full newspaper coverage, including the painful picture of Hank down and his mother and others standing around.

I knew he was going to the cemetery, and I wanted to accompany him. Some small way of showing that I know his pain and want to share it in our isolation up here in these neighborhoods.

Dave had already visited the grave once today with some of the young fellows from around his house and an aunt of Hank's and her children. He said he wanted us to go out later alone. This second trip would be his more meditative or prayerful visit, although he would not use those words. He could talk coming and going about Hank and untimely death and the unfairness of it all and ask what the mystery we call God has in mind, allowing such tragedy among poor people whose lives are already harsh enough with such awful disappointment. And he knows that I will sit alongside him *en route* and absorb his lament. He does not want answers. He knows no answers exist. He just wants a patient, attentive ear. Someone with his own cultural and formative background who knows whence these questions arise.

In the middle of a cold, damp afternoon, we stood beside this grave in a cemetery lost in the shadows of huge gasoline tanks not far from the airport. Contrary to expectation, the headstone had arrived in time for the anniversary and included a primitive carving of a basketball going over the rim down into the net.

"That means to express how Hank went out," says Dave, "doing a slam dunk. What an incredible way to go. So much better than, say, falling over while sitting on the bench."

The raw cold was penetrating my thin coat, and perhaps my almost shudder was the pathos of everything getting to me as well as the cold seeping in. I did not want to make any gesture to leave until Dave was quite ready. A lonely sorrow this. He has been grieving this loss with the grief of losing his own son, if he had one. He talked about Hank and how special Hank was, how contagious his energy and vitality, his cheer and generous, good spirit.

Hank's mother was in California and not there to see that her new gravestone lacked the action photograph of Hank attached to a niche carved into the stone itself.

Dave had brought a photograph, some heavy transparent tape and scissors and we attached the picture to the stone as carefully and neatly as possible. An improvisation until the more permanent arrangement. Dave just wanted to do something like that for this anniversary. Below the stone were the flowers he had brought on his earlier visit.

Eventually he did discard his second cigarette and we returned to the city. I believe the black cemetery is just outside the city limits because until WW II or thereabouts black cemeteries were all outside the city limits. On our return we stopped for a drink, lifting our glasses to Hank, and Dave having still another cigarette. With this anniversary coming up, I knew his Lenten abstinence from cigarettes would never last; as for my effort at abstinence from drinking for Lent, I thought joining Dave in this small ritual to a fallen friend seemed necessary and appropriate. Lent enough some moments without our needing to attach anything else.

# 2

Again downtown and a chance to pray or sit or whatever I do at the cloister. Here at home the church is attached to the house and convenient enough. But at the cloister the Blessed Sacrament is "exposed," as we say. Visible. And I have discovered that I am a visual person. Locking something into view can command my attention much more than, say, listening can. Besides, the cloister chapel is comfortably warm, far warmer than the church chapel here on weekdays. And at the cloister I am unavailable for the interruptions which define my life here. Here life is interruption. There no one knows my whereabouts.

Except today. Some homeless street people have discovered the chapel. Not many. The place is warm and clean and quiet and you can even stretch out in a pew, and the sisters seem to let it happen.

A fellow who comes frequently to our door saw me from his rear pew as quickly as I saw him. I pretended not to see him, quite sure that he would make a move. Here I was someone he knew, a priest, someone whose *raison d'être* is to be available to fellows like him. He would wait to see how lengthy my stay was and accordingly would either plan his departure for a meeting or give me some minutes before approaching my pew.

Finally, he did come up the aisle. "How you doing?" he asks. "Fine," I answer. He shows me his feet dressed in thick white socks and rubber overshoes without any undershoes: "Give me a ride down to St. John's Hospice so I can get a pair of shoes? Besides, I need something to eat."

Determined not to be completely detoured, I mentioned that I was going to sit here for a while, and when I was leaving, we could discuss the matter further. I gave him three dollars, half hoping that he would disappear into some neighborhood shop and I would not see him again until some further visit back home.

He was not going to waste this good fortune of our meeting so easily. I could tell from body movement that he had returned to his rear pew, still waiting for my departure.

His presence was a distraction to any other attention I might attempt. The weary sense that the mystery is as present in my friend back there as anywhere. I cut my time short but not too short, and there he was at the door as I was leaving.

Shoes were on his mind. Now in my car, he invited a closer look at his inadequate overshoes. His destination now was, he said, his "hut" back in North Philadelphia, a few blocks beyond my place.

Driving along, I decided the time was ripe to discard that older pair of handsome sport shoes. I possess two pairs of these hiking or climbing shoes, and one shoe of the older pair has a tear where the upper shoe joins the sole. However ungenerous of me, my friend would get the older pair.

I stopped the car at my front door, telling George I would quickly return. Inside the world of people and phone calls and other needs are waiting, all the reasons why I go and hide in the cloister. Before attending anything else, I fetch the old shoes and return to the car. George notices the tear immediately and looks at me with a knowing expression. Off we go to the few blocks farther and out he gets, at sure enough, a "hut," an old downtown corner newsstand transported somehow to this desolate narrow lot between two row houses. "Keep in touch," he says as he leaves the car.

# 3

An article in the diocesan newspaper about church attendance. Last October we were all asked to count attendance at our Sunday Masses, and this is the report. Mass attendance is 33% in the archdiocese, with variations from 61% down to 13%. Affluent suburban parishes seem to have better attendance than older inner-city places.

Amazing how in the analysis almost no consideration of what is going on in the church that would have people come or not. Much discussion on the religious practice of different age groups, ethnic parishes, parish size and geography, whether people live near the church.

Nothing about what people hear by way of homily when they attend or the music or the aesthetics of architecture, as though these things are unimportant. Catholics are conscientious and go or not because they are dutiful or negligent.

Simone Weil says that "the Greeks looked at their temples. We can endure the statues in the Luxembourg because we do not look at them." Often in church one has the impression that nothing is going on or happening, and we do Mass so often because we do it so poorly, repetition as a substitute for reverence or substance.

I know about the theology that the sacraments are substantively full whenever the essentials are present but that cannot be an excuse for the dull routine which Annie Dillard laments. One sits through these uninspiring celebrations and imagines the possibilities of the Church which is itself a sign and speaks only through signs. A local bishop has no real earthly power beyond the vulgar intimidations of authoritarianism over priests and religious. His only power concerning people would be the signs he makes by what he says at the altar or by where and how he lives. The signs, like the miracles of Jesus: "If you do not believe me, believe my works. They bear witness for me."

The miracle of Oscar Romero of El Salvador, the sign that his life has become "the voice of those who have no voice," and his words brought down on him the death at the altar by which his life and death become a sign of hope for suffering people.

How I yearn for the miracle and sign of a bishop here who would come and live among the abandoned poor of North Philadelphia and suffer the car theft and burglary and hazards that these people suffer every day.

Why does such a miracle seem so impossible? Why do our bishops avoid any mention of Oscar Romero? Why recently was the Oscar Romero Interfaith Coalition unwelcome in a diocesan building? Perhaps the answer is very simple: the Church in this country lacks the substance or seriousness or courage or urgency or whatever even to consider Archbishop Romero straight on. Here the reverse of Simone Weil's example and afraid to look at the terrible on a Greek temple lest we be transformed by what we see. Instead we cultivate the mediocrity and repetition to insulate ourselves and avoid the conversion that serious notice would require.

So instead of talking about what happens when people come to church, we get endless discussion of how old the churchgoers are or how close-by they live.

# 4

Yesterday at Sunday Mass, I tried the lesson on faith of the man born blind, how the Gospel and other readings are instruction for baptismal candidates on faith as a "way of looking at the world" in the images of faith of William Lynch, SJ, one of those writers like Simone Weil to whom I keep returning. He shares with her a love for the classical Greek literature and world.

Out there in church I see a Temple University graduate student who is here only because the Catholic center is closed for midterm break. Once before he came here thus and was so offended by some homily of mine that he sent me a very critical letter, hostile even, putting me into a liberal stereotype as someone supporting even abortion.

I responded with a mean enough letter of my own, telling him how judgmental his letter was. Later we became friendly enough. He even did music here some summer Sundays when the church pianist was on vacation.

This Sunday I could tell from his body language that my homily offended him. Amazing how 25 pews away I can feel his withdrawal; closing me off later at Communion, he could hardly receive the sacrament from me. In those new personality tests I must be a feeling person more than a thinking one. Immediately I sense his hostile reaction.

What I said was that faith needs nourishment. The flame must be fed as in the parable of the wise and foolish bridesmaids with their lamps. Every morning, rising, I grasp a phrase from John of the Cross, not Sacred Scripture, but light on the dark night within and without, difficult times. I told how during this Gulf War I found more Gospel in the *New Yorker* than the Catholic press. Leaving church, he could hardly look at me. Something about never before having heard John of the Cross called "fiction" or the *New Yorker* "gospel." I was annoyed at his unfairness. I neither called John of the Cross fiction nor the *New Yorker* gospel, and it seems less than honest for a philosophy student to manipulate my words for some purpose of disagreement.

Yet my discomfort which lingers these several days says something about me, so sensitive to how others think or feel or respond to me, even to a fault. Not easy for such a fellow to do the prophetic thing of thinking something through and being faithful to that no matter what the cost or what others think.

I remember once doing civil disobedience. The plan was that we were to fall limp in the Federal Courthouse on Hiroshima Day so that the security police would have either to arrest us or remove us bodily. When the time came and going limp was about to make his job more difficult for some poor minority guard, I just could not let him lift or carry me out. The idea of being a burden to anyone is intolerable.

At first this sounds like virtue, not wanting to impose on anyone. Yet like the heroes or antiheroes of Flannery O'Connor's stories, our virtues are also our weaknesses. My convictions become dissolved in what sometimes is little more than hypersensitivity to what others think. Too much regard for human opinion. The old spiritual manuals called it human respect. I guess we all have weaknesses which cripple us and waste good energy. This is one of mine. Something I have to work out without ever quite winning. The human condition. We must be as patient with ourselves as we know we should be with others for all the same reasons.

Annoying though to know that the criticism of that fellow leaving church on Sunday was unfair and what I said was properly said. Humiliating to be so easily intimidated within when angrily you even know you are right.

Years ago I refused an assignment when I was appointed *pro tem* teacher in a Catholic school on the eve of a lay teachers' strike. I managed with knots in my stomach to hold out against the authorities who told me my resistance was disobedience to ordination promises of obedience. Somewhere in my mixed-up insides I knew that this obedience had limits like everything else. Somewhere even St. Paul says that "our service is a reasonable thing," and I know I was no intruder who could be moved in to break a strike.

The authorities came on very strong, but I knew I just could not do it, whatever the cost or my interior conflict. As I say, years ago now, but a moment that gave me some assurance about my shaky self in hindsight. I am still very angry that the fellow leaving church can affect me so deeply. Much ado about nothing. One reason I doubt is that I fear I talk too much about large grandiose matters and neglect the spiritual nourishment which the people before me need to cope with their more immediate, coping lives. Yet even as I say this, I know it is not true. I do try to tend the needs closer at hand. Even talking about John of the Cross is evidence of that.

# 5

Hospital morning: the sacraments of Reconciliation and the Anointing of the Sick.

Usually a Sister accompanies me, and I move very quickly. Altogether too quickly, I fear. The old manner in priests which people can complain about quite reasonably: using the ritual of the sacrament as defense or barrier from any personal involvement with the patient who needs human comfort as well as ritual and sacramental grace, who needs grace through sacraments expressed in signs that are fully human and full signs. The sign that is hurried or clipped or impersonal is not a good sign nor a proper administration of the sacrament. I guess why I am falling into bad habits here is the sense that each one of these people lying sick in bed has a story and need that could last all day, and now that listening is the responsibility of the two Sisters and not mine. My journey here simply to do the ritual that the Sisters cannot do. Allowing myself the relief from this former care no longer mine.

Today a Sister did not accompany me. At one bed an old woman buried deep in her sheets asked me in a weak, sad voice whether I was from Saint Malachy.

She then told me how when she was a child in this neighborhood, her mother would take her there to church. Her father was in Baltimore, and she and her mother were poor and lived here and there in rooming houses.

What hard, sad lives these people had. Things have changed so much in these last 50 or 75 years. Difficult to imagine how people managed without welfare and pensions and the free medical care now available sometimes.

The woman deep down in the bedsheets seems so alone in the world. From her few words I suspect her whole story: she never married and has no children, might even be an only child, and in her old age with mother gone, she probably has no one in the world and is still in and out of the rented rooms of her childhood.

I wanted to lift her small, aging body from the bed, hold her in the embrace of a caring son or daughter whom she does not have. Somehow communicate to her that even when we have no one close or near, we are each of us beloved of God who counts our hairs and knows our tears and sad stories and loneliness.

But how do you do that without being presumptuous or preachy or saying things you only shakily believe yourself with hardly enough conviction?

I tried to slow down somewhat. Heed the woman quietly. Let her know that I was truly listening to her story. Madeline is her name. I shall have to tell the Sisters to pay some special attention to her. Somehow she seems as humble and lonely as ever I have seen here.

# 6

Holy Week coming. How I envy those priest friends who because they are teachers or retired or simply do not have the feeling for it all never get into all the preparation. All my life I have been wishing that I could escape all that detail work of preparation: the music and the servers, the preparation of palms and outdoor speakers, the basins and towels and place of repose for the Blessed Sacrament. Then the liturgy of the Lord's Passion on Good Friday is so different, so unfamiliar, that I must actually study the sequence and make certain the servers do not appear lost or confused up there in the sanctuary with me.

And all of that is nothing compared to the preparation for the great Easter Vigil where the 24 people to be baptized stand, either themselves or holding the children to be baptized. Who will do the six or seven readings and what are their cues for coming forth?

"God is in the details," says Mies van der Rohe about architecture. So with liturgy or worship also. Important to make these signs well so that they speak worthily of the grace they celebrate and bring about.

But the detail work bringing it off is demanding. Those few years when I was at the Cathedral as an assistant, the seminary students came and did the detail. With that exception, I find myself with this responsibility every year. Several meetings already, and with Holy Week just one week away I have to set my mind to it. A rather predictable responsibility given my choices and fate as a parish priest.

I certainly do not have the interest and enthusiasm of earlier years—particularly those years of liturgical reform following Vatican II when we were enthralled with the possibilities of the new English liturgy and the restoration of such practices as the washing of the feet. In our excitement we thought that the beauty and meaning of these new forms would simply win the hearts to the Gospel, much as Simone Weil says that beauty is what brings us to grace. She made her parents take her to the great Benedictine Abbey of Solesmes and was motionless in church for hours and hours listening to the Gregorian Chant.

So Holy Week can be important between all the detail work.

Most of my lay friends who shared with me the enthusiasm for all this now surrender to the exigencies of family life. This is all too long and esoteric for children, and they must build their own church habits around the children.

Or simply all of it is too much. More ritual and worship than anyone needs. The truth of the Protestant reaction.

Next week I shall try to remember that in all those services which require my bodily presence, as they indeed do. On Good Friday, when I place my lips on the rough wood of our huge cross, I shall express physically by that gesture an acceptance of the cross in my life which is still far from me. Perhaps the physical gesture will pull me along.

# 7

A late night call from a street friend of 20 years. His light-hearted manner and voice told me that he had been drinking earlier. Not drunk, just lighthearted and less depressed than his usual self, alone in that rooming house watching television or whatever.

He called to make some sense out of religion, that important but impenetrable reality which I represent to him. His own religious origins only some fierce fundamentalism of an aunt, which he abandoned as early as he was able.

His question was about heaven. That later happiness which makes up for all the misery now. Expanded by his few drinks, he was trying to imagine heaven—all those people of all those centuries. And what do they do with all the time on their hands?

The hour was late, and I did not have the time to get into it all. He sensed my reluctance—annoyance even and let me off easy: "I'll call later in the week," he said and hung up.

I guess I am even threatened by the heaven question and was annoyed by the late hour of his call. Heaven talk is the most frivolous part of the religious talk. People living well do not seem to need that hope anymore, and people who do believe seem too negligent or indifferent toward this life and its reality. Alienation, the Marxists call it, but now they are gone too. And religion remains. Invoked even to help us win the war in the Persian Gulf.

The only thing I can do with heaven is what Simone Weil says we are to do with truths of faith: they are to be embraced with the heart more than understood in the head. Holy Week is coming, and again I will hear the Gospel of Good Friday when Jesus turns to the thief beside him with the promise: "Today you will be with me in paradise." The whole scenario unbelievable, one dying man seemingly as helpless as the fellow next to him making such an outrageous promise.

So. In recent years that promise does not figure large in my own prayer or work here. It would seem a betrayal of my real task, which is to make life here a little easier or better or happier or manageable. What happens to them in some other life is a mystery and something hidden in the mercy of God.

# 8

Sometimes I wonder about my interest in saints who seem so preoccupied with suffering: Thérèse of the Child Jesus, Margaret Mary Alacoque, John of the Cross, Simone Weil. Even Dorothy Day and her bleak view of her world from the Bowery.

Psychology has us wary of pain as anything attractive, and I can see pathology at work in the cultivation of trouble and pain in my little anorexic friend.

Indeed, friends often chide me humorously about my own bleak sensibility. People have come to expect such sad questions from McNamee. So I should be aware enough of my bleak side to be wary.

Yet when I hurt—and I am hurting now—I am pulled to prayer as I am no time else. Most times my hurried, frantic self gives prayer short shrift, despite my complete conviction that prayer is important and essential and the exercise of our highest and best selves.

When I am sitting in that cold church because I hurt and do not know where else to go and what else to do, half of me is feeling sorry for myself. Sorry that I hurt so, that I am so weak and fragile and not tough and able as I imagine others are.

Another part of me senses obscurely and without much comfort that the call here is a rare gift. Most churches and chapels which I haunt are quite empty all the time. Precious few people in our secular world are inclined to seek these places out and want their hurt somehow to pull them in closer to the Mystery that we call God.

I think this is what those saints sense when they welcome pain and say they are even grateful for it. They have that same sense of themselves as I, do only more refined and acute. They know themselves deeply and discover that the pain makes them more aware of their own fragility and dependence on grace and prayer. They welcome whatever brings them to that awareness. Yet pain is pain, and our sensibility recoils from the hurt. The deeper the hurt, the more we recoil.

Pain would be easier if we could imagine ourselves heroic and suffer nobly. Most often the sense prevails that we have brought the trouble on ourselves and are even a burden to others. Henri de Lubac says in that small book, *Further Paradoxes*: "When we really suffer, we suffer badly."

# 9

The last stop on a run through the hospital is a 36-year-old white fellow about to be transferred from the medical unit to the drug and rehabilitation unit.

I am tired because I had a late night last night and a longer run here today than I expected, and Holy Week is almost upon us, and I am always on edge around Holy Week.

Big problem. The patient is over the edge. His one task from all the social workers around here is to travel by public transportation to an adjacent county where he resides, obtain the welfare card more or less waiting for him at the public assistance office, and return to the hospital.

Well, the whole project is so beyond the fellow still in a bedgown and in bed smoking a cigarette that he lapses into some lament about his parents putting him out and how he does not know what buses to take him there.

Suddenly I am over the edge, wildly calling a friend at the transit authority about bus routes, fiercely taking a phone call from his weeping mother telling her how he can only deal with one thing at a time, and right now getting into rehabilitation is the priority, not his relationship with his father.

Finally I turn on the fellow himself: "Look, you have all day and only one fairly simple, if lengthy (four buses each way), thing to do. I have a thousand tasks back at the church. All you have is this one thing. Get it together and get out of here. Here is five dollars to supplement whatever bus tokens the social workers here give you."

I leave him, and the Sister accompanying me on the bed tour marvels at my energy, suspecting correctly that more adrenalin than compassion is at work. Meaning a compliment, she tells me that I should be a social worker. In no mood for a compliment and annoyed at my own display, I say to myself: so concern for the realities of this situation is social work and I guess religion is giving the patient warm fuzzies or something.

Before I leave the hospital and while Sister and I are having coffee (I hardly need caffeine) in the cafeteria, a page for me on the public address. Back we go to the fellow's room where nurses and security guards and social workers have gathered. It seems that just before I met the patient, his upset over buses and routes had him say something suicidal which the nurses heard and had to report.

Now the wait begins for the psychiatrist in another building who may or may not arrive, and the patient may not get started early enough to complete his travels, and we are into the weekend so that he is more distraught than ever about where he will spend the weekend since his parents will not have him at home.

# 10

A trip downtown today with our resident Haitian family. An early start. Father and mother and three daughters instructed to arrive at the Immigration and Naturalization Services at 8:30 a.m.

So much easier for them if I go along. An automobile rather than guiding a shy foreign family through the intersections of subway and bus and walking crowded streets full of people hurrying to work.

And the clerical collar helps. Clerks and security guards and immigration officials are so much more helpful and courteous.

Amazing the violent juxtaposition of life in a modern city. Here just adjacent to a luxury hotel an overcrowded, overheated waiting room full of Oriental and Caribbean and Central American people looking for green cards or extensions on their visas or the next step in their laborious immigration procedure. No privilege or amenities here—just the endless waiting, the restless children, someone taking fingerprints and another taking passport photographs, people who cannot speak English talking to clerks who cannot speak Vietnamese.

Nothing dramatic, just the sense of visiting a vast underground adjacent to a luxury hotel. The world of refugees who are grateful for a job picking berries in New Jersey for a few dollars a day, while next door people are spending more for a continental breakfast than the immigrants' day wages.

Money is the bottom line. Worth and acceptance, importance and nonimportance are all measured by whether one can afford that continental breakfast or not. Two buildings away, on the far side of the luxury hotel, is the diocesan office building where the bureaucracy of word processors and photocopiers and bulk mailings flourishes as fiercely as in the hotel, and ignorance and indifference to this subterranean world of refugees and immigrants is just as obtuse. True, Catholic Social Services has an immigration agency and even cosponsors an office here where a patient Polish woman takes photos and fingerprints. I am disappointed they charge those refugees for this service; the Church is generously supported by freewill offerings.

Even my presence here is more symbolic than real. The only priest who can really minister to these immigrants must be a refugee himself. Someone whose finances and future, whose precarious status and lack of privilege is as real as their own. I am here as a visitor, an extraterrestial in this circle of *Inferno*. Never for one moment of my life have I been so completely at the mercy of bureaucracy as they. Never have I wanted for a dollar or any necessary assistance. My clerical collar and privilege enables me to help my refugee friend and his family here enormously, but I am far from sharing their life, their ordeal.

Indeed the Church does not even want priests living that "low." No problem with priests becoming lawyers or teachers or even physicians. All these are professional people. But the Church would have immense problems with a priest becoming a sanitation worker, say. The suppression of the Worker Priest movement in the 1950s an expression of that problem. Respectability and professionalism and affluence are as unquestioned values in the Church as they are in the luxury hotel next door. All this despite the unprofessional cast of the first disciples and apostles, the origins of the early Church in the lower classes who were attracted to the Church because the Good News seemed to preach the end of the world and some cosmic deliverance from the social injustices of slavery and poverty which oppressed them.

# 11

A dreary March day and walking to the hospital for some dreary dinner meeting where half of the nearby clergy, Catholic and Protestant, who said they would attend will simply not show up. During my walk I notice how desolate and forgotten this shabby neighborhood looks. Across the rooftops you can see the bright new tower downtown outlined in designer lighting. Not far away, yet a million miles away.

I also notice that my fatigue is not the weariness of an aging body toward evening of a busy day. More the long-haul, weary feeling which sleep does not relieve. Even some heaviness which I should honestly call depression or anxiety thrown in. Holy Week is part of the story but not the whole story. More psychic strands than I can unravel. Just have to be patient with all this. The self I have to work with right now.

The religion inside is not going to suit me. Not something I am comfortable with, but I should attend just for reverence to this modest struggling place trying to provide health care to this poor neighborhood.

The half who show for dinner are all women except one elderly preacher there with his wife. He is dressed in his full clericals as I am—black suit and Roman collar and an elderly dignified wife on his arm.

Here in this seamy neighborhood these not-old-or-young women who volunteer faithfully, visiting both medical and addict patients here, are as happy and grateful for this modest dinner as if they were in some expensive restaurant high up in those buildings downtown, nor do they show any sense of being at an unimportant event in a forgotten corner of the city.

Their every sentence is followed by some religious exclamation, like "Thank God" or "Praise the Lord." For them importance has nothing to do with location or affluence or whatever. The sense that they believe in this work and the privilege of visiting the sick poor or sick prisoners here is a great privilege, a joy even. They see Divine Providence everywhere. The chance meeting with some responsive patient, the chance happenings that have them doing this work these months or years.

I walk home reeling. Beyond or beside the fundamentalism which I still cannot handle, something else going on here altogether missing in me. More than one way of being poor.

# *12*

Holy Thursday. Perhaps those years as an assistant at the Cathedral parish were enough for a lifetime. Whatever the reason, I do not attend the priests' gathering today when most priests come together with the Archbishop to celebrate the Mass of the Oils before going back to their own parishes to celebrate the evening Mass of the Lord's Supper.

Dave Hagan does not do any of Holy Week beyond showing up on Easter Sunday morning for whatever Mass he is assigned at the parish he has been serving on weekends these past 10 years, and my Irish friend across the river in another diocese observes the fraternity of priesthood by visiting me on Holy Thursday. We have coffee and cake together.

My reasons for not going to the Cathedral are probably the same Dave Hagan has for not going or Michael visiting me rather than going to the Cathedral gathering over there. Perhaps we should be more tolerant and accepting, less righteous or arrogant or indifferent or whatever our absence says. God knows the Church with all its nonsense and frailty is no less perfect than all those other institutions and associations which we participate in as well as suffer: nation and city, peace organizations, interfaith groups, neighborhood efforts. . . .

I don't know. First of all, an economy of energy. Living as a priest within the Church, the need to keep at a distance some of the ways it would absorb you. One could live in the Church as though it were a complete intramural world.

Simone Weil says that Roman Catholic worship still retained an aesthetic restraint lost in the excess of modern life. I am sure that remains true—more or less—with the reformed Holy Week. However, she says these rituals are unrelated to the rest of life. That also remains true. The Holy Thursday liturgy is so elaborate, so involved, so arabesque or something that things become "disconnected," as Dave Hagan would say, a favorite word of his.

Again, the insertion of some reaffirmation of celibacy at the Holy Thursday Mass of the Oils is a problem.

Not even celibacy or the recommitment to celibacy. I suppose renewal here is as healthy as renewal of marriage vows. Rather the identification of priesthood with celibacy and the Vatican trying to use liturgy and liturgical spirituality to resolve a question that should stay open: are we going to make celibacy a value more important than the Eucharist? I examine my conscience on this: would I object to other uses of the Eucharist to make a political statement, the Eucharist as a war protest, for example?

I would. Here at the parish we never pray the intercessions for causes or programs. We pray for people afflicted by causes and ideologies.

Anyhow. Today is Holy Thursday, and I regret that I am so limited, and the Church is so lackluster that I cannot eagerly gather at the Cathedral. My fault as much as that of the Church.

# *13*

Just as I was about to put Good Friday to bed as indeed a good day in Church and on the street where Catholic Peace Fellowship does a Stations of the Cross downtown, we came out of church into a pleasant evening to discover that a car had been stolen.

All of Holy Week, a suburban couple who came to the church almost every Sunday now came to services with their two grown children. Seeing them, I am always both encouraged and embarrassed. Encouraged that they come so far and thus we must do something right to attract them. Embarrassed because I know how often my pulpit words or the whole celebration is not everything I wanted or anything worth traveling 20 miles to share. Dave Hagan says I am too hard on myself, that I should simply accept that our work on Sunday or Holy Week is quite good and that people come simply because they are enriched by their visit.

On Good Friday night, the suburban couple came out of church to find their van gone. Police arrived, the usual note-taking and card-checking. I was reminded how after Christmas Midnight Mass an entire family of visitors was held up at gunpoint and robbed of wallets and watches and rings.

The lengthy police action afterwards only adds to the letdown. One faces the truth about how little Christmas or Holy Week mean just outside a church where we are celebrating the immense meaning of these feasts. One realizes how little one is reaching or touching the neighborhood despite the endless food lines, the parish school, the neighborhood.

One is always grateful that the armed robbery or theft was not worse—that no one was injured.

One also wonders whether these friends will ever return or whether we shall become more and more alone and isolated in this neighborhood, deprived of the presence and help of the visitors who are such an encouragement to the parishioners and myself. I know the parishioners are pleased to see the visitors, whose presence is evidence of our good effort here at choir and all of worship.

Amazing too the resilience of people. I guess after a Good Friday liturgy when the Cross is venerated and the Passion of Christ is read again and celebrated, the loss of a car seems small suffering in the scale of things or the larger realities of this neighborhood. The visitors suffered the inconvenience easily and even with humor. They took my own car for their journey home, and I know they will return tomorrow for more reason than to return the car.

# 14

For lots of reasons, all the way from childhood, I am not good dealing with all the preparations of feasts and holidays. The edginess inside me is always on the brink and I can fall over into impatience or anger all too easily. People sense this and are wary or careful with me. An embarrassment this fragility, a humiliation even. In recent years I am more conscious of this fault and do whatever I can to ease things.

Holy Saturday is a difficult day. The Easter Vigil requires infinite preparation of detail, ceremony and church decorations, books and candles used only on this one night, clues when church lights go on or off, vital statistics for the 20 children and adults to be baptized, arrangements in the hall for some refreshments after the long Vigil and Mass. Over all this the sense that I should have something to say at homily time worthy of the Feast and all the effort of others to bring the Vigil together.

Foolishly I also arranged to see a college student who is home for Easter. She must write a paper on the 60s, and her mother asked me whether I could see her. For an hour on Holy Saturday afternoon, between phone calls or whatever, the young student and I talked about the Catholic left and draft board raids and Karl Kabat, the Catholic priest spending still another Easter in jail for antinuclear resistance.

Still the interview is not foolish. Allowing time for other things away from the detail may be just what I need to become more calm and be easier on the others around me. Thinking of Karl Kabat in jail for trying to make Easter happen more in our world might be just what I need for a better homily.

# 15

Easter Sunday. The daytime Mass is a muted "alleluia" after the Great Vigil when we were in Church for about two and one-half hours and baptized three adults, the rest children and infants. Something in me wants this long, complicated story of creation and Abraham and the Jewish people and Moses and the Red Sea crossing as image of our baptism to wash down into the hearts of ordinary people as the story of the love which made the heavens and the stars reaching into many wombs, making each of us by an act of Divine Love fleshed out in the lovemaking which made us also.

I wish all could see and hear the disorderly splashing around of 25 awkward, confused, shy baptismal candidates as further love. The rebirth, the call of faith, the summoning of hearts to God that follows sooner or later the bodily call to existence.

Even while I am splashing them and praying over them and rubbing oil on them, I know it is all too much to believe or absorb or understand.

Yet what else do we have except these strange myths and stories, bread and wine and water and oil? I am up there like some modern painter, wildly throwing colors onto a canvas and telling people what these strokes and shades mean.

Along the way, all these years I had to make some effort to understand all this. I know the whole configuration is utterly beautiful and awesomely deep, inexhaustible. Meaning within meaning. Jewish Passover lamb whose blood on doorposts spared the Jews became the Lamb of God whom we put on at Baptism like new Easter clothes. Only Gregorian chant had the genius to contain the whole wondrous mystery. Simone Weil said that Gregorian chant and Romanesque architecture were expressions of genius. I recall that her mystical experience came during Holy Week while listening to the Gregorian chant at the services in Solesmes and in the midst of a migraine headache. Her biographers say her father was unable to move her away from the chapel for any moment of the services.

Of course, Simone Weil understood every word and symbol and was transfixed by the wondrous beauty and truth of the mystery being sung and celebrated so elegantly in that elegant place. A far cry from my clumsy efforts, and besides, there are few Simone Weils around. Even while celebrating the Great Vigil, the wonder and obscure joy of it all together with the futile sense that most of it is being missed.

# 4.

# *Going Away and Coming Back*

# 1

Off to Ireland today. Easter was fine at Saint Malachy. The Church looked great and we sang "Alleluia" at the Vigil and again at the late morning Mass. One hardly knows what to say by way of homily. I shared the good news that our prayers and work trying to get Steven Blackburn out of jail were answered; the governor will pardon his life sentence. The new life of Easter for Steve who became a Muslim in prison.

# 2

*En route* to Dublin, U.S airports are full of black people tending the security checks, the baggage chutes. The airplane maintenance that has us mostly middle-class people, up, up and away. One is always reminded of the privilege in which one lives. One should always remember the privilege that travels mostly on the backs of the poor.

Nevertheless. The road to Dublin from the airport is banked on both sides with bright yellow daffodils. Both sides of the road all the miles or kilometers into the city. Easter week with this yellow clamor. The hour is early morning, and soon I see people coming and going to weekday Mass in numbers unimagined elsewhere. Belloc or Chesterton called Dublin the last outpost of Christianity. George Bernard Shaw called it the world's largest outdoor lunatic asylum.

Something in the genes must draw me here. I love every crowded corner, the doubledeck buses reminding me of Dublin history as a provincial capital, a little London, Anglicized and less Irish for centuries now than those areas beyond the pale. Even something in this aging celibate self responds to the lovely faces and forms of the Irish women; smart or casual, who wait at crossings or at queue lines for buses. Bookstores and Trinity College, the General Post Office where on Easter Monday 75 years ago the troubles began. Again I am home here. Or I would want to be at home here. Again it must be the genes.

# 3

The luxury of reading on the morning of a day when other people are out working. Just as I notice the sounds of a hammer on wood somewhere beating nails into the joists of a new doorway or whatever, I come upon a line of Seamus Heaney in an essay on the poet Patrick Kavanagh: "the inexplicable melancholy of distant work sounds" (*The Government of the Tongue*). Something registers in me. I have had the experience as described by Kavanagh: "all caught in a language that was both familiar and odd."

And the catching is a very observant hold on a small sliver of life—the melancholy of work sounds. Melancholy why? Inexplicably melancholy. Why? More important than any answer, the careful noticing of life in its infinite and minute detail and trying to catch the detail in words. Heaney or Kavanagh or someone talks about the "boldness of going at the blank page." Hopkins would walk around the Welsh countryside, catching in his notebook descriptions of clouds rolling in and out, the color of spring flowers or the wings of a dragonfly. Not many with that urge or talent or discipline. Graham Greene said somewhere that a writer had to be spectator of life even more than a participant. The writer cannot even have much more purpose than to catch the life sliver which no one else might catch if he does not. In the author's note to his own collected poems (1964), Kavanagh wrote: "My purpose in life was to have no purpose." Earlier in the same brief piece he wrote: "I have a relief in poetry as a mystical thing." Well, if life or writing has no purpose, then the only alternative is the mystical.

# 4

What luxury, these retreat days. "The morning has gold in its mouth," the saying goes.

I am at table in retreat silent with a gentle Irish Sister also here on retreat. We did converse our first meal together and then agreed on silence.

That first conversation and even her appearance have me comment further on this tragic, dying Church. Perhaps the real Church worth saving or belonging to is the Church represented by my table companion. She belongs to an order long cloistered. Years ago they took wayward women and girls into their cloister by way of court remand and rehabilitation. A kind of holy jail, I guess. They even had a side order of "Magdalens," street women or delinquent women who so decided to turn life around that they became contemplative Sisters themselves.

No doubt this tradition fostered much madness—excess and even tragedy. Yet the idea of Magdalen cannot be unacceptable. The term is biblical, and Mary Magdalen is an honored Christian saint. Nothing wrong with a Charles de Foucauld or a Thomas Merton either.

Nice to share that table and one full conversation with the Sister during these days of Easter. Her presence gives the sense of someone who has left her earthly self behind already. She works among the very poor of Belfast, in and out of homes of abandoned, neglected women burdened by children without ever learning the emotional or physical resources to run a house or mother children. She only talked about her work in answer to my questions or comments on the conditions of North Philadelphia. She spoke with such feeling on the plight of these families, the wonderful opportunity hers to be among them, share their life and suffering somewhat, the satisfaction of helping a young mother to learn cooking, say, and thus care for the children better. Her lowly, unsung work seems her life in the best sense and she seems to need no other life or love or children of her own.

Oh, I am sure this impression of mine is an idealization of a stereotype which some feminists can and would resent. I would want to say the same things were she a Brother or some volunteer layperson working in prisons or an AIDS hospice. And I am sure the picture is not so clear or undimmed as I would have it. Perhaps, like me, the Sister doubts it all and is whining to the retreat director about her weariness of the work, her poverty at prayer, her unbelief or yearning for some more romantic life—a home and children of her own before it is too late.

What I want to say is that a piece of this Sister—and all human life comes in pieces that do not fit neatly together—represents a tradition, a piece of the Catholic Church which I can believe in. A piece which I hope we do not lose as we discard so much along the way. A piece infinitely more important yet invisible than all the hierarchical and even theological nonsense. The New Testament is, after all (and according to Simone Weil), a way of life much more than a theology.

Nor do I want the hierarchy using the selfless miracle of this Sister, her life and work to sustain and bolster their church as though we could not have her without all their bureaucratic nonsense. They live off her like parasites. The people support them and their nonsense because when those who still do believe and contribute see the working church, they see this quiet Sister, and they as well as I can believe in her.

# 5

A retreat can be difficult. The salt of your own tears and stewing in your own mess is not easy. That might be why I avoid retreats. Often enough I am not good company for myself. One needs the comfort of friends, the distraction of things to do and places to go.

A great help during this retreat were the Patrick Kavanagh poems which my friar friend showed me and even mentioned in our most helpful sessions. A wonderful help, this director. A wonderful work, this spiritual direction. Not a phrase that would have much cash value in the fast secular world. Yet an important, even crucial work in helping us discover and befriend our own depths where all our trouble comes from as well as our gifts. A good director—Teresa of Avila says they are rare—can help us find ourselves there and do the gentle patient work we must do to change wounds into blessings. Like Jacob wrestling with the angel. There are good and bad angels. And in the darkness, difficult to see what we are wrestling with or where it is going. All we know is the fearful darkness down there so uncomfortable that we are not inclined to delay there.

# 6

Sunday Mass in a huge, handsome church in a small Irish town outside Belfast. This earlier of two Sunday morning celebrations is so prosaic, without music or much joy even here at Eastertime.

The priest, I am told, is gentle and good, but timid and has poor health. In the homily he even says something about the people there not having much if he is all they have. Painful, that sense of limitation. I can feel it out in the pew. Someone uncomfortable with himself doing the best he is able with the difficult task of praying and speaking and inviting and gesturing in matters that can make someone very self-conscious—and uncomfortable, especially if the person is uncomfortable with self already.

So the mystery of the Church. Or the pathos of the Church, that grace is communicated to us through these often limp signs and celebrations. Little talk more than a new seminary burse in memory of the recently-deceased Cardinal.

But maybe that sense of the sacraments is too mechanical. Maybe the people there have some sense that their priest is fragile and timid and his effort up there connects with their own sense of themselves as poor and weak and failing often and coming here for mercy. One can imagine or hope for so much more. A work of joy or hope in this Easter season. A word of reconciliation or healing here near Belfast in Northern Ireland in a week in which there have been political murders almost everyday. The Church is as human as it is anything— more human than it is anything else. If people do not get a good spirit here for their violent world just outside, where are they going to get it? But God is patient, and the mystery of Grace is a mystery mired in human clay—myself or that priest up there or the parents and children on every side of me here. I would want to be very patient with the parents' limitations, knowing that their own childhood story deeply affects their own parenting. I should bring the same kindness to the timid priest perhaps stuck with a task quite beyond him, at least according to my expectations. And finally the retreat tells me that I should be kind even with myself—for all the same reasons that I need to be kind with these parents or that priest up there. The mystery that we call God is larger, greater than this lackluster Mass. These people know that better than I. I live so upclose to the Church that I give it too much importance. Yet all this does not mean to dismiss the great yearning in so many that the Church be the healing and comforting presence among us that we need. As much here in the north of Ireland as anywhere.

# 7

This evening visiting an Irish cottage which two years ago I visited with a friend who called it the most beautiful place he had ever seen.

Tonight I am writing by a window looking out and down a hill to the River Foyle. Across the lough, the sun is lighting up a headland mountain with a last orange blaze. Sheep and cattle graze on the green fields which fall away to the lough where I can see small waves breaking on the beaches of small coves and the tidal pools. One field or patch near the water is lined with the furrows of a farmer whom I saw yesterday making the furrows with his tractor. So distant is that field that I could only see the tractor moving without hearing a sound. Every sheep seems to have a lamb or two suckling, and there is the occasional black lamb, like the other lambs no larger yet than a housecat.

The fishing boats return from a day or days out in the Atlantic. Smaller boats sit at this mouth where river widens into lough and lough soon empties into sea. Across the water another Irish county. Earlier today one could see Scotland some 50 miles across the water.

I am so alone here that the silence can be ponderous. I will go outside to hear the wind in the trees or the bleat of a distant sheep on the chance that might happen. Now the orange has left the mountain and lingers on a large dark cloud. The wind is brisk, cold really. I shall wear a coat to stand on the rise to watch darkness descend so slowly but finally so black that the lights far across the water or on those fishing boats seem like stars on the horizon.

# 8

Morning on Inishowen. The splendor framed by this window is beyond belief. Visual contact is not enough. I want to take my coffee and stand just outside the cottage where the land falls away to the water, and with the blowing grass feel this wonder in the brisk wind which must be constant here, yet diminished by the hills of Donegal rising behind me just beyond the road.

The morning light on the water—a vast opening of river into lough into North Atlantic has the earth as bright as the sun, which here is bright, there dark on the water because of the swift clouds. Fishing boats come and go seaward or homeward. Again all this such a panorama that this place is far distant from any sound but the rise and fall of the wind.

The sheep and cattle seem to stand in the far field just as they were last evening. Again so distant that the new lambs with each ewe so small one could not see them unless you knew the lambs were there because of the season and seeing them at closer hand along the road.

Surely I have seen sheep before, yet never being in Ireland at lambing time I never saw these little ones so little or closeup. Utterly innocent and fragile, they have a young, frisky and playful manner lacking in the watchful protective mother who seems so intent, so vigilant that she allows yet hardly responds to their nudging into her for milk.

One can only imagine the meaning and feeling in John the Baptist when he saw his cousin coming and pointed to him: "There is the Lamb of God." One can sense also the way I should mean and speak when at Communion I hold Him up saying also: "Behold the Lamb of God." Such a wondrous image, we would hardly have chosen something so lovely to bespeak or express a mystery so mysterious. I am in awe of the image and sorry that I do not bring that awe to every Mass. "We are his people, the sheep of his flock" (Psalm 100). The people need this nourishment as much as those lambs need their mother's milk.

Years ago I was at a monastery for retreat. The time was before the new Catholic worship and we were all eager for the Mass away from Latin and in our own tongue. There at the monastery an old German couple who were friends of the prior were living in an old farm guesthouse and helping the monks with their music. In conversation the old music scholar expressed to me his sadness that we could lose the Gregorian Chant and lovely old Latin hymns altogether. "Yes, but now the people will understand their prayers," says the eager I. "Father," the old gentleman courteously answered, "I am not sure that if we do not take time to learn what *Agnus Dei* means, whether we shall understand what Lamb of God means either." More fair and thoughtful than to offer this as some full or final reason, the old man merely wanted to sound a warning about easy solutions.

# 9

Bunbeg is within the Irish-speaking part of Donegal. A wild and barren stretch through the Glenveagh wilderness of bogland and mountains.  A brown and beige field of nothing but sagelike grass bushes going off into the hills which are constantly in and out of the late afternoon clouds.  Now and then a spit of rain on the windshield.  Here and there a pond or small lake beside the narrow road where you can see your only route for miles ahead.  A strange and desolate place.  The kind of desert that would attract those early Irish monks so drawn to deserts where the spirit can be tested as the Lord was tested in the desert.  Kenneth Clark says in *Civilization* that this earlier, wilder Irish monastic tradition died or gave way to the Benedictine tradition because the earlier was built on a heroic image.  Saint Benedict came later with that Mediterranean sense of moderation, a discipline available to ordinary spirits.  The thought of those early monks half freezing or starving in places like this or out on those forsaken rocks like Skellig Michael, eating seagulls or whatever sounds spartan and muscular, and perhaps it was the warrior of a primitive society transformed into a spiritual warrior.  William James says that before society can do away with the military, we must discover something to replace the discipline which the military provides.

But I think those rugged old monks were about something deeper still than warrior discipline.  The *Writings of the Desert Fathers* reveal a great wisdom and spiritual achievement.  A wild place like this eerie, beautiful bogland is a mirror image of the wilderness within, the maze of emotion and mood and ego and libido and superego which Freud travelled much later.  The monks knew the truth of Ram Dass: "The only work we have to do is on ourselves." Whatever good we are to society or others is finally the overflow, the abundance of some gathering within.

Just the sense that the early monks knew this wilderness within and put themselves in this bogland as proper setting and image to reflect on for their lifelong journey within.  Self-mastery not for its own sake but for discovery.

# 10

Saturday night at a pub in rural Donegal looking out on the sea.  The locals are all Irish-speaking and include all ages from very young to very old.  A man dancing with his daughter; "Shoe the Donkey" is the dance.

An Irish musician in America once said how remote and beautiful Donegal is, "not like the rest of Ireland at all—a place completely apart." I recognize types—faces and hair and sizes I see back home because so many Donegal people came to Philadelphia. I can see Eugene McFadden in that tall fellow or the white head of Charlie McAneny in that other.

The music is quite traditional and the absence of rebel songs quite noticeable, save for singing "A Nation Once Again" at the very late conclusion of the evening. Everyone became quiet and stood at a relaxed attention.

I asked the woman beside me, who turns out to be the owner, if the rebel songs are put aside because the troubles just next door in Derry are so fierce, with murders almost every night. She nods yes as though to agree that this is indeed the reaction. Donegal is very close to the troubles because Donegal is the hinterland of Derry and people are back and forth very often. One fellow whom the IRA killed last week in Tyrone was killed because he was identified as part of a Unionist attack or bombing in Donegal a few years ago.

Anyhow. The huge worn hands of these farmers, their workshoes and ever-present cigarettes, their quiet ways even among themselves conceal a huge gentleness. One thinks of that line from Hopkins from "Brothers":

Ah, Nature, framed in fault,
There's comfort then, there's salt;
Nature, bad, base, and blind,
Dearly thou canst be kind; . . .

These hard-working, often hard-drinking farmers and workers do not sing the rebel songs for fear of stirring a pot which hardly needs stirring in the counties next door.

# 11

To begin with, they should heat the place. I do notice radiators in the small old stone church sitting on a brae over the sea, lovely as a sea gull on a rock.

Indeed the air outside is fresh enough, yet warming in the good morning sun. Inside, without the sun, the cold is quite uncomfortable.

All this conspires to bring one into the presence of some cold gothic God this Sunday morning. Again the earlier of two Masses and again no music, no lay readers; the priest goes on in that dull recitative voice that we bring to this routine. The mood is flat and moralistic, that linear presentation which accepts the fact that this is a Sunday obligation. Obligation it is and little else.

One comes back out into the fresh morning wanting still to do something joyful, festive—relieved to be out of that cold, lifeless place. A good breakfast with warm coffee and good talk to give some substance to this grand, still quiet morning.

Something joyful, festive should have happened there in church. Again not the priest's fault. He seemed a kind, gentle, middle-aged man. And he did try to do something with the Gospel story of the Good Shepherd on this Sunday of Easter when the Mass readings present the Risen Lord as the One who leads us safely through the Valley of the Shadow of Death. People are going to come to this only because they have to, and fewer and fewer feel they have to come. The whole recital is so flat that attention is quite difficult to sustain. Nothing there to hold you.

That priest up there is about my age. His seminary training would have discouraged the artistic and creative. The tone was moral and impersonal. One was to communicate objective moral and doctrinal truths which had nothing to do with feelings, interpretation, incarnation.

My experience in the black community these years now is such a contrast. Black people come to church because they want to come to church or need to come to church for strength and inspiration for another week. The singing, the swaying and praying, the fervor are all an effort to *feel* Sunday morning. I do not do that part of it very well. Much inside me conspires against giving feeling and display such importance. I do try to be honest about more *mental* feelings, if you will: compassion for victims of war or the difficulty of believing. But I could not be there these years and not let the people take over somewhat, assume the parts and music which they came to express, the cry of the heart which is religious joy or need.

We do not have Saturday evening Vigil Mass in any of our parishes in the neighborhoods back home because no one attends them. So absent is the sense of Sunday as an obligation that one either comes on Sunday because one wants to come or one does not bother at all. Operating more out of impulse than superego, I suppose, and the larger picture back home is that neither my parishioners nor anyone else in the neighborhood attends church regularly or in great numbers.

Again the Church failing to do well that most important thing she is about—gathering people to hear the Word and celebrate communal faith. To hear the Church talk about herself, you would think that she does this and most other things magnificently well. Again during the evaluation of statistics back home which showed that only 33% attend Sunday Mass, the quality of the celebration never was mentioned. Implicit acceptance that obligation and linear morality are the rule just as they are here this morning.

Simone Weil says somewhere that our ordering is backwards: the beautiful should invite people to its inherent goodness, not asking people to be good and telling them to believe in the beauty of that goodness.

# 12

That awesome rock phenomenon, the Giant's Causeway, only a good walk from here. A stack of stone cylinders reaching out in the direction of Scotland, which can be seen across the water on a clear day like today.

The folk tale is that the hero Finn McCool was building a stone causeway connecting Ireland to Scotland. Nearby is Rathlin Island where Robert Bruce retreated and hid out in a cave. More recently, the very first radio transmission by Marconi was made from the Irish mainland to Rathlin Island.

The Giant's Causeway has the appearance that a huge side of a mountain just fell into the sea. The pyramidal rocks still sustain the steep high cliff. One part has the name and appearance of a pipe organ, the long slim rock table visible high up on the cliff retreating from the sea.

The sense is that of being lost in the mists of prehistory and time so unlimited that a human size and the years of my own human story seem insignificant. Everything about me is threatened. I am lost in immensity of space and time. The cosmic terror which Pascal felt looking at the heavens.

The terror is just the opposite of everything else here in Ireland where human problems, like the "troubles" in the North or unemployment or urban decay or the environment, seem human scale.

Back home in the United States, the devastation of the South Bronx or North Philadelphia has the scale of the Giant's Causeway, problems beyond human capacity and containment, society run wild; North Philadelphia goes on and on and the quality of life so wounded that we would need the impossible, a full-time therapist or teacher for every drug addict or prison inmate or disadvantaged child.

Here in Ireland a sense that imaginative faith and creative effort could in fact and in a short while handle these very human-scale difficulties.

William Lynch, S.J., says somewhere that the real terror of modernity is not the cosmic terror of Pascal rather the nausea of Sartre. The idleness, the proliferation of things and talk, the excess in all direction caricatured further in the writings of the absurdists.

# 13

Dave Hagan fetches me at the airport. Getting from Kennedy International Airport in NYC to Philadelphia as difficult and delayed as ever so that my arrival home was quite late.

The weather too was an adjustment. A warm spring night had the city as alive as a night in the middle of the summer. People everywhere. The affluent in the restaurants and bars, the poor out in the streets, young and old. Here the beginnings of a quarrel, there some youth running from some trouble he had just started. Crowds of young people out looking for action or a few dollars.

After Ireland, all this is like a blow to the head. From a small society where evening means sheep out on the hills and morning means the same sheep quietly feeding on the same hill, seemingly in the very same positions, to this scene which is something like a huge overcrowded outdoor brawl.

A good part of me resists this return. Soon I will be back in the heart of this vortex. People at the door, old street friends awaiting my return and looking for the few dollars available only from me which will suspend—certainly not resolve—their most recent crisis.

Dave is always puzzled by this Irish gravity in me, wondering what questions it answers, what resources it offers. For Dave there are no answers, and the only seeming resource is a dogged, immense compassion. We stop somewhere for one last Irish whiskey—he a Southern Comfort Manhattan—before the full return. He is completely undone by my airplane companion whom we dropped off in the suburbs, an illegal Irishman with little more than a high-school education, in this country only three years, who has a successful contracting business, a new panel truck and two employees. All this with a North of Ireland brogue so thick that when he talks fast you can hardly catch a word. Dave is in disbelief. The fellows who pass through our lives are for whatever reason unable seemingly to pull anything like this off. At least neither of us have seen a single example of this kind of success or achievement in 20 years. Dave had one spectacular success abuilding: his part in the college career and superstar professional prospects of basketball player Hank Gathers whom Dave guided through high school and California college. And Hank Gathers falls dead on the court last year before 4,000 people. Something in Dave went down with Hank Gathers and it shows in every phrase.

"Take a good look out there, John," he says as we finger our drinks, looking out on the clamorous city streets near midnight. "You can go to Ireland and get in touch with your origins all you want, but here you are back and out there is home and summer is coming—which you and I dread—and you will have to deal with the craziness of it all somehow." Nobody sums it up as awfully and as truthfully as Dave. I cannot imagine what I would do without him up there, despite his brutal, painful, accurate vision.

# 5.

## *Aesthetics of Asymmetry*

# 1

Here, even in the old city, streets dressed in pink dogwood and other lovely colors these few brief weeks before the great greening. Hopkins somewhere calls it "a May-Mess," but I cannot find the poem . . . well here it is, not his wonderful "Spring" but his equally wonderful "The Starlight Night" where he actually is looking at the night skies and sees stars so many and in such clusters that he calls it ". . . a May-Mess, like orchard boughs!"

While I have Hopkins out, I shall look at his "The May Magnificat" also, a more pious and traditional poem summoning memories of May Procession in childhood and May Devotions during seminary years. Memories both pleasant and unpleasant, yet inner space to be revisited just for fuller understanding of my whole story.

My own melodrama needs me to notice spring here as well as in Ireland. Perhaps more here than in Ireland because the pace, the stress, the abandoned houses and littered empty lots everywhere require that kind of relief.

So I shall notice the trees along these streets, the azaleas now so scarlet and pink and purple as close as the small lawn out front here at the church.

"The beauty of the world," as Simone Weil calls it. The lilies of the field where Jesus pointed. I notice the faith or confidence or hope or whatever ebbs and flows inside me is more precarious here by reason of geography or leisure or attention, I am less connected or in touch with "the beauty of the world" which helps us to believe.

Simone Weil says the beauty of the world is like a work of art as opposed to an artifact.

Ten years ago I tried a poem of my own around that idea. I was in New Mexico and had just visited the Grand Canyon and was overwhelmed by the beauty of canyon and desert. Out in the middle of nowhere my guide and I stopped to share a lunch he had brought along. At a turnout for a panoramic view somewhere between the Sangre de Cristo mountains and the red clay canyon country of northern New Mexico, a small bird of the most extraordinary plumage and coloring stopped momentarily on a closeby cottonwood tree.

Both the bird and the Grand Canyon seemed mysterious in that their beauty had some meaning even larger than human viewing. I thought this tiny bird might never again be seen by human eyes, that other birds like this lived and died without ever being seen by a human glance. Like the Grand Canyon. The morning I was there the sunrise, the light reaching down those different layers of rock to the river, was so beautiful that I thought of the immense age of the canyon and how many such mornings came and went before human life even existed, much less any human eye saw that light.

What did all that mysterious beauty mean, those magnificent passing mornings never to be repeated or seen? I guess we can say the tiny bird's color exists for mating, but even that phenomenon is beautiful and mysterious also.

# 2

Downstairs this morning to the news that someone apparently smashed a truck or whatever through the chain mail fence of our schoolyard parking lot and made off with a new leased car one of the Sisters in the convent has with her job.

The school building sits between me and the schoolyard, so I heard nothing. The Sisters did hear the crash and were hesitant to venture out. They reckon that the car was stolen later in the early morning hours and that the smashing of the gate was the preparation for the theft.

Hard to imagine that such mayhem can happen and people just glance out and return to their beds, but apparently nightlife has been fierce during my weeks away. The other priest here mentions hearing gunshots frequently at night from the public housing tower just across from us and police sirens are nightly fare.

Hard to imagine what kind of vehicle could come crashing into the two huge, swinging, steel-wire gates without becoming a wreck itself. The gates have an inch-wide steel pin which goes into a sleeve sunk in the concrete. Of course someone could lift that pin by reaching through the mesh. The impact sheared off the steel plate welded to one of the gate frames so that the padlock was left on the other gate unopened.

So the morning becomes busy with calling the welding company which dismantled our deteriorating flagpole several years ago, police reports, trying to repair the situation so that cars can enter and leave the school yard without encountering the loose gates, also a hazard to the children playing in the schoolyard this bright May morning. Amazing how the children absorb all this as though it were normal morning fare after a pleasant spring night when people are out and around and the neighborhood is alive.

Even I am doing well in my gray hairs. I absorb it as well as the children. Again the premonition that I will just have to pull my belt a notch tighter. Summer is coming. . . .

Later this afternoon I see the Sister heading out with a companion to the police station. They call out to me that the stolen car has been located. No sense from here what the damage is.

# 3

The blood-red azalea on the front lawn struggles with the world news for my attention. May so breathtaking this Saturday morning, and because I am back from Ireland only a week, I have not yet scheduled leisure out of my life, so I have the time to breathe in the morning, the blue sky, the cool fresh air and that azalea out front around the pedestal of the concrete Ladyshrine.

I brought down to Mass a poem Hopkins wrote for May, something also intended for the front of a Mayshrine like the azalea. Amazing how Hopkins took in every blessed detail of his May morning at the Jesuit house in Stonyhurst. Hopkins writes:

and azuring—over greybell makes
Wood banks and brakes wash wet like lakes.
                              "May Magnificat"

The other reality which intrudes, clouds the May morning, is the news from Bangladesh. Indeed the dead from the cyclone are 100,000 with thousands upon other thousands without food or clothes or drinking water and suffering all the diseases that follow such a catastrophe.

The issue of *Commonweal* magazine dated yesterday has a fine remembrance of Graham Greene, giving me some words of his to put on this disaster: "Clumsy life again at her stupid work." The phrase hardly seems large enough for such colossal suffering, but the self seems so small and powerless in the face of such an event that the Graham Greene shrug seems to express our powerlessness.

The *Commonweal* author puts Greene in the camp of the Spanish philosopher Miguel de Unamuno, whose words describe Greene's shaky belief:

Faith is in essence a matter of the will, just to believe is to want to believe, and that to believe in God is to wish, above all and before all that there may be a God.

I guess I shall have to put myself in the camp with de Unamuno and Greene. Wanting to believe. Keep my eye on the wondrous azalea while I am being assaulted by the Bangladesh tragedy.

# 4

That quiet Saturday yesterday went well until about noon. An old friend, a now-married priest, was in the neighborhood and by telephone said he would be stopping by. With the doorbell I put aside the deskwork to learn that the caller was a familiar street person. The expected caller was still coming up the walk—past that wondrous azalea.

Together in the foyer, friend and I heard the street fellow out. Deep inside I am annoyed that he comes on Saturday when little can be done to help, even if his problem can in fact be helped. Perhaps unfairly I am also annoyed constantly that these city and social agencies operate according to the convenience of the social workers rather than according to the need which feeds the job. Finally, the school or agency begins to exist as employment for the workers rather than the "human services" of the needy, as they say these days.

Of course any mention to the fellow that today is Saturday is out of place. He might not know and certainly does not care what day it is. He knows that he hurts and this is a church and I am able and should be willing to help him. Good Samaritan and all of that.

And the fellow rambles on, nervously and erratically. I notice that he is not asking for food or money. Deciphering his shallow phrases, I hear him asking if some judge would give him permission to die. He does drugs and drink and is homeless with both his parents dead. They lived just up the street here, but when I asked where he slept last night, he said something about a box or hut or crate on a lot at Franklin and Jefferson, just a few blocks east where the neighborhood looks bombed out.

He keeps repeating phrases like "no use" and his "life is over" and "nothing can be done. " He says that he does not have the courage to take his own life, but perhaps some court or judge would do this for him.

My intention was to run out to lunch somewhere nearby with my friend. Saturday. Indulge yourself. Get back into things slowly after the weeks away. Besides the long, hot summer ahead of you.

Not easy to do that now. A few words or dollars to the fellow here and then business as usual? Hardly. Human decency and guilt and image require something. I begin the predictable calls to predictable places and persons. No avail, of course.

Next we take the fellow somewhere I had not been able to reach because the phone was busy. No room at the inn. And I am edgy for my visitor. This is not his thing as it is mine from living here with desperate fellows like this all over out there. This is what I am going to be doing and should be doing.

Dead end. I honestly do not know what to do except to give him five dollars. I hesitate to write this even. The left hand should not know what the right hand is doing.

My only justification is that these exchanges and experiences should be recorded so that people out in the suburbs, people like myself or my visitor know how bad and desperate things are in these neighborhoods, hidden now beneath the interstates as we speed over them off to the beach or a workshop.

I beg the fellow to return Monday morning. I have a few names and places and resources to help him if he is able and willing for help. He can survive until Monday. He is a street person, better at living by his wits than I am certainly. I have no great hope that he will appear on Monday.

The thought always occurs to me simply to take him in here. Doing that so immediately or spontaneously seems mad, crazy even. This place is a functioning parish. Tomorrow is Sunday and we have the Masses and Sunday school and all the regular traffic, and my man is a dysfunctional person. He needs even short-term to be in a place where people have as main job taking care of him.

I do have to work at this. Even after 20 years up here I excuse myself from the direct manual hospitality of Dorothy Day too easily. I have to work on this. Do it better, more generously.

My friend and I do get to lunch and around to talking about his interests after an hour of time and travel on my concerns or should-be concerns.

He is very active in organizations and efforts to reactivate married priests and broaden the concept of ministry to include others besides priests. All this a worthy concern indeed. The neglect and indifference and worse for these men from a Church which throws words like reconciliation around so easily is outrageous.

Yet somehow after the hour with the street fellow, all this seems so middle-class. Conventions in California, assemblies in Europe, the whole business seems cast in the mold of professionalism and academics and what the bishops think.

Who cares what the bishops think? You don't need ordination or marriage or unmarriage (maybe unmarriage helps) to jump into this crazy world of beggars at the door asking to die and no room in the inn. God, I hope that fellow comes back on Monday.

# 5

Thirty-two years ordained today, a fairly keen memory of that day. Never capable of much religious excitement. I think I was worried that I could not share the ecstasy of my classmates, most of them anyhow.

Years later, a classmate who has since left the active priesthood interpreted my calm or whatever as a sense of foreboding, some intuition of mine that later on this was going to be more difficult or complicated than we could ever imagine.

Indeed it has. Hard to imagine anything that has come apart more thoroughly than the priesthood package conferred on me under the hands of arthritic old Cardinal O'Hara those years ago.

A few days ago, I tried to dismiss the Church questions as unimportant—celibacy unimportant up against 200,000 Bangladeshis drowned and thousands more dying.

That does not keep the lesser questions from being a great burden and anguish to people, including myself. That married priest friend who visited me left me several issues of his *Diaspora*, a magazine of priests who have left to marry and miss deeply their ministry as they yield to other human needs—the needs of home and hearth and human love and parenthood. Things quite integral and necessary for full human life and not easily put aside, or at least not so easily put aside as we imagined 32 years ago. A lead article in *Diaspora* is "Beyond Traditional Priesthood," where a married priest assembles a line of awesomely-important theologians who are saying and have been saying for sometime now *Eucharist without Ordination*: the Eucharist is real not because the celebrant is real but because the gathering is a real gathering of the Church, and people have access to the Lord's supper whether an ordained person is available or not. I am not learned enough in theology to discern all this and have to stay within the traditional framework until this all plays itself out. Even the possibility of this certainly undermines most of my earlier images of being a priest and all the sweat and effort seminary and years since have cost me. Whatever. Let it be. As John of the Cross says: "One who has lost all is ready to be born into all." What seems spiritual disaster can become precious spiritual opportunity. What I am doing these years in North Philadelphia has precious little to do with traditional sacramental ministry anyhow. I am on the edges of Church life by reason of neighborhood anyhow. Learn to live on the edge better. A question of balance.

The Sunday newspaper had an interview with a priest my age whom I know from his long and distinguished standing in the Alcoholics Anonymous community. Not an alcoholic himself, he says that his addictions were food and work, and his losing 100 pounds and marriage and recovery from burnout were part of his own recovery, learned from his work with recovering alcoholics. He discovered he did not need to be a priest to do the work of these years, that he became a priest for many wrong reasons, that without the priesthood he is just as able for his work, that hard-earned freedom after lengthy therapy of some kind or other gave him finally the freedom to put aside this burdensome dimension of himself.

Well, I shall just have to live with all these changes and reports which threaten me deeply around this 32nd anniversary. Modern life places great value and priority on human freedom. That priority might go back to Sartre or Camus or further. The idea that life is absurd and what we do or choose so meaningless in the end that the only value is that we act freely, since freedom is so exclusively human. We who stay—who would choose the isolation and loneliness of the priesthood for no good reason—are caught in the dilemma that only by leaving can we ever really know whether we are staying or leaving freely.

Yet freedom is not an absolute either. People act as destructively and foolishly pursuing freedom as they do from constraint or unfreedom. If I were a married man with children, I would want to be unable to walk away from someone to whom I pledged my life or children whom I had brought into the world.

We are all so different. The freedom of one can be the compulsion of another. The person who runs off to something or someone new can be as compelled by his anxiety as the person who stays home and unhappy because he lacks the conviction or courage to leave.

And none of us is so free as we think or desire. Freedom is not some ultimate state beyond all compulsions or anxieties or guilt. Freedom is a small fringe on our humanity. Small areas which we can own in the midst of our larger pathologies and compulsions.

So what we do because we need to can be as valuable and salutary to ourselves and others as the gallant, daring thrust of freedom. Simone Weil thought the only human actions worthwhile are those done from necessity. I know she means external rather than inner necessity, but they are related. We must accept who we are and where we are, the real world but also our real limitations as we go along. I do not want some heroic grasp for some ultimate freedom to consume me or become the sole meaning of my life. Something to be said for staying here, doing what I am doing, accepting myself as I am in all my freedom and unfreedom. Realizing also that being a priest in the traditional sense has great value in that people are nourished by this traditional ministry or work. Being unmarried has meaning also. I could hardly live here and be with the people here as I am—clumsily—with them unless I am alone and not responsible for others in some familial way.

Sombre, ambivalent, even painful thoughts for an anniversary. Given the times, given what has happened out there since I was ordained 32 years ago, what other thoughts can I have? A difficult head place, but a human one if only that my head is there. Again our whole tradition says that the falling away of old forms and certainties is a precious new opportunity. Eventually we have to get around to playing the hand life is dealing us. Welcome it even.

# 6

A wondrous May day and a trip to Princeton to visit a friend who is teaching there this semester.

I cannot believe the beauty along the way: the white dogwood, the pale pink dogwood so delicately, so exquisitely colored that no painter has ever caught all those shades which come as the sun climbs higher. The wisteria are such a light purple, almost gray or blue gray, and I notice that the azaleas even this tiny distance farther north are just cresting, while the azalea bush on the small church lawn has already peaked.

The beauty of the world. The green explosion. No explosion is too mean a word . . . the trees breaking into green and all of them different shades of green and the underside of the new green leaves of one tree still a different green from the shiny side.

The ride is enough to lift me from the heavy thoughts of yesterday, of being 32 years ordained and quite older than most everybody around my life. The beauty of the world this cloudless May day. No matter age or aging or loss of old certainties, we live surrounded by a beauty that we must absorb so that we can even endure the news from Bangladesh or the grime and decay of the streets I drive through to reach Princeton. The color, the magnificence so abundant, so unbelievable that I cannot not notice it, cannot not be overwhelmed even. I am pulled into it despite my doubting, bitter, hesitant self which says: don't be drawn in by all this; most people can see this spring spectacle and absorb it for what it is—something that just happens in season, something worth driving through. No need to let it take you anywhere. But this May day takes me somewhere, reassures me mysteriously about the love and grace in which we live, that also is gift. Perhaps a gift given me and not the others who need not take it anywhere. Just as their gifts of wife or children or whatever are not my gifts. Accept what is yours, what is given. Be simple, grateful. Welcome this lovely May day.

# 7

Ascension Thursday and my birthday.

As glorious as yesterday was, today is cloudy, cold and overcast. And I had to spend a great part of the day at police headquarters bailing someone out of jail. Waiting the interminable wait of those places. A young woman—the unmistakable look of what we call "poor whites"—waiting with me to bail out the boyfriend she had locked up last night for beating on her while he was drunk. She asks: "You a Catholic priest? I never seen a Catholic priest in a place like this before."

So on my birthday I am overwhelmed by how drowning I am in the chaos of my neighborhood after only a week back from Ireland. I feel fear: can I do this again . . . will I make it in the long haul . . . is this all too crazy to try . . . . is this sadness in me pathological . . . have I wandered off the deep end submerging myself in this bedlam? Even here at the police building people begging a dollar from me . . . no peace, no quiet, no hideout . . . too quick the drowning in all this only one week back . . . as though I were never away.

Whether I make it or not, better here than elsewhere. The remark of that woman; "I never seen a Catholic priest in a place like this before," says much. Better here even if I do not survive in any traditional sense. Better failure here than success somewhere not at life's point, as Dan Berrigan once said.

# 8

Last Sunday such a lovely day. The eastward scene framed in my morning window quite perfect. So perfect that I walked outside to the church entrance to vest for Mass in the vestibule. I wanted to pass the azalea bush on the front lawn at the foot of the Lady statue. The azalea is perfect, as though creation herself had arranged a Mayshrine like those of a Catholic childhood when we stole flowers from lawns on the way to school to dress the small Mayshrine in every classroom.

Walking past the azalea bush and shrine, I am pulled into the beauty of the flowers, while another side of me pulls me into shadows and doubt: how can you go on like some Victorian about a flowerbush when 200,000 Bangladeshis might be dead? Back and forth. A roller coaster ride.

Walking up the aisle gowned for Mass, I still am unsettled enough inside not to know what to say for homily. I am unable to get up there after the Gospel and say prepared things—I prepare very little—less than honest up against my doubt and confusion.

So what I shall do I decide as I arrive at the altar. It is Ascension; it is the time when the Easter One is leaving "for a little while" so that we shall weep, and then He will return "and you shall rejoice."

So I will tell them about my little melodrama walking along the side of the church a few minutes ago. My struggle, my doubt, my confusion, how He comes and goes like the Christ who in Flannery O'Connor is "the ragged figure in the back of my mind darting from tree to tree."

I tell them about my retreat in Ireland, how by kindness of my Irish friar friend and Patrick Kavanagh I am learning to discover the mystery within as well as the mystery without, in tabernacle or pictured in great stained-glass windows to which I gesture. Anyhow, one of those windows is the Agony in the Garden, when even the Easter One explored or experienced all those dark tunnels I talked about yesterday: will I drown . . . is this all futile . . . will this kill me, and for what . . . ?

I hope these ramblings mean something to someone else besides me. At least because they are efforts to take as honest a look at myself and my insides as I can manage.

# 9

Another wonderful spring Sunday morning. And also Mother's Day. A day when more local people might come to church than usual.

Not the case as things turn out. Both Masses are rather slim in attendance, and I fall back into my never-far-away doubts about this place and what I am doing here.

More of my marginal Catholic friends from elsewhere than local people—by far. Not that the marginal Catholics—among whom I number myself—do not need a place also and we are close enough to downtown for their convenience. Some place has to harbor Catholic Peace Fellowship and married priests and former sisters and Catholic Worker people and those who want to connect with that kind of Church.

We serve by default. So little of that Catholicism is around that people wind up here—or at St. Vincent's in Germantown—by their personal gravity. Not in great numbers either or with any regularity. The few and their unsteady churchgoing habits say something about the situation also.

But the reality of this neighborhood is black and poor, and the foolish hope persists that we might more abundantly serve the neighborhood by way of Sunday Mass as well as food distribution or finding jobs or drug rehabilitation or bailing people out of jail.

Foolish because the realities are that so many around here suffer such chaotic, disorganized lives that regular churchgoing is as unlikely as regular bill-paying. They come when they can or feel the need or are feeling kind about this old place for some other momentary service, like the kindness of burying a parent.

I could say Mass standing on my head. We might have a magnificent musical program at Mass. The church can look as lovely for Easter as this May morning. Still only the few; the regulars will come.

So. That sense of failure reoccurs. Especially on a Sunday morning lovely as this one when life and nature and everything seems full—except the lovely old church.

The thought occurs that someone more than myself able for the happy, emotional black celebration might do better. Yet I suspect that other Catholic churches where the priest does more of that suffer the same empty pews. I even suspect that the large successful Baptist church nearby attracts mostly elderly people, that those churches do not reach the poor, the project people, the single parents any better than we do.

So the wandering through the day and the neighborhood wondering just what you are doing, if anything.

A little light on the subject: the other day when a project woman sent our Sister social worker a letter thanking sister for her work "in continuing the education of my two daughters at St. Malachy's."

The letter goes on to talk about how these nine and ten-year-old students would cry every morning and beg their mother not to send them to the public school. At first our principal was hesitant to take them because of very poor test scores and "they didn't even know how to write in cursive."

And she is very grateful. She goes on: "If you have any doubts about the values of a Catholic education . . . I now have happy children who sing in the morning while they are getting ready for school."

So. Encouragement for my doubting self. Especially the supernumerary or administrative part of me—the fundraiser even. Often I walk around sensing that I do little more than field phone calls. "What do you do all day?" Often enough an honest answer would be that I talk on the telephone.

At least going on next door is a Catholic school with 200 students, 85% of whom are non-Catholic, and the place would not survive without the many friends who are generous here because I beg or visit or because they find here a Catholic worship or effort they can support.

We have no corner on excellence or dedication, nor do I have any feeling for extolling our operation by running down the local public school or dedication there. This is a smaller, gentler environment. We do not have to take all the impossible problems the public schools must take.

The letter of the grateful woman assures me that the place is worthwhile, worth even the dubious role of fundraiser, although beggar sounds more acceptable: "Woe to him who has not begged," says Leon Bloy. Some relief then about being here and doing what I do between phone calls. "Better here than not here" was our appeal letter a few years ago. Better Saint Malachy School than another empty lot up here.

Even with the Sisters of Mercy needing finally to withdraw their very last Sister and our having a fully-lay faculty, still the work is worthwhile. More difficult, more expensive but worthwhile, even with the further begging required in September.

# *10*

A busy day and a busy evening ahead, attending what will surely be an interminable Baptist funeral. The brother of a wonderful teacher in our school who is herself a preacher.

I try to plan a precious 45 minutes after dinner for this entry before going off to the funeral. I know that I will be too tired upon return tonight.

Inevitably the phone rings, and my temptation is to get rid of the familiar voice quickly and get back to my plans. The caller is a long-time acquaintance from the streets. Years ago she lived with her mother and many brothers and sisters in an abandoned house just across the street from a rectory where I lived. I could look out the window down onto the litter-strewn porch. In summer I looked through closed windows (because of our air-conditioners) on her and her sisters and brothers out on that porch on a bruising summer day, searching for a mouthful of any air cooler than the squalid inferno inside.

In winter I knew they were in there huddled around a kerosene heater because five dollars now and then for kerosene was a big item in our relationship with Sandy and her mother and the other children. No electricity, no heating system, no plumbing, no running water.

The grandmother lived up the street and I just presumed they all went up there for toilets or washing. The grandmother ran a speak-easy from her home, an unlicensed bar where people could gather and socialize and buy a drink.

Sandy called me just now to say hello: "Just want to tell you I have been clean of drugs for one year and two weeks. My children came over from my mother-in-law and we celebrated my being off the stuff . . . hard for them. They seen me when I been on."

I had no track of the ages or number of her children, so I ask. "The oldest is 15," she tells me adding that she just had her own 30th birthday. Her youngest, "my baby," is eight, and all together she has five children who live with the mother-in-law because she was unable to tend them those drug years, and her common-law husband has been both alcoholic and drug addict all these 15 years. I ask about him and she does not know his whereabouts. Word is that he is in jail again, she adds.

She is calling me just to say hello and "keep in touch" and to let me know that she is doing "just fine" in some house away from here provided by some subsidized housing agency. She lives with a friend. I know her well enough to ask whether he is a male friend, which he is, and she is on public assistance because she is attending school learning to be a meat cutter.

Sandy and I have a stormy history. Sometimes her drug problem made things impossible. Once I had to cart her off to a hospital because she had taken so many pills that she was falling asleep standing up or falling down or however. That was the time I came back to take those children—younger then, of course—to her mother-in-law where they have probably lived ever since.

Again she was living in an abandoned house which somehow she managed to obtain from the city. A suburban friend of mine put a roof on it—no big deal, only a thousand dollars, but the new roof kept the rain out.

Later, while the children were still with her, that house became a crack house. Some druggies around began using it for drug deals: a sexual exchange behind a curtain that was the only privacy in this place without inside doors. No money exchange: drugs for sex, sex for drugs.

Often enough I drove her off to some emergency detox unit or some residential program. Inevitably the stay was short and she was back out on the street again, soon calling me again in the middle of the night in some crisis.

Eventually I gave up. We get older and tired and discouraged or cynical. I lost all trace of her except for those occasional calls "keeping in touch." In recent months and years I tended to give her short shrift, not even asking about her children. Tonight I tried to be a little different, more patient or caring. I asking all the questions which gave me childrens' ages and husband's whereabouts. We were on the phone about ten minutes before she signed off saying: "I love you."

# *11*

From early Sunday Mass in Ireland to a funeral service in the Church of the Deliverance in North Philadelphia is a trip to the moon. Farther even.

The church is a huge old theater. The congregation is building a real church up here in North Philadelphia, the largest church built in this city in a hundred years. I cannot fill or even heat this old place here and the black church can finance a huge place that will cost millions.

The service so emotional, so charged, so lengthy that the sisters and I left after two hours, and the main eulogy was still a long way off. People sing and wave and jump up in the middle of a song or reading shouting "alleluia" or "thank you, Jesus" in such an altered state of consciousness or something that time does not matter, does not exist.

Nowhere have I seen a Catholicism that can connect with that level of feeling. Nowhere. Never.

I realize the congregation is still a small enclave in a brutal drug landscape. Even that fierce feeling and enthusiasm wanes just outside the doors. The larger reality the drugs, the street life, the broken families, the brothers stealing cars and breaking into stores and going to jail.

I do not understand it. People there can go into and out of some ecstatic state four or five times during three or four hours—religious feeling or something that I have never experienced for one moment of my life.

I cannot even say I admire it or trust it. What good when it goes no farther than the church door? Everything in my culture and training and background has me distrust such intensity. I guess I have learned to believe in intellectual intensity, but what good is that either? I have no more answers than the people I was with there in that church. And I do not have their joy, their faith or whatever it is.

I remember that Simone Weil haunted churches like that when she lived briefly in New York after leaving France with her parents in flight from the Nazi occupation.

My friend, Simone, was a mystic. She could look at it more deeply and directly than I. She could see the movement as an invaluable way of bringing some people to the Mystery that we call God. She had no need to see it against her own inadequacy.

This week before Pentecost I had been thinking of a Pentecost years ago when the very first black African cardinal visited Philadelphia. Monsignor Mitchell, that frail and heroic priest whom I was later with as my pastor, was so excited in his almost pathetic way. He arranged a great Mass at the Cathedral and the black Catholics gathered. I remember the responsory antiphon of the still-new English language liturgy for that Pentecost Mass sung triumphantly:

The Spirit of the Lord has filled the whole earth.

We sang it over and over. The feeling was that this new, vigorous Catholicism could finally be true to its name, Catholic, and embrace the whole world. And here we are 25 years later with any such hope or illusion as far from me as the exuberance of that fundamentalist church tonight—from my tired, distant, even discouraged self.

The Church is so far from being any practical solution to the problems of this city or the world that that earlier experience with the African cardinal must have been some altered state of consciousness itself and an illusory one at that.

# 12

The subpoena reads 8:30 a.m., and Family Court does not even open or allow people inside until 9:00 a.m. A rough wait in winter but on this early summer day in May, I can sit on the front steps with my parishioner in big trouble and look out on Logan Circle, that most lovely part of the city modeled on the *Place de la Concorde* of Paris, with the Swann Fountain geysers representing the three rivers of Philadelphia surrounded by trees and bushes and tulip beds all aflower and people moving briskly to the tall towers and up to their offices.

I am part of the horizontal action, not the vertical ascent. Just beside me the archdiocesan tower filled with priests and religious who should be everyone of them, including the cardinal, here with some family rather than at the word processors or photocopy machines which they operate all day. A priest friend says that if we stopped all that paper-pushing for one day we might discover or rediscover the Christianity lost as early as Constantine or whenever the Church became just another self-serving bureaucracy like the corporations whose taller towers shadow the archdiocesan building.

I shall be here for two hours before the judge appears inside. If I am lucky and a clerical collar has any clout left, I shall be summoned among the first, receive the continuance which our most helpful lawyer wants and be on our way home. Two hours just for the defendant's signature on his new subpoena.

A memorial service at the hospital I tend for an employee who has taken his own life. Not a name I can put a face to. No wonder people come to dislike priests. We get rolled out for occasions where we are complete strangers, intruders even. But that does not stop the words. Out they come. As often as not words that do not help the situation very much. Better that some coworker speak to the situation. Some personal, memorable remarks about the deceased.

The service was on me before I had time to work that all out, so over I go. I borrowed some things I said the one or two times I have been involved in such a tragic death. Those remarks borrowed in part from an Irish priest friend who had to speak about this on a still earlier occasion.

I mentioned how life is very hard for all of us and even impossible for some who at the center of their being are so fragile, hurt that they just cannot endure that hurt and loneliness not always visible or verbal. Their plea to us: "Listen to what I cannot say." In the end, only the Mystery that we call God can hear that. I borrowed my Irish friend's metaphor of a child home from school early through fear or sickness, and the parent greeting him: "Stephen, you're home early, too soon."

I explained that living in these neighborhoods 25 years, I seldom use the expression "God." I use rather Karl Rahner's phrase: "the Mystery we call God."

All I said further was that we really should not fear for Stephen home from school early. Despite all the dread that we bring to suicide, God is greater than our dread. The Mystery that we call God, Father of the Prodigal in the parable of Jesus, is even more welcoming of our fragile, even foolish selves than the caring parent who finds the child home early from school.

I surely hope it was presentable. I felt so distracted, hurried from all that went before during that day. I felt so the intruder into a gathering larger than I expected. No one said much. I hope I was not offensive. I hope I was some comfort, especially to the young fiancée of the deceased whom I did not know was there until I was introduced to her afterwards.

# 13

A cup of coffee in the hospital cafeteria with a drug counselor at the hospital who is a seminary classmate of mine and long departed from the active priesthood.

I am here because this afternoon I went to fetch my longtime street friend, who became sick at work. This classmate has been his weekly counselor. Of course we come to talking about my "codependency," the $20 or more I seem to feed my street friend every two weeks, more or less.

He has to learn to live within his means, not take on more responsibility than he can handle or afford, pay his bills and even save something if he wants to live differently than crowded into the single rented room with improvised kitchen and bathroom where he now maintains his younger unemployed brother and the children back with him because their mother, who is his former common-law wife, collapsed under drugs and is in a hospital somewhere.

I know that co-dependency is a real obstacle. The Alcoholics Anonymous people who meet here are very strong about it and discourage me from any handouts at the door—especially money.

Yet when I think of my street friend's transit fare to work—two or three zones between city and suburb—his expensive methadon maintenance clinic fee, which is either $40 a week or a month (which shows how much I know or don't know for all my years up here), the pull on him from these penniless children of his for spending money for new sneakers, I wonder how he can manage at all much more than I question his always needing help from me. He has rent and food for these children, the expense of the laundromat. When I was home on Sunday for Mother's Day and my birthday, one sister slipped $20—the most recent of many—into my coat for "gas." The birthday card from mother and another sister had two $50 bills. That kind of care has never happened to my street friend for one moment of his impossible life.

I remember once visiting some friends at Christmas. Several handsome and beautiful children home for the holidays from expensive colleges and out and around with friends to expensive restaurants and theaters, presumably at parents' expense.

Uncharacteristically, a parent said something unfeeling about all the lazy young people back down in my area living off welfare.

I went for the jugular, pointed to her lovelies heading out for an expensive evening. I said: "Don't you think your own brood here have their own very profitable welfare system going?"

Dave Hagan who visits and tends his aged mother so faithfully was years ago so hurt when she said something about his "spoiling" the fellows around his house. He saw a double standard: ordinary parental love she saw her grandchildren getting was an excess when seen in Dave and his surrogate children.

I know too the need to bring some intelligent discernment to the human mayhem all around us up here. Yet somehow that calm professional sorting out which the counselor and I do in the hospital cafeteria is so short of the reality of my friend's harsh impossible life.

I do not want to be up on the professional level, detached, distant, reviewing his chaotic problems as the material of my 9 to 5 workday. His situation is overwhelmingly the result of the racial injustice and neglect that sent his father under and drove his gentle mother, as I knew her, to drink. The schools he attended, the opportunities he did not have, the absence of stable family life and incapacity for sustained relationships—all these things have him poor and sick and barely employed. And $20 or talking to his drug counselor is little more than patchwork, meaning nothing beyond itself.

I guess I believe in just being here, stuck here as he and so many are stuck here, not being able to see beyond the transit pass he needs immediately. I hope my being here with him means something to him. More than once he has said it does. I shall continue to try to make that enough for me. At least in that respect being poor like him is not seeing or being able to see beyond the present crisis, content to do what we have to do to ease the crisis somewhat. That is as far as I can see these days. I shall have to be content with that. I will not even try to make the situation easier by bringing God into it. That mystery eludes me in all this right now. That poor, I guess.

# 14

Friday morning convent Mass. I should get around to telling the Sisters that the hebdomadary (how's that for an archaic term!) should include a brief homily as part of her preparations. We could move that much toward a more woman's worship.

As it is, I had to say a few words, and the Gospel was that post-Resurrection story about Peter being free to come and go early on. Later his hands will be tied, and he will be led around.

The business about freedom and necessity must be stewing inside me because that is what came out. How we *a la* Sartre and Camus say that life is so absurd that the only meaning is acting freely, whereas Simone Weil seems to be saying that only necessity brings out the best in us because constraint is more free of ego, self. Staying with a marriage because you said you would or raising sometimes un-grateful children because you brought them into the world in the first place are as good reasons and choices as any.

So the events that washed my life into this difficult corner of the world are as decent a reason for being here as any. You are here because you're here just as people around here are simply here. You cannot not be here because this is your place. Simply. I don't know what the Sisters thought about all that. It has not been stewing in them all week. Probably sounds too much like stoicism and stoicism sounds too much like cynicism. Simone Weil says Greek stoicism was not cynicism until the Romans made it so. She says Greek stoicism was *amor fati*. Profound love of the Mystery that we call God as that Mystery unfolds in any life story, like Mary at the Annunciation. The only possible response: "Be it done unto me according to thy word." Whatever. All is gift.

# 15

Some of the love of "awful necessity" should have accompanied me yesterday to the meeting of urban priests.

I was looking for reasons not to attend. Reasons such as the schoolchildren's May Devotion earlier that morning. Finally I went. Something pulls me into the fraternity of fellows managing these im-possible places like my own. We need the support and encouragement of one another. Sometimes I wonder about the increasingly rapid turn-over, fellows in and out of these places in five years.

Besides, I wanted some sense of what is required of me by the archdiocesan fundraising campaign. Here I am strapped with an addi-tional $8,000 yearly as assessment for the archdiocesan high schools which none of my children can attend because they cannot afford the tuition. Now comes still another effort to raise money where, to the best of my judgment, there is no money. Just this week a sister here begged a thousand dollars for a St. Malachy pupil to attend the local Catholic high school. His single parent mother so grateful because he is small and fragile and she says he would be ground up in the public high-school environment. The suburban friend wanted us to find a student for something more exotic, the outbound wilderness adventure which he thought would be an awesome experience for a ghetto youth. We turned his attention to funding something more practical.

The fundraising part of the priests' meeting was something like a pep rally. I should be easier on all this. The Church does need money to operate and the schools and agencies and parishes do good work.

Just that the fundraising fellows look and sound like people from a casting agency. No, I am being unfair. All of them made a concerted effort to speak sensitively about inner-city realities. Some had valuable experience in places like Harlem and the South Bronx. And an archdiocesan effort which did not invite the poor themselves to contribute would be condescending and patronizing to the poor.

Stop. Put anger aside. Awful necessity. What gathers in me here are many other things. Disappointment of many years that the Church is only this, not more than this. If this were some small part of a larger, more caring Church, I could accept it. The Church reduced to this vulgar effort and little else. So hard to take.

# 16

Sometimes I am running so that if an idle hour surfaces, I am thrown off guard and don't know what to do with it.

The tendency is to run from one task to another always back there, waiting for the time or leisure you promised to it.

Mind and body resist such intensity. Yesterday after Mass, several couples who needed attention about a summer wedding somewhere and the high school friend dropped in from Maryland and an Irish couple were brought here to meet the priest just back from Ireland. Some hospitality is required. Coffee with the one couple at the end of the table, then walking to their car with them, and returning to the second and third couple still waiting.

I am like "Holy Joe" Colman, the legendary priest of my time 20 years ago in Chester. Not like him in being holy, but his practice of filling up his room every night with callers whom he had socialize with one another while he slipped off to another room with us one at a time for confession. Amazing the crowd, mostly men, in his quarters every blessed night. The banter was that his not requiring "a firm purpose of amendment" was the reason for his popularity. Utterly devout and childlike, giving me once a holy card of St. Lucy because it was her feast. Holy Joe was the real thing.

When everyone left, I could hardly climb the stairs fast enough. The luxury, the leisure of my rooms such a lure. When I arrive, I always imagine that I shall forthright get into the things waiting on my desk, including this notebook.

Nature resists. Sunday morning is a workout, and I wind up falling onto the bed, shoes and all, or collapsing into a chair watching whatever is on television, hoping it is something Sunday afternoon soothing like ice dancing on Wide World of Sports.

Just when I begin to feel guilty about this hour of indolence, the phone rings. No need to feel guilty. The wife of a new immigrant who hardly speaks English begging me to come quickly. Her daughter "has a bleeding eye," and after Mass here the husband went off to a meeting.

Oh my God, a bleeding eye. Off I go to the house in a car and discover with relief that the accidental wound is a deep cut under the eye, not the eye itself.

The local hospital rather than the farther eye hospital will do, and off we go to the emergency room. I have to translate and interpret and decide whether the doctor attending the emergency room can do the sewing rather than find a plastic surgeon for this facial wound on a Sunday afternoon.

In the midst of all this, a breathtaking little Hispanic girl appears and disappears and appears again from another area of the emergency room. I discover that her still, small cousin is the little fellow on the table with stomach pain and vomiting, and this little woman has all the presence and calm and understanding one can imagine. She even seems to be a reassurance for an older woman who must be mother to her or the little fellow under the sheets on the litter with the big wheels.

"Rose of Spanish Harlem," that song of years ago, comes to mind. Thin and lovely, dark with long flowing hair, the child is on the threshold of early womanhood. Seeing her here I know she must be from the awful streets around here. I am sad for the ordeal that awaits her as soon as this summer. She will have to toughen to protect herself from predatory men. Men who are as overwhelmed by her fresh young beauty and innocence as I am.

Riding home I see others like her, slightly older, on corners with tough young men. Hair is teased; bluejeans are tight, drugs are around, cars spinning, screaming tires, babies. I wish somehow I could throw "Our Lady's mantle" or some gossamer of traditional Catholic childhood over her to protect her from the harsh realities coming down on her as soon as school closes next month.

For better or worse the mantle or gossamer is not there for this little Spanish rose. My priest's shirt and collar seemed to mean very little to her. These Spanish Catholics who fill these streets have fallen through the gossamer. They are so poor that they are unimportant. The Church hardly notices that they are there.

# 17

A day when I went outside only late in the day to vote at the parish school just next door.

The feeling that I did little more today than field phone calls. Nothing very urgent or important. Just the usual traffic.

Late in the afternoon, a summons downstairs. Someone "wants to go to confession" and thus bypasses the others who parcel out food or carfare. Going downstairs, I was already suspicious. The neighborhood and the reality that almost no one goes to confession anymore.

"A white male, about six foot and 40 years old," a police report would read. His dress, his manner told me what I already knew: a fellow down on his luck needing a few dollars to buy a bed for the night at the shelter.

Annoyed and tired, I tried to listen. He was up from Baltimore looking for work.

My manner was enough to shame him. He started or feigned leaving, apologized for the confession trick, talked about his radio news work in Virginia, his marriage, his wife becoming a Catholic in the RCIA process. I was impressed by his knowing all the terminology. RCIA is the acronym for *Ritus Christianae Initiationis Adultorum*, the Rite of Christian Initiation for Adults. A fairly new phrase in the world of Church.

He went on about his marriage coming apart, his own emotional breakdown. He is out on the street, homeless, no one but a brother who is down South and is not about to help him.

No signs of drugs or alcohol. I begin calling shelters and hospices, knowing before I call that I never succeed. The places are always full or nobody is home. The hour is approaching 5:00 and daily Mass here. I want to take the fellow in myself but distrust my own judgment. After the workday, I am more or less alone here. No staff to supervise residents. No security to speak of. I would need more acquaintance with the fellow, some sense that he was honest, fairly functional and the rest. Tomorrow is another day, and when people arrive to work, the presence of a total stranger whom women and others might understandably fear is a real problem.

Something inside me does not want to let myself off so easily. I call Dave. He is straightforward about these things and, like myself, wants to err on the side of being generous and careless and even take a risk. Dave says I am too old to deal with this kind of traffic. These kinds of problems washing up here more and more rather than less. He suggests giving the fellow a few dollars and the address of the place where I was told they might be willing to take a look at him tomorrow.

Just a few days ago, a visitor at the daily Mass at this same hour put $25 in my hand quietly: "for someone needing food."

With the money, I give the fellow the address for tomorrow and see him to the door. Vaguely I tell him that should nothing work out, I will try to help him further.

# *18*

Still the Pentecost thrust. A phone call from the young fellow whom I asked on Sunday about his unemployed cousin.

Both live with their grandmother in the projects down the street. Projects which sprawl for blocks and are known as among the very worst in the country. Several years ago, my very dear friend now in Washington D.C. who has given his professional life to public housing was in Philadelphia for some federal hearing on public housing. He wanted the Chief Counsel for the Congressional Joint Committee or whatever on public housing to see the places they solicitously but abstractly talk about.

We visited the unit where the two cousins live with grandmother, the still high-school twin of one of these cousins who has two children at 18, the mother of the other cousin—the small child left by the mother of the twins when she died from drug abuse. All these people in two bedrooms, a parlor with completely broken-down sofa and chairs and a kitchen hardly more than a closet full of insects crawling from sink to empty pantry.

The one cousin was here on Sunday, escorting his two little sisters whom I forgot to count as also residents of the small unit. Their mother is the woman who wrote the most grateful letter about our taking these two little girls into the parish school tuition-free. The girls are preparing for First Communion soon, and I am so distracted that I do not even notice the devotion that has them here every Sunday since Easter in their white baptismal dresses, according to the lovely custom of the newly-baptized wearing the white, all "clothed in Christ" all the Sundays until Pentecost. And of course their baptismal dress will also become First Communion dress of Corpus Christi Sunday and First Communion.

Such a touch of tender, traditional Catholic beauty for these two little sisters against the harsh, dreadful, concrete reality of the public housing courtyard where they live with their older brother now in the Army and soon off to Hawaii. They say they all must dodge crossfire every single night. Nobody ventures out after dark. A big lockup, especially in summer. About 10 people jammed into those four rooms. Just the heat, the crowding, the summer . . .

Imagine me so "out of it" that I do not notice their devout presence these Sundays in their white baptismal gowns, now becoming First Communion dresses. Of course, I was away in Ireland most Sundays since Easter. Try not to be so hard on myself. . . .

The visit of my friend and the congressional counselor brought about some high-level attempts to find larger, better quarters for this family. The effort almost made things worse. The local public authorities coming down on the family for having more residents than allowed for a two-bedroom unit.

Back to the phone call which came from Sunday and church and my telling the cousin in the Army and soon off to Hawaii to call me about bringing his unemployed cousin in about finding work. Both cousins are out of Catholic high school a year now and the one not in the military just around the concrete courts down there. One more mouth for grandmother to feed, one more dependent for her beaten, overwhelmed self. I see her weary face, gracious and generous but weary, at the meetings our parish social worker Sister has for the project women. The Catholic high school principal was quite generous with these fellows. When I described the family situation as more than poor, destitute even, he waived tuition for both cousins. My hope was that the fellow would be doing something with that education by now.

After the phone call, the two cousins came to the rectory and I come on strong about the one cousin still a burden to the grandmother, not working all year, hanging around and not much help. Even as I attack, my sense or hope is that my annoyance is seen as a form of caring, upset or annoyed or disappointed that he is not coming through, getting it together. My clumsy version of parent examining the poor report card of his child. I do it with fair confidence that this affection is coming through. I can somehow step back mentally from the exchange and see the two of us—myself attacking and the youth defending himself.

Weary the process. No job because he has no decent clothes, no carfare, no idea where to begin to look. A brochure about some minimum wage city job as a "park ranger" not aiming high enough for his years and time in life. He needs a real job with real wages with a company that will not be out of business next budget cuts, as will the park rangers for sure.

Some talk about a resumé, graduation pictures. If I had his resumé and a photograph, I could send them around law firms where friends might be looking for a courier, small business friends who might make room for him in maintenance. The job would mean a whole new world. Up early every morning, the downtown vitality, dressing up, money in the pocket, feeling good about oneself. . . .

All the fantasy and enthusiasm is mine, not his. He once had a resumé; a counselor back at the high school had it. Perhaps he could get it next week. . . .

Next week? why next week . . . he should have several copies, hold onto the original, photocopy the page or pages.

Finally something personal. The lethargy and whatever, an emotional low these months, a depression he is unable to get a handle on.

And as I leave the cousins with their promise that they will have this pitifully poor and brief resumé with me very soon, I am ashamed and abashed and appalled at my brisk cheerleading with them. Depressed indeed. I know where they live and sleep and eat. The real marvel is how any of them can any morning even get out of bed, face the morning.

# *19*

A casual visit to the home of a close friend. I was in the neighborhood on an errand and stopped by just as remote preparations were beginning for Senior Prom. The daughter and her out-of-town date, the dress and the arrival of two other couples in a huge limousine for a small party of prom-goers and parents and me, as it turns out.

At 58, seeing the parents gather with cameras, I notice how different my life is, how removed I am from the familiar worries and joys and excitement of human life. No children of my own. I notice how these parents are much younger than myself. I could in a few years even be the grandparent of these prom-goers. How much of life has passed me by. I am tempted to say that I chose some other path quite decisively and even confidently. My sense is that would be less than honest. Life happens to us more deeply and even ignorantly than any choosing.

Off to the seminary at 18. I gave myself this project and goal. I shall be a priest. There was even a meditation of the French priest Lacordaire which many printed on their ordination cards:

> To live in the midst of the world without wishing
> its pleasures, to be a member of each family yet
> belonging to none. . . .

Long time since I thought of the choice in those terms. The eager, generous reach of young years. Now I might choose rather a thought from Trappist Thomas Merton, who said later on in his choice that although he never wanted to be anything but a monk, if he had to do it all over again he would never be a monk.

A monk was very much the image of priest that I was choosing early on. Sometimes I sense that many others were not so monastic. The seminary regime was rather eight years to be endured until you could be out and around again in natural, worldly ways. For me and some others the seminary was a nearby chapel where I could often go to be "alone with the alone," *solus cum solo.* A library full of books, an exterior discipline which puts aside concerns like senior proms and seashore vacations, a small room where one could have full privacy: a single bed for necessary but minimal rest, a desk for study and more casual reading, a crucifix to remind me of the essentials, the "one thing necessary" or at least the few necessities of the Gospel.

This quiet evening of a holiday weekend has all the solitude, the isolation even of a monastery, even here in the midst of the city. Quiet now, yet a few minutes ago I heard sirens and fire engines, and soon again I will hear the shouts of children or the squeal of car brakes. Right now I am happy—or at least content—with the removal from *famiglia* or *familia*, the company of a home and spouse and children, the excitement of someone preparing for a prom.

Within the hour I hope I shall be faithful to my plan to slip into the church here for a quiet hour or half an hour. And I hope afterwards I can come back to the desk or the half dozen books I am reading before that empty hour of television which has become my way of going off to sleep.

I feel no desire to join the seasonal rituals of beach or cookout. These hours when the house is empty and the weekday traffic lessens or even stops are precious.

Most of my life I have been exploring this landscape. Even during summers when I was home from the seminary, I was mostly to myself. I worked in maintenance at the parish school closed for the summer. All day I would be alone in an empty classroom, varnishing a hardwood floor in summer heat. The drudgery was immense, yet somehow hard physical labor seemed required along with all the books and whatever.

The parish church had a hand-rung Angelus bell, and my final daily summer task was to ring the 6:00 Angelus and go home for dinner. I gave myself that last hour—5:00-6:00 in the evening—to sit alone in the darkening church, as dark and alone within as I was without. The same dark aloneness will be my companion tonight. It has never been very different, except those times when I have stopped formal prayer altogether. I always seem to return. Alone with the Alone. Whatever it means.

# 20

Almost 20 years up here in the neighborhoods and still I never expect or accept it. Some months ago, we were very attentive to a family where the father was dying. All of them are Catholics and live quite close to the church. After the funeral the wife was so grateful, so comforted by our attention and care during the last illness and the Mass of Christian Burial there, she all on her own began all kinds of assurances that she would never miss Mass again. She would be there every Sunday, she said, week in and week out. Good news. The extended family so gathers around her that her coming has them all here, including the grandchildren who sorely need some regular, attentive religious habits and instruction.

This holiday weekend manifests the erratic church habits which really should not surprise me but which, in fact, leave me so disappointed. No church for any of the family because elaborate preparations are already underway for the Memorial Day cookout in the backyard. Their liturgy this Sunday is the cookout.

Despite my lifelong attachment to the Eucharist, all the theology which says how sublime and important the Sacrament is, I must live with the reality that for most people Sunday Mass—or any Mass—is low priority. A fellow goes in and out of the rectory here often who shares very much my images and vision of the Gospel. His whole work is gathering churches into community that will tend the needs of these deprived neighborhoods and cities. His whole story is as Catholic as my own, and I know he takes his family off to Sunday Mass. Yet when I leave him at five o'clock of an afternoon for Mass with the elderly sister who always attends and the others who may or may not show up, he is simply out the door. My sense is that the daily Mass is part of priest routine, not his.

So here am I full of the wondrous hymn-poems of Thomas Aquinas, especially the *Panis Angelicus*, which in image and succinct word strike me as a perfect poem to say nothing of the sublime musical setting. Eager for Corpus Christi next and First Communion, I must learn to live better with the realization that the Eucharist has been so lost by repetition and poor celebration and whatever that it means little more than a minor obligation to most, a concern far behind a Sunday holiday cookout.

I think we do modestly well with Mass here. The music, the beauty of the old church, the faithful flowers, even by report my effort at the homily come together in a celebration worthy of the inner truth of what Aquinas calls so eloquently: *O memoriale mortis Domine* (O memorial of the Lord's death).

Yet I know that we could celebrate Mass standing on our heads here—or more reverently with full orchestral music—and still we would gather only the regulars, those who already come. Despite my childish impulse to blame the neglect on my inept self, I know more deeply that the empty pews are not my fault. The world has passed all this by. Despite the awesome theology and poetry of Aquinas, despite the attachment of myself and some few others to the Pink Sisters' chapel where the enthroned sacrament is simply there visible and available for prayer, the consensus is that all this is not important any longer and even that the earlier importance was at best an illusion, at worst, an ecclesiastical pretense.

And this consensus which leaves me as alone in the dark church as I was and felt those years of seminary summers threatens terribly that fragile faith of mine. I am still alone with all this. More alone than ever. Possessor of an obsolete religious sensibility. A museum piece. An anachronism.

# *21*

A dance troupe visiting the parish school. Despite my benign neglect of the school, I hear about the visit because the school secretary phones to interrupt my clumsy morning effort at prayer, saying she needs our portable public address system for the occasion.

New season beginning the day after Memorial Day. Easy does it, time for new beginnings, gently put aside the psalms, respond. Be gracious. Blend more easily and effortlessly into these thousands of daily requests. Stop fighting it, the having two lives: the nurtured self of books and poems and journals and literary purpose. Go in and out of it more easily. Go and find the unit for the secretary. Interrupt your cherished plans for a quiet morning hour enough even to stay for the dance performance. For teachers and students and visiting dancers your interest and presence important. Stop fighting it.

Good show. Black people and white people dancing together, ballet and modern dance, tap dance and flamenco and whatever. Beauty too in the lithe young bodies of the dancers. Good for these eighth-grade fellows here to see a man doing modern dance. A modification for their sullen macho stuff.

As I sit in the rear of the auditorium, also a cafeteria needing new tables and chairs and new lighting, I remember the one mental tape I am playing with another dozen: finding some agency or foundation to make that lunchroom a more human space. Round tables rather than the long narrow ones. More attractive aluminum stacking chairs rather than those noisy steel folding chairs. An attractive wipe-clean colorful table cloth and each table with occasional or regular flowers.

Soft music also. I have noticed how high the noise level is at lunchtime. The hundred-year-old building has almost no kitchen resources, so we are reduced to a fast-food, packaged, convector oven system which hardly makes for attractive eating.

Yet this luncheon with all its flaws is the closest many students come to sitting around a table for a communal meal. Desirable that we provide round tables and flowers and a tablecloth of sorts with music to quiet things down. A foundation fellow visiting soon. His foundation funds food, shelter, clothing for the poor. Perhaps we can persuade him to help make something decent of this dreary old hall.

Anyhow. Seeing the delight of 200 children watching the dance troupe makes all this weary thinking and planning and proposal writing and begging for funds worthwhile. A small effort but an obvious achievement. And I have been part of these precarious fragile shaky operations called inner-city Catholic schools for so long now that I am infinitely weary. I know I am weary because I cannot, do not extend myself as I did years ago as a young priest, driving a van, hauling a dozen off to basketball somewhere, planning and producing and directing plays for Christmas and Easter, teaching religion in one or another classroom each morning. I have none of the energy for that anymore.

All I can say is that I try to keep the school afloat. An infinitely small island of gentle Catholic stuff and dance troupes and holiday pageants without my direction. And the glee of the children this morning clapping to the music and dance sends me back to the house realizing, despite myself and my weariness, that all this should continue—impossibly and interminably and faithfully.

# 22

Someone here needs a huge loan to pay delinquent tuition or else his child cannot graduate from the local Catholic high school.

The borrower is a working man, hard put to keep it all together. The wife is unemployed since her firm left town, and no doubt they are having to manage on one income for the present. So they borrowed, only two weeks ago, a substantial amount for mortgage and car payments. Now the tuition crisis. So much effort seeing this student through high school. A pity that he would not graduate because of money. Yet I can understand the school policy. The poor with fewer options walk away from debt as did our school parents several years ago when our mild sanction late in the school year was that no student could return the next year with delinquent tuition still unpaid. What happened was that many parents simply walked away, so many that the school almost went under for want of an adequate student body.

The parent asking for this further loan borrowed once before and did quite dutifully repay the loan in full and in proper time. This time the amount will be enormous accumulatively. Something of a strain on our accounts and a real worry for me as well as him.

Yet where can the poor go for money if not to the Church? They do not have the collateral, the access, the resources of others for the financial crises which are part of life everywhere in this culture. How many affluent parents must be in real debt for college tuition— thousands and thousands of dollars? But they have homes and insurance policies which make these large loans available in a way not available to poor people.

My responses are quite cultural. An impulse to lecture the borrower on budgeting. Something I would not dream of doing to a more affluent person in need. Simone Weil says that the charitable exchange which remains real charity and does not enhance the mutual roles of humiliation and superiority is rare. More a miracle than walking on water.

I know part of my weariness with all this is that the draining never ends. Again my paranoia is cultural: I see the situation as the perception that white people and white institutions have money, even if we say we do not.

And that perception is fairly and relatively accurate. We do have dollars or somehow access to dollars in a way the poor do not. They see cars in the schoolyard; they see us coming and going from retreat to vacation. They see a new vestment in church (which is a memorial to someone's mother really). They see bag upon bag of hardly-worn clothes coming in here and a reasonable conclusion is that the suburban folk who sent them are still out buying more clothes. And they even see this whole operation going on in a poverty area: church, school, convent, rectory, fuel and utility bills, roofers and plumbers and electricians. The money must be somewhere. . . .

The other side of this picture is the endlessness of it all. Nobody has the funds to respond to all the financial need and crises around here. The inner city is an abyss of colossal human need which expresses itself in the endless stream of people to the door for food, for carfare, with stories so long and sad that you cannot bear the telling. And for all the stories here, another hundred over in the school: aides who need their check early this week, a grandmother who used the money saved for tuition to bail an older grandson out of jail.

And the poor live with all these problems. Never the plateau of security, only the few dollars that will prevent the telephone being turned off today and then facing whatever dollars tomorrow requires. And being at the target end of this endless stream of need, the rich guy or white guy in charge of the money bags of the white institution—which must have money or all of it could not be here—has me weary, exhausted and as often completely exasperated with anyone at the door with still another story.

# 23

Morning at a public elementary school honors convocation and noontime off to a rally or vigil or protest at the State Building. Both events closeby.

I was asked to the public school gathering by my friend of 20 years—Eugene. Through family trouble, his young son is back with him in his one-room apartment. He is so proud of the achievement of the little fellow that he spent yesterday trying to get appropriate clothes and shoes for an honors assembly. Something other than the sneakers which now cost more than regular shoes. The wardrobe cost me $20 and the invitation to the affair. This season of graduations of our eighth grade and kindergarten and the local Catholic high schools and children of friends' graduation here and there. I hardly need another school event. Yet I so admire the responsibility that Eugene brings to his shattered dreams of his own spouse, children, home that I want to be with him. I could see his surprise and smile when I did meet him in the foyer.

And I was touched by the assembly. "Holy Mother City," as Dorothy Day called her, trying to do the impossible job of raising these children in the absence of family life or safe streets or adequate funds and facilities.

Just the ethnic sensitivity of trying to include Spanish and Vietnamese greetings, eastern European or Jewish dancing. No prayer, of course. The national anthem and Pledge of Allegiance to the flag instead. I thought of Simone Weil and her disdain for Imperial Rome where the only religion was civic religion. Caesar as God. I have a difficult time with this civic religion or patriotism.

When I see a tiny Hispanic student at the rostrum, I think of the Church and her absence from all this—except that I am there and some of these teachers are certainly Catholic.

Otherwise a seemingly total absence of the Church from this world which is the real life of the city, the real effort to bring all these diverse peoples and races together in peace.

The Church has her own world, her own schools which are becoming fewer and fewer, her own agenda, her own distractions: our graduations, our ordinations this month, 118 priest changes in the diocesan newspapers, Catholic Life 2000, which is the big fund-raising project. And since the archbishop was named a cardinal this morning (or yesterday morning, I do not even know), that excitement and planning or travel to Rome for the honor and some public celebration back here will consume all the energy of the Church for the next two months.

Yet the idea is that the Church is the yeast in the dough of the world, not a separate mass of dough. The Church does not exist for itself, for an intramural agenda, nor can the Church be a world apart, unto itself: "The Son of Man came not to be served, but to serve."

Nor am I anything near the first to be saying all this. Father John McKenzie, then a Jesuit, had trouble with censors for saying that the only basis for authority is service. I remember the papal visit here and the cortege of limousines arriving at the Cathedral with Vatican diplomatic flags on the front fenders, and my hearing in my head the Gospel verse which was in the Mass today or yesterday: "Among the Gentiles, people lord it over one another and their mighty ones know how to make their importance felt. Let it not be so among you. . . ." Church authorities have an unbelievable capacity to absorb that kind of criticism.

The reason this public school affair happens here today as a world completely separate from the Church is a profound and inaccessible ignorance. The Church authorities are not even accepting or aware of this world as a place larger and more real and important than their own. Their immersion in the smaller, more immediate world is something like the play I saw where a family is so absorbed in a family problem that the historic moonwalk crackling through on television is ignored. Of course, another reason for ignoring public schools and city and being absorbed in cultural intramurals is the illusion can be more easily sustained, the illusion that the Church is doing her job.

# 6.

## The Margins of the Church

# 1

A somewhat quiet Saturday morning and Dave Hagan lumbers in. For about 10 days he has been harassed by phone calls from the local prison by one of his young friends wanting out and wanting Dave to pay the substantial bail deposit. Dave has a hard time saying no, despite my encouragement to say no. Sometimes I assume the custodial role of keeping Dave in the ballpark. He tends to have no limits with these fellows in his care of them. Without much knowing what I am talking about, I give him occasional lectures on setting limits like a good parent should and would.

For Dave, the matter deserves the same treatment as our brothers would give if their son was in jail. Of course our brothers would bail him out. It is as simple as that. We should do for anyone what we would do for our own. As simple as that. Simply.

"I know you don't approve," says Dave, "but I paid the bail. Want to hear my 'theology' behind it?" I nod in the affirmative. I am going to get this theology, want it or not.

"I figure all the money that will be spent on this archbishop becoming a cardinal, going to Rome to get the red hat, the entourage traveling there, the parties in Rome, the big parties back here to celebrate the event. When I think of all the money that will be spent on travel and partying, I can easily justify the bail." An argument *ex convenientia*, the old theology would call it. An argument saying, "all things considered, it is the right thing to do." I had no immediate answer or objection for Dave Hagan; it's as simple as that.

# 2

*Corpus Christi.* A favorite feast and also First Communion Day here. At Mass I always tell the story about its origins. Thomas Aquinas requested the feast as a way of avoiding being made a cardinal. Instead he asked the Pope to establish a feast in honor of the Blessed Sacrament since the Eucharist instituted on Holy Thursday is somewhat overshadowed there in Holy Week by other events, such as the Agony in the Garden and Crucifixion.

The Pope agreed, provided Aquinas would gather and compose the readings and hymns for the feast. Thus we have such wonders as

*Adoro Te Devote, Panis Angelicus,* and *O Sacrum Convivium.* Worth knowing Latin just to appreciate *Panis Angelicus.* A marvelous distillation. A perfect poem.

The legend says that Aquinas agreed to the task on the condition that someone else also compose hymns and poems in case those of Aquinas were not satisfactory, worthy of the feast.

So Saint Bonaventure, the Franciscan, later called "the Seraphic Doctor," was given the task together with Aquinas, "the Angelic Doctor." The story continues that Bonaventure was so overwhelmed by the work of Aquinas that Bonaventure threw his own work into the fire.

Eighteen children. Faith and sense of sacrament so lean in these last years of the century that I hope their First Communion is not their last. I find something in Thérêse of the Child Jesus about her First Communion when she was 11. She says how Thérêse just disappeared into an ocean of love so that only Jesus remained. Sentimental and Victorian, I guess, but not very different from the phrase of Paul which brought Augustine to his knees: "Put on the Lord Jesus Christ and make no provision for the flesh."

We gave each communicant child a small woodcut print by Robert McGovern. A saint nicely framed so that he or she can sit beside each bed or wherever. Perhaps someday the child will want to know who Elizabeth Ann Seton was, and the saint can be further extension of the "daily bread," the grace begun today with First Communion.

Looking out on the children, I know the odds are against the life given today in the sacrament surviving any length of time. These children live in mean projects in a brutal world. What will happen to them seems all too predictable. So brutal the realities that this sacrament and feast of the Lord's Body seems hardly real by comparison. The Eucharist appears as an anachronism, an outdated piety. Even the dreadful casual frequency of communion suggests that no one believes very much about it anymore.

Perhaps we believed too much. Repetition as a substitute for quality. We celebrate Mass so often because we do it so poorly. Dave Hagan often quotes me as saying that when the Church or priests do not know what else to do, they say Mass.

Yet the promises are that the gift is stronger, greater than the brutal world. The trouble is that the Scriptures have the same fragile, unreal quality as the Blessed Sacrament.

Anyhow. I was quite satisfied with myself and the idea to give each child an original work of art by a distinguished artist. Something very attractive in knowing that children living in the harsh concrete heart of the Richard Allen projects—at least two of the communicants—have their very own original work of art. Each one different and individually signed by the artist. Different and individual as the face and story of each of the children. ". . . for Christ plays in ten thousand places, lovely in limbs, and lovely in eyes not his" (G.M. Hopkins).

# 3

The light, bright weekend of a fancy wedding and an Italian wedding anniversary downtown and the lovely feast of Corpus Christi became comedy or farce before Sunday was over.

As I was settling in on Saturday for a few hours of desk work before the wedding down at the Cathedral, our wonderful Haitian refugee borrowed my car to go shopping with his wife for food and drink for his many Haitian guests coming for the First Communion of his youngest child.

Down at the famous South Philadelphia Italian Market our Haitian had his pocket picked: wallet, bankcard, driver's license. So on Saturday when money is completely scarce around here—the secretary leaves absolutely no money around over a weekend—I had to come up with dollars for the First Communion party and hurry downtown to see whether the wallet was around. Just the hope that the wallet was lost rather than stolen. It was stolen.

Early Sunday afternoon, two Masses said and the alfresco First Communion cake and punch gone, I was settling in. News arrives of an impending disaster. The Haitians innocently consumed all the wine and beer stored in the school cafeteria for still another party: the graduation party of a Sister who resided in the parish convent and just received her master's degree from nearby Temple University.

The lilt of Corpus Christi and First Communion and I in a handsome old silk chasuble faded into my chasing across the Delaware River Bridge to "The Booze Shop" where Pennsylvanians go for spirits on Sunday, because package spirits are unavailable in Pennsylvania on Sunday.  Going and coming I am hoping that the law does not catch me.  The penalty is confiscated spirits and impounded car.

Yet I know I was better with all this.  The confusion, the crowding of crises into already-crowded hours.  Since the retreat in Ireland, I ride the rapids more smoothly.  The deliberate and calm acceptance that these things happen.  If  I am going to live and work up here where life is in fact so chaotic, I should stop fighting it.  It goes with the territory, as they say.  So accept the very minor poverty of being robbed of time and plans and privacy and the inevitable return of all cares to yourself.

How else would I want to be here . . . some God living loftily on Mount Olympus, reaching down to assist poor mortals in their clumsy, confused striving?  Or rather poor myself, all the disorder and chaos which eats into the lives of the poor—grandmothers starting all over again with babies because the mother too young or irresponsible and the like.  I should accept some of that as part of being here.  The only real way to be here.

# 4

Well over one 100 priests' changes in the Archdiocese.  Every year this furor after ordination.  Fifteen newly-ordained this year which, of course, proves that the conservative, even reactionary hold-out is vindicated:  things will return to normal after the madness of the last years of the century.

So long as enough people crowd the churches for a few Sunday Masses, the illusion is sustained.  No worry about reading the larger world of the disaffected, the secularized, those who do not or cannot believe any more.  Their alienation is their own fault.  The thrust of going out "to the highways and the byways and compel them in," in the language of the Gospel wedding feast, is lost.

Either people accept the Church on her own terms—Restoration Papacy and the traditional oppressive forms of the Latin American church, say, rather than the newer forms of Base Christian Communities, or let them go.  Bishops and priests are in charge; we set the rules and all of this canonized by an imperious theology which says this is all divine institution and not something to be resisted or questioned.

This posture lacks full reverence for the Church which is the people in whom the faith resides and is transmitted—John Henry Newman and his "Consulting the Laity on Matters of Infallibility"—the massive disaffection and practical departure of many is either ignored or even unnoticed. Ignored or unnoticed because the old guard cannot fit massive defection into the theology. Years since I visited Rome, yet my sense even then was that the whole top-heavy Church was busy enough with Roman congregations and meetings and general housekeeping that the organism can function without the participation and interest of ordinary people. So long as the funds are available from worldwide support or Church banking adventures, the indifference of people out walking the Via Veneto or Trastevere every evening might not even be noticed. And when public indifference to abortion appears, say, in a Catholic country like Italy or Spain, you ignore what that indifference is telling you and move to the United States to attempt the political and moral clout that proves you are still strong and relevant.

So the ordination of so many priests here and the seminary population "up 45% over the last two years has reached 220, the largest since 1974" (*Philadelphia Inquirer*, 3 June 1991), proves that the world is coming around again from secularism to faith. All the Church must do is wait. The prodigal children will come home.

And the hundred-plus clerical changes the local version of Roman Curial meetings. Busywork, housekeeping as reassurances of health. I mean no criticism of the fine priests managing these changes. They try their very best to maintain the well-being of "boneweary" priests, as a recent official bishops' study described our morale status. Just that fewer and fewer priests make this frantic effort to cover all the bases looks more and more desperate.

And the poor neighborhoods and the poor suffer in the process. A revered idea of pastor is someone wedded to his flock. Indeed according to the Gospel of John, pastor means "the Good Shepherd who lays down his life for his sheep." Being wedded here should mean being "stuck" here, the way the poor are stuck here. The frequent turnover has the look of "the hireling who is not the shepherd . . . abandons the sheep and runs away." I mean not to give this harsh judgment some literal or absolute force. Here among the poor, the seeming irrelevance of the Church is most visible. The frustration for a pastor trying to make it all work is overwhelming. Burn-out, as they call it these days, is always just around the corner, especially when the priest brings here familiar expectations of tribal Catholicism that still work elsewhere. Sometimes a sane, healthy judgment is to move on, move out . . . the tribal expectations do not work so well out in the more Catholic areas these days either, but if you reduce the number of Sunday Masses so that the numbers for five services now crowd into three, the church still seems crowded, and we are reassured.

# 5

The Feast of the Sacred Heart. I slept late this morning, asking the Sisters next door to excuse me from the weekly Friday convent Mass.

Yesterday the muscle aches that have been with me for more than a week were much worse and a trace of fever appeared. Just that extra hour of morning sleep might make a difference. Keep me on my feet for a busy weekend. Kindergarten graduation today. Eighth grade graduation on Sunday. A few social obligations in between, including Sonny's funeral tonight.

Sometimes the sense that I am in a sound studio having to manage or mix five or seven tapes that must be played all at the same time.

Sleeping late, I usually succumb to the temptation to put off morning psalms until I get downstairs. The secretary is already in the office just outside my bedroom and I seem too available. I am distracted by the activity already started and the idea is that I can make it to the quiet church for a half-hour.

What a wonderful space. So often around here I feel without space, physical space or time space. The church is busy, or my room is busy, or the phone is ringing, or I am expected at the school for kindergarten graduation, and afterwards the Sister needs me at the hospital for the anointing of seven sick people.

Meanwhile a half-dozen clipboards crowd the desk. My strategy is to keep order and play all the tapes: Hiroshima Day and the Catholic Peace Fellowship Concert, the poetry reading for the Irishman whose great-grandfather was married here, the fall appeal folder and letter, the flyer for the annual benefit concert by my Irish musician friends just set for November, my poem about Graham Greene needing more work.

Going downstairs to church, I meet the women going off for a retreat day. I need to greet them and see them off while getting in a cup of coffee before the kindergarten graduation.

Of course, this matter of space is minor for me. Marriage would mean even less space or privacy—not even alone in a bedroom and children needing and wanting at every turn. And the poor: I think of the family whose two little girls made First Communion last Sunday. About 11 people crowded into four rooms in that concrete courtyard in the projects. And I surrounded by all this wanting more "space." I should let the crowding of my life consume me even more, then I might know what being poor means or the demands of marriage. I could learn better to be "poor in spirit" at least.

# 6

A dressing down by a good friend. She says I am critical and haughty and harsh with everyone. That I behaved very poorly at a recent meeting. Nobody does enough, nobody follows through, nobody is helpful enough. And so on.

I try to hear the truth of what she is saying. I know she cares for me very much, so the "fraternal correction," as we used to call it, is done in love. She is not confrontational by character and trembled as she scolded.

I remember a sentence from an essay years ago. Something on conscience and superego: "Even anger and embarrassment are evasions of insight." We would rather do anything—become angry or ashamed even—rather than face the truth about ourselves or change or put aside our defenses.

How fragile and thin the ego or whatever is. As she talks, I try to hold onto the truth of what she is saying. Other remarks surface in me, intrude like a boxer fending off blows to the face or stomach.

I certainly see all these faults in others: the irritability, the whining, the preoccupation with self. No question but that these things are also in me. *Nil humanum a me alienum.* Augustine, I think: "Nothing human is foreign to me."

I rage in part at the impossibility of my life. The rage is always there just below the surface, even when things seem smooth and I feel in control.

This morning as example. Three calls back to back from street friends. One wants residential detox—right away, of course. The other needs money or a letter to excuse him from a big utility bill which he thinks he can avoid if I certify his need. All of a sudden I was so abrupt with him that he tried to get off the phone quickly, asking whether he could call tomorrow when I am in a better mood. The third was a domestic problem. Someone wants me to help keep his children away from his estranged wife's boyfriend.

And the other night a suburban woman wanders in from no-where. She is feeling guilty about her neglect of a daughter since the family came apart through marital separation. Now her daughter, whom I do not know, wants to marry and I am the fellow who can pull it all together.

So I do rage at the impossibility of my life. I never cry, but if I could cry, I would have done so after Mass this evening. Those calls, the last day of school, an awards ceremony and a funeral Mass at a distant church, where I arrive, only to discover they do not need a priest at all. A family friend showed up, but no one had bothered to call to say that I need not come halfway across the city.

Nor do I mean that my life is impossible and others are not. The strain of family life would surely send me under often. How do fellows my age deal with a son or daughter costing $20,000 a year at a university and not studying? A whole dimension of life, impossibility that I have had to deal with.

My rage at the impossibility of my life is not impossibility mea-sured against some other life. It is just the impossibility of these neighborhoods where so much is in chaos. So many fractured lives, so many crises, everybody looking to me for dollars or direction or a bailout or detox or carfare. And all this happens in crisis. Nobody does anything until things fall apart and then they want or need me right away.

What happened after Mass is that I thought I might just steal into the dark, empty church and stare at the windows for the half-hour be-fore dinner. All day I have been looking for a half-hour when some-one did not want me, and here I am stealing it, and in walks a fellow with a long report that needs discussion and he drives halfway across the city to see me because this is an hour when he can catch me home. And my tears also come from the sense that this has been going on for days and I just cannot take another phone call or someone looking for me.

And I know my rough, arrogant manner at these meetings, for which I am criticized, is transference or something. I am not angry with the people at the meeting. I am enraged at the impossibility of my life. I hardly know what to do with it all. The half-hours in church are some hope that prayer or gazing at the windows or whatever it is can absorb some of the rage, and I am unable to get the half-hour in.

Most of my 58 years at this and whatever is at work in me is hardly noticeable.

# 7

Arrived at the funeral yesterday to hear the younger priest already there say that I was rumored for a change. Nothing better, just bigger. I had not heard the rumor myself, but I am tempted to call the priests downtown, telling them to leave me here just in case the subject does arise with them.

I am on the edge, the margins of the Church. This is as much of Church as I can handle. Both Newman and Ronald Knox were Anglican converts and stayed away from Rome. Something about staying "out of the kitchen if you cannot take the heat." Well, that phrase gives the situation too much elegance. The "heat" is just the irrelevant fallout of officialdom. I can hardly read the diocesan newspaper because the "news" is so trivial, so unimportant up against everything going on here everyday.

My presence here in these neighborhoods these 20 years is in part self-interest. I am here because this is as much Church as I can handle. The neighborhood with people poor and needing jobs and in jail and needing detox is real life. Only part of the Church relates to this. Most of the Church is about bishops and clerical changes and a fund-raising campaign and whatever.

The part of the Church that connects with everything here is the Gospel, and whatever else the Church gives or does not give, she does give me the Gospel, that strange story about publicans and prostitutes coming to the wedding feast while the obvious candidates are cast out. The Good Samaritan is the fellow who helps the bleeding man, and he is neither priest nor Levite. The Roman centurion has more faith about the cure of his servant than any faith appearing in the Chosen People.

No promise that you will have company or support among the marginal people. No promise except that this is the right place to be and the right thing to be doing or at least trying to do.

So I hope they allow me to stay here in the peripheral zones, doing what I do—like tomorrow morning taking a friend to the emergency room first thing so that he gets the first available bed.

All so precarious. My relation with the Church depending on my removal to the edge these years. And on the edge finding all those situations and people who inhabit the Gospel. So I stay, aware nervously that staying depends upon the distance which so deludes tribal Church life that I can get the Church down—like needing water to swallow a pill. Again that book I read in Ireland. The contributions by a priest living on the Aran Islands on the edge of Europe describing himself as an "*a la carte* Catholic" and justifying it by claiming that Jesus was an "*a la carte* Jew," someone who could take his Jewish tradition only from a distance. Just as I can take the local Church only from the immense distance of this neighborhood where the agenda and concerns are a million miles from the tribal Church and thus distant and manageable for me. I have the Gospel, and the Gospel comes from the Church, as does the Eucharist—which is not meaning a lot to me these days, but I can wait upon better times.

I think any rumor that younger priest had about me and a new parish is just rumor. My source says that they are content to leave me here "doing my thing," where what I do or not do is not important because of geography. These neighborhoods are not important. What anybody says or does here is not important. The people are not important. What one says to them is not important. I could be preaching Maoism here and they would not care about that—or me—unless it made the morning paper. No money. No Catholics. A world of Samaritans and publicans who do not count.

# 8

At it early. Cha-Cha called to say that he needs to be off the street, to be hospitalized, detoxed. Of course all this has to happen right away.

These fellows live by crisis. Nothing happens until something else is completely falling apart.

His wife goes along with us. Denise is the best thing to happen to Cha-Cha. A second marriage. She is more middle-class—steady work of a rather sophisticated kind. She has him working, and together they are even buying a home. After the wedding she insisted on a honeymoon cruise, and he had to go out and buy street methadon because his clinic does not have "take-homes" and he could not be without the drug for the cruise week without getting sick. I had to help buy the street methadon.

Apparently he fell into something more than methadon these last months: cocaine. The recreational drug of the white sophisticates they say. Cha-Cha and friends do more heroin.

I know all this because when we arrived at the detox intake at 8:10 a.m., we were told that his Blue Cross covers heroin addiction but not cocaine. His impulse is to go out on the street and do some heroin so that his urine will show heroin.

An alternative is to try the group insurance his wife has instead. She has him covered on her work policy, so off we go to West Philadelphia to "Recovery Intake, Inc.," an agency that does referrals for several insurance carriers. No luck. We need an appointment there from his primary physician or whatever. They call the designated doctor in these insurance plans. Farther out into West Philadelphia we go and there we hit a stall: the designated doctor is a fellow back in North Philadelphia.

By now I am amazed at two things—how supportive and unangry his wife is and how patient both of them are with all this referral.

I would not have her patience maintaining this relationship—again. My sense is that she knows what these black guys are up against and responds with understanding. She is a sensible woman, not an enabler here, I sense. No nonsense about her. Driving to West Philadelphia, we stop for a light and Cha-Cha says to me: "Hey Mac, how come white guys have to do the whole thing, have all the gear?"

I did not know what he was talking about until I saw the biker just beside us at the traffic light—the whole gear of helmet and correct shoes, gloves and spandex pants, and sunglasses with the little rearview mirror.

All three of us laughed and when the light changed, I had to wait for a truck sitting in the middle of the street because the white driver was returning from a run to the sidewalk for some reason. I said: "I was sure that driver would be a black." Again we laughed.

By the second West Philadelphia stop, my patience is gone. I just do not have the patience of the poor who are used to lines and delays and confusion.

I had on my clerical collar and called the hospital looking for some administrator I might know who can short-circuit the system for us. Of course it works or looks like it is going to work, so we return to North Philadelphia and the detox intake waiting room. The clerk shows that someone called her, and she tells us to sit down without any indication to the others in the waiting room that these latecomers are going to get preferential treatment.

After 15 minutes I return to the church, promising to keep in touch by phone to be sure that the admission is happening. Cha-Cha was admitted at about 3:00 in the afternoon.

I have no idea how the insurance matter was worked out. All I know is that the wife called to tell me that the detox stay will be a few days only, and Cha-Cha needs to be in some residential rehabilitation program and off the streets for about a month at least. Today is Friday—that will be a problem for Monday. I can see it happening already—Cha-Cha discharged from detox and me with no place for him in a rehabilitation residence. I can hardly wait. Monday morning coming down.

# 9

The retired bishop of Camden died at age 77, and before they could put him into the ground, they waked him in the Cathedral rectory; during the night, a 13-year-old boy and a homeless man broke into the house and stole the ring and pectoral cross off the corpse.

You can imagine the newspapers and television local evening news. I saw one headline on the local tabloid—"Is Nothing Sacred?"

Hard to know how real the outrage is. Not much news around except the boiling weather, and the newspeople have to fill those pages and television half-hours.

Hard to believe that the dismay could be serious if people have the least sense about life in these neighborhoods of Philadelphia or Camden across the river, which has the worse economic statistics of unemployment and such in the country. Philadelphia is, of course, just as forsaken and the desolation is even larger. But Philadelphia has some upscale and working-class neighborhoods that pull things up on the statistical charts. Camden is just an extension of North Philadelphia, the wreckage of urban sprawl without relief.

Perhaps the dismay is not so genuine or fierce. If people know the conditions of these neighborhoods, people wandering the streets stealing or taking anything moveable, hustling, scheming, conspiring, hanging out, drugging, there should be no surprise.

The only messages are the symbolic—the unimportance of a bishop or the Church on the bottom of society and the facade-like movie-set quality of Church pretensions: moving pastors around and evangelization schemes which ignore the conditions which make life impossible and evangelization in any traditional form futile.

# *10*

Mindful that Cha-Cha is over at the hospital in detox and that the three or four-day stay is about over, I take up the task of getting him into some month-long residential rehabilitation program. After his admission to detox, his wife called to ask that I stay with him in this because he needs to be off the streets for a longer time than the few days of detox. The doctor who was helpful told me to have her explore what was possible with his coverage on her work insurance. Nothing possible on his own because Blue Cross does not recognize physical addiction with cocaine. Heroin, yes, cocaine, no.

I also call the woman who helped with his admission last week and she explains that residential rehabilitation with methadon maintenance is difficult to find. Most residences do not want the added problem or care of dispensing methadon or making the necessary connections with the methadon clinic. The protocol would involve "take-homes" or having a medical person at the often nonmedical facility or having the addictive substance of methadon around an environment where the other residents need a completely drug-free situation. Life surely is complicated.

So we begin the weary search for a residential program that will accept a methadon-maintained resident. I call one friend who is a counselor at one place. No luck. I also call the wife to inform her that I am working on this matter with her. She tells me that her husband is already home. Our search continues. You would like to believe that you could spend the day doing things that would help many or several people. Just one of these situations can sometimes be a full-day job, and even at the end of the day you are nowhere. Two fellows just out of prison calling me for jobs, and jobs are very scarce right now. I try to imagine what being just out of jail must be like. Hanging around home or some room "waiting for something to turn up," like Dickens' Mr. Micawber, or even out there looking for work and learning that most businesses or people want to stay very clear of ex-offenders. So you try to help these fellows with the phone calls, and the results are the same as trying to find a residence with methadon maintenance.

At least checking the system for a rehabilitation facility, I can ask about another need—a seashore friend did say she would take in my vacationing friend with his two sons for the second week of his vacation, beginning next week. He will need "take-home" methadon for his days at the seashore. Perhaps I can facilitate that. Someone at the clinic said the alternative would be to connect him with a seashore clinic. "Take-homes" sound more convenient and manageable.

# *11*

A whole week or weekend can come apart suddenly. So many calls and obligations or invitations that life must be rearranged. Before noon I was in three different hospitals. At the neighboring hospital, the Sisters looking for me to bring the sacraments, especially Reconciliation and the Anointing, to about seven patients. Another parishioner calls to ask me to visit her father in a hospital downtown. He is non-Catholic, and I find myself in the room of an unconscious man near death. She requested my visit because he is her father from a distance, because her parents have been apart for years. She is a Catholic, and one way she can respond to the news that he is dying is to ask the priest to see him. The vague sense that the "hour of death"—as in the prayer "Hail Mary"—might be an important moment if we are passing over into judgment or whatever. Just in case . . . so I go. Important that I go even to find there someone unconscious. According to a venerable theology—Aquinas should not be casually dismissed—I can lay a hand on him and say the words: "Shalom, whose sins you shall forgive, they are forgiven." They say hearing is the last sense to go, and who knows how a touch and the words of absolution might lift someone's heart and hope in a desperate moment. Who knows what it means or does not mean? In any case I go.

While downtown I also visit the third hospital where two tragedies lie. One a young man who will seemingly be a paralytic after diving into a swimming pool last weekend. His own father has such precarious health with his heart trouble. This is a terrible tragedy for a family already stretched by sickness and worry.

The other a still-young mother of college sons who has every reason to live. Her diabetes is ravaging her body. Next week she faces extensive surgery, frightening even to consider . . . .

I try not to hurry these visits, despite the press of the day and the traffic downtown and the difficulty of parking which makes the trip much longer than I anticipate. Each one of these people is a story, an individual, a human drama, not a name on a list.

Years ago in the old Church of confessional lines, I recall the advice of an eccentric-enough seminary teacher "Take all the time the individual on the other side of the screen requires. Your only immediate obligation is to that penitent, not those still waiting in line."

So I put aside the pull of a frantic weekend just beginning to be in that hospital room with this patient. I bring her those formidable poems of Barbara Sigmund, *An Unfinished Life*, poems about her dealing with a fatal illness, and I read a poem or two because I am a priest and this is what I am to do for people.

# 12

A nothing meeting with fellows whose main job is to host or attend meetings. They call us pastors to a parish farther north to say that we are going to plan pastorally. I am reaching a point where I should for mental health just presume that the meeting will only enrage me and stay away. Occasionally I weaken, feel that I must soften my cynicism, make a contribution or something. So I attend and know why Jesus became enraged at religious leaders or rabbis or whatever. He was shouting at them that publicans and prostitutes would enter the kingdom before the clergy.

The fellow who called the meeting knows that the authorities are completely inaccessible and uncooperative and admits as much in private, yet looks out at us and says how different things are from some former administration in that full consultation and collaboration are desired. How can he look us straight on and talk like that? Maybe words are just words, do not connect with reality. Perhaps people just talk and we are not supposed to hold their words to any truth. We all just talk through this meeting and then have drinks and dinner because we have filled up the empty day hours with empty meetings. Are things that bad? They seem that bad here.

During the meeting, another priest who quite unwarrantedly claims competence in these inner-city matters pontificates. His funding committee is studying the inner-city Catholic school situation and questioning the expense because so few Catholics are served. Here at St. Malachy—financially independent and unfunded by his committee—only 20 of 200 children are Catholic.

My impulse is to lunge across the table, lift the priest from his chair by his shirt lapels and ask: "What has Catholic got to do with anything? I just drove through North Philadelphia to come here, and the whole landscape and the conditions of everybody here are a catastrophe, Catholic or whatever! What has Catholic or non-Catholic got to do with anything?"

The most casual reading of the Gospel shows good Samaritans who care more than priests, Roman centurions who believe more than Israelites. The whole point of the Gospel is that these tribal concerns or criteria mean nothing.

I do not lunge across the table, in part because I do not want to fulfill their stereotype: this is what we expect McNamee to say, how we know he will react. Stubbornly, I do not want to fulfill their expectations.

Nor do I think I will attend the next "planning meeting," my time better spent visiting sick parishioners in hospitals or getting friends into detox. In any case, I did not write down the date of the next meeting.

# 13

The heavy rubber-backed inside doormat stolen. No big deal. Just a sign of what people have to endure around here. And most of them endure it with an unbelievable patience. Just this morning our religion teacher who lives nearby was near tears because someone again broke into her car and stole everything from radio to glove compartment items to battery to air filter. She was near tears but did not cry. She did not even mention her troubles to me when I came downstairs this morning. She knows these troubles are frequent enough right here in the schoolyard without her mentioning what happened to her car down the street. Thoughtful of her on the brink of tears not to make her trouble a worry for the rest of us. Besides, these things happen so often.

The stolen doormat is also a sign of the desperation around here. The mat sat in a small closet-like foyer with doors on three sides: the outside door, a door into the rectory proper and a door into the 30-person meeting room which is used constantly by AA and other groups.

Often when you enter the front door, you notice the smell of the poor, as Dorothy Day called it. You know that people have been waiting in the foyer for the emergency food or carfare or whatever they come for. Hard to describe that smell. Dorothy Day says it follows the poor everywhere, even when they have access to showers and clean clothes. Sometimes the smell is perspiration, sometimes stale beer or whisky smell, or clothes worn too long without washing.

At least the foyer is a more elegant place to wait for food than the front steps. At least a bench is there for sitting. And on the wall even a small drawing of St. Malachy in a plastic box frame. And until now, a large bright-blue doormat.

Someone must have been waiting for food and decided that the floormat was a better deal. Something which could purchase two drug bags rather than the one which some cans of food might bring. Vaguely I remember this happening before. Again the warning to do something about the heavy, three-foot marble statue of St. Martin de Porres also in the foyer. Only the weight prevents the little mulatto from Lima, Peru from disappearing into the pathetic underworld of desperate, petty drug deals.

And a call today from my street friend, who with his brother and two sons is at the seashore home of my hospitable friends. Forty years old and he was like a child on the phone, telling me about being in the ocean for the very first time in his life and how those waves "knock you around." Forty years old and 60 miles from the ocean and he is having his first ocean swim. I wonder what he thinks of the spacious seashore house coming there from his third floor, single-room apartment here where four share an improvised kitchen and bathroom. I know my seashore friends have renovated the summer home and now it is more than a casual vacation place. My street friend would not steal a doormat or anything else. Desperately poor, he just has that honest edge. He does not steal. I do not know his children well. These years they have been out of state with their mother. I hope they do not steal, or at least steal nothing from that seashore house, or drown in the unfamiliar ocean or get arrested shoplifting in a convenience store in that white seashore world where they are so obvious and so suspect.

I really can imagine myself seeing that affluent world of second homes and nearby ocean and bay and easily stealing a doormat or whatever. . . .

# 14

The morning newspaper has story and picture on Page One about our neighbor and former parishioner, home from prison for a week before his pardon release to a halfway house later in the summer and full release this time next year.

Inside the paper, more pictures and the continuation of the story. Former parishioner because during 16 years of his life sentence he came upon Islam as a new faith which has been an immense strength to him. As I have mentioned before, his dying mother entrusted to me the task of getting him out of jail. An impossible task at that. The article says only about a dozen pardons in many years.

Deep within my vain self I do think a letter of mine might have turned the whole thing. After the Pardons Board recommended the fellow for pardon, nothing was happening at the Office of the Governor—even after election day. Ever since the Willie Horton affair which George Bush used to defeat Michael Dukakis, no politician wants the fame of letting felons out of jail.

Some friend of mine contacted a close aide of the Governor's telling him that the prisoner attended the same Jesuit high school as the aide. The instructions came that I was to write still another letter to the Governor's office, directed to the close aide. Within a few weeks of my letter, the pardon was announced.

Reading the newspaper article this morning, my vain, vulnerable self was looking for some acknowledgement of my crucial part in the liberation. Alas, no mention of the devoted priest. I could use the publicity because time is approaching for my annual appeal letter and the newspaper mention would help.

More deeply, I was looking for a mention just because a deep and larger-than-I-want-to-admit part of me wants to be recognized and appreciated for the impossible work in this neglected neighborhood. Just last night I was so harassed and impatient with the Sister chaplain for calling me to the hospital to see a patient in the prison unit who wanted and needed the priest.

I had just returned from a 100-mile round trip to the funeral Mass of a classmate, and trying to squeeze in an hour to rest or change before something that would require the entire evening. A dead classmate already had me low and one more thing pushed me over the edge. So I was off to the hospital, wondering how I painted myself into such an exhausting corner of the world, angry that authorities or whoever worry so little about the poor sick in the nearby hospital that they just leave them for me, already weary with so much else.

So needy and embarrassed by my behavior, I was profusely apologizing to the fine Sister by the time I got to the hospital. I need and want the morning paper to give credit where credit is appreciated. Namely to me.

Yet more deeply still than the fundraising publicity or the need for recognition, I do know and recognize further that I cannot and do not want the recognition.

I have to be here and do whatever I do. Succeed or fail. Honor or dishonor. Fame or obscurity because somebody should be here and Saint Malachy ought to be on the corner and the Catholic Church can justify her existence only by some Christlike presence to the down-and-outers. And in this instance, I am the Church because I am here and this needs doing. End of story.

So. This modest or not-too-modest yearning in me for credit or recognition needs to be recognized itself. Accepted as something quite human and understandable and then gently but firmly put aside. A lifer who should be out of jail is out of jail. His Islamic faith and not his earlier Christian faith sustained him through many of the 16 impossible years, and my real or surmised part of his release is not mentioned in the morning paper—again!

Better that way. A chance to be here more purely, more deeply, less trying to prove something to others or to myself. Nice to win one after losing so regularly. Nice that something like this can happen. Better for me that any part in this win be secret. The Gospel is filled with invitations to that kind of obscurity: "When you pray, go to your room and pray in secret; when you fast, wash your face . . . do not let the left hand know what the right hand is doing." I should welcome this small opportunity and invitation to live more deeply. I should even be embarrassed that I am so vulnerable to such obvious vanity after all these years and prayer and effort to live more deeply than my fragile ego self.

# 15

Another big win. Almost as big as someone getting out of jail after 16 years into a life sentence. Another big win today that made for a frantic afternoon but the win was worth the frantic.

Over the weekend I was at the bar at a wedding reception, having a drink with a young lawyer wonderful to me here in this old place where his Irish grandparents married. The wedding was one of a lawyer from his prospering law firm. These young Irish fellows are in the passing lane. They asked my help with the marriage because the bride is a staff lawyer in the firm and the marriage needed special assistance. Hard not to return a favor when people are so good to me.

At the bar, the young law partner tells me that Michael is doing very well at the office. Michael is a young fellow from the projects whom I scolded in church three weeks ago when he appeared for the First Communion of his two cousins who live with him and his sister and his sister's baby and his aunt and her two lovely daughters and an older son—all in the same crowded apartment in those concrete courtyard projects where the brick apartment units around the concrete remind me of burnt-out fireplaces and the residents the timber burned up in them. Michael says they all just stay in the apartment after dark, even on torrid summer nights, just to avoid the crossfire.

I scolded Michael in the church three weeks ago not because he is so seldom at church but because he said he was unemployed. Getting Michael through the local Catholic high school was a fast financial maneuver. Each time the grandmother received a tuition bill, she came running to me, and I would run to the high school principal who always told me that I need not raise the money elsewhere. Somehow he would waive tuition or something.

Michael finally graduated, and I scolded him because a year after all the effort and graduation, he is unemployed, "hanging out" in those concrete courtyards. At best dullsville. Nowhere. At worst a war zone. In either case, going nowhere.

The day after First Communion, we hauled him into the rectory, required and demanded a resumé, however modest, high-school band and such. Later we sent the resumé here and there—including the law firm whose young partner suddenly tells me that Michael is doing very well after a week. I am amazed. Somehow they contacted Michael and he came and it all is working out.

Today the story takes on epic tones. The young lawyer calls to tell me how bright Michael is and how he should be in college. I agree but remind my friend that college costs money and Michael still has no high-school diploma or transcript because of a huge tuition debt of $2,700. Apparently the tuition waiver was not a waiver. What goes around comes around, as they say in jail.

Lawyer friend and I agree to divide the tasks. He will explore college with my warning that a local community college is the only real option for many reasons, especially expense. My job is to talk to school or diocesan authorities about an amnesty for the delinquent tuition.

Before I accomplish my task, the lawyer is back to me saying that because of friends at his own small, liberal arts, Jesuit alma mater upstate, Michael is in, free tuition, bed and board. A miracle.

So I call the high school, then the diocese, and the reception is cordial enough. Policy on delinquent tuition requires some payment, a gesture, as little as $500.

Before the work day is done, the transcripts of Michael are faxed to the lawyers who fax them upstate to the fine Jesuit school, and

Michael is in. I knew some worthwhile use must exist for those new fax machines.

About 7:00 this evening, Michael is at the door with a young woman who is obviously a girlfriend. He is beaming, rejoicing, and just wants me to know how happy he is, how unbelievable this all is. He tells me how wonderful these lawyers are to him and that he wants to obtain the diploma too and surprise his grandmother. I fetch a Pennsylvania map and the three of us look for Scranton and the distance from Philadelphia. Michael can hardly read the map because his eyes need glasses and the appointment the young lawyers made for him with the optometrist on the ground floor of their offices is not until tomorrow.

# 16

An inevitable call from a journalist looking for an angle on the new cardinal since the events in Rome are filling television time and newspaper pages these days. I take the call with such weariness, annoyance even. I am so tired of being a loyal dissenter. Some battles I do not want to fight anymore. Nor do I want to rain on any parade, especially the honors given our still-new archbishop here.

Yet the call forces me to express even to myself feeling and opinion which I want to ignore in myself.

Last week in the breviary for the feast of St. John Fisher, some mention that the Pope made him a cardinal when he was a prisoner in the Tower of London before he was beheaded on 22 June, 1535; thus the distinguished office used as protest against injustice—the imprisonment of a decent man because he would not lie.

Dressing early one morning last week, I saw the new cardinals getting their red hats from the Pope one by one. Close together were two new cardinals: one a very old Chinese bishop who had spent 30 years in jail, the other a Vatican diplomat whom a priest friend calls "the war criminal." He was Papal Nuncio in a country where there was terrible oppression from a military regime, including political torture and strategic murder of dissenters by death squads. By all reports, the new cardinal regularly played tennis with the generals who ordered or at least tolerated these crimes. To all reports, no protests or even tennis refusals from the Papal Nuncio now become a cardinal.

Some would say that he was the ultimate diplomat then. Invisible, trying to prevent murder by suave diplomacy that none of us would know about because it was so suave.

Whatever the contrast of two cardinals side by side, one perhaps suffering persecution for the sake of justice and the other perhaps silent in the face of screaming injustice, says something about the Church which is embarrassing and more.

That Church spectacle or ceremonial is mostly style without substance. Able to embrace and honor anybody, not because of worth or courage but because someone is on the right career track, or on the other hand his courageous story can be used to bolster Church image.

No question but that the ceremony is an extraordinary spectacle. Years ago, in a television show derived from his book, *The Italians*, Luigi Barzini mentioned the pathetic little demonstrations of post-World War II Italian Communism and showed a few placard carriers at some village piazza. "Italians love a show," he said, then flashing to a scene of 2,000 bishops in St. Peter's Basilica for Vatican II. He added, "and in Italy, nobody puts on a show like the Church." Dressing the other morning and watching the spectacle, the whole affair seemed obsolete to me, the pomp of another age. Louis XIV court flourish to which the papacy has never taken second place.

And that reaction or response of mine seems fairly common. Many Catholic people seem indifferent or even embarrassed by this costumery and flourish. Of course the hierarchy and clergy can be oblivious to this disaffection. So isolated and insulated they have no idea or even concern what ordinary people think, and there are always enough of an entourage to fill the papal audience hall and assure them that "the people like it." Even if they do, what is it they are liking?

Dave Hagan took offense at the headline over a picture of our new cardinal archbishop in the local press: "From Pauper to Prince," referring to his immigrant origins. "Should be the other way around," says Dave. I was in the home of a sick parishioner the other morning when all the ceremony was about to start. "I am surprised you are not in Rome, Father," said her non-Catholic daughter, coming down the stairs and seeing me. Our subsequent conversation was my first notice that the events were beginning that day or the next. A long way from my days as a Cathedral curate and necessary involvement in such matters. Surrounded everywhere by affirmation of the importance of these affairs, I probably did believe in that importance. The only importance I would attach to the College of Cardinals now would be historical—the fact that Richilieu or Cramner were cardinals or even Borromeo or the great Spanish humanist, Cardinal Jiminez. And the ritual over some nuncio who was silent during government political torture in a Third World country saying ceremonially that he is ready to shed his blood for the Faith or the Church strikes me as empty ritual, ceremony for its own sake. As far as I can tell, the modern world is not impressed with empty ritual or ceremony for its own sake.

# 7.

## *Tired of Losing*

# 1

The Feast of Thomas the Apostle, the doubter, the disciple who had such difficulty believing the whole impossible story of the Resurrection. I know that difficulty. I can feel in myself the effort necessary to believe anything. Most often I do not know whether the difficulty is my own insides—the deprived oldest child, often a lone self who even when I go to pray just presumes the possibility or likelihood that no one is there. Never was, in any satisfying sense.

Or perhaps the difficulty is my geography. These desolate neighborhoods where people have nothing; nothing works; mayhem is frequent. Most often life seems accidental. No beginning, no end, no middle nor sense. The other evening I took an Irish visitor into the concrete courtyards of the projects, which are quite hidden from the street as you drive past. A torrid evening and people were sitting out or walking around, noise and glass and an aborted tree sticking up through the asphalt. Of course the people thought we were police or bill collectors, and I had to assure them that I was the priest who lived up the street. Not sure, they still refused to point out the apartment. I was searching. I was even embarrassed to have my car—any car when you are in the midst of people who have nothing.

I wanted my Irish friend to see my reality here, to know something of what pulls me down so. More deeply, I probably wanted to see how he would interpret it within his own faith, so real and mature and yet without any illusions, it seems to me. I also wanted him to meet artist friend Bob McGovern, a nourishing grace in my life, like the Irishman himself. At the McGovern home we met activist friends who knew the Irish friars in Central America. My Irish friend commented how friars in Central America fared better than friars suffering similar ordeals over the years in Zimbabwe because of the geography of community; the Christian base communities in Central America provide immense communal strength and support. The suffering is great, but the ordeal is shared around and the individuals nourished and sustained by the faith and courage of one another.

So my difficulty is probably both inside and outside. I carry the emotional pattern of being still quite alone with it up here, quite away from mainstream Church, and lacking also the daily sense of being together with others at this.

None of this means that I do not have wonderful friends who give me immense support and encouragement. I certainly do have that. Nor should I presume that the fragile sense of faith which I do experience is not gift also. St. Paul says that everything is gift, which means that even the deprivation has possibilities. To feel fragile, to hold on, to find self often drawn into the Church, to be "alone with the alone" as they call it, this might be a very great grace. A divine invitation which might not come any other way except through the experience of need and fragility.

The feast of Thomas the Apostle reminds me of Graham Greene who is dead two months now; the lengthy obituary which I read in Dublin in *The Irish Times* said that at his Baptism in 1926, he chose Thomas as his baptismal name. "Sadly, he chose well," the article commented.

Today at Mass the few who came got some Graham Greene as a modern brother of Thomas the Doubter, as of course I am myself. I came to Mass with my Irish obituaries and a two-year-old interview with Greene from the *London Tablet* where Greene says: "In a curious way I've always believed that doubt was a more important thing for human beings. It's human to doubt." He goes on to say how the present uncertain Marxism is a more humane Marxism and how a less certain Catholicism would be a more humane Church.

Graham Greene and his lifelong struggle help me more than new cardinals reminding or pledging that they must be absolutely willing to shed their blood for the Church. "Isn't it lack of doubt that gives rise to fanaticism?" asks Greene.

At Mass with me and my Greene obituaries is a woman who just yesterday was annoyed with me for my few shaky words at that Mass then. I confessed what trouble I was having with all the new cardinal ceremonial endlessly on television from Rome Today as I was mentioning Graham Greene, I felt her discomfort again. I do not do this to annoy her or anyone. It just comes out. My honest insides on the feast of Thomas the Doubter. I even mean it to help as I believe it helps me to know that Graham Greene had such trouble believing, and he took Thomas the Doubter as his patron, and the trouble was lifelong.

It helps me to know that this man, almost 87, had to suffer lifelong the wounds of his childhood and the experience of being a student at the British school where his father was headmaster and he was quite alone and suspect to his classmates. It helps me to know that at 87 he was still holding onto the Church, despite his keen disappointment with the Pope and recent Church policy so disastrous for the Third World which Greene so loved. His clumsy handling of his disappointment helps me handle mine, even to be more patient with my own clumsiness.

After Mass yesterday, the woman in a gentle scold said she was going to pray that I receive the gift of joy. Fair enough. Joy is one of 12 fruits of the Holy Spirit and I certainly can use more joy and patience and charity and all the rest. I do recognize some lack or defect in me, and I do not like this wearing my heart on my sleeve. I am a priest to nourish the faith of people, not to assault their faith with my doubt as though they should anguish or doubt as I do. Two years ago when I tried this journal, several readers commented that my view is indeed too bleak.

Well I do not know how to throw the bleak out. What we feel is what we feel, and I do not want joy at the expense of the truth of what I see. Another visitor today was someone involved in Church planning. I told him I disagreed thoroughly with any theology that would create a specious distinction between our several responsibilities to people up here according to whether they are Catholics or not. He said that room exists for various ways and methods. I added that my worry is that in the back and forth some are winning and some are losing, and a classmate left the priesthood years ago because he was "tired of losing." My fear is that the Church can be unfaithful, and that I thought a benign, reflective pessimism was compatible with a theology of grace.

I hope I can come to joy. Perhaps I should complain less, share less my own anguish, reveal myself less. I think the only way that will happen is if I can come to some joy deeper and beyond the ups and downs of life. Just today, the breviary psalms and antiphons for Thomas the Doubter were coming together for me so that I was getting a brief, elusive glimpse of something wonderful.

The glimpse was partial and so brief that I wonder whether it happened at all. No doubt I saw something. Perhaps joy is available down the road, a joy not drowned by what I see in the projects or inside myself. I shall be patient, hoping that joy may come and accepting if joy never comes. Meanwhile I shall try not to wear my heart so open on my sleeve, not allow my difficulty to make the struggle of others more difficult for them. Life is difficult enough for any of us. Let providence measure out whatever. Keep my struggle more to myself.

# 2

A torrid summer Monday morning and the Sister here beginning an improvised day camp for the children of the projects in our rectory meeting room. Arts and crafts, video cassettes, lunch sent in from some nutritional agency. Good attendance. Even the mothers come and spend the morning doing craft projects with the children.

The weary sense that I have seen all this before. Twenty years almost up here in North Philadelphia and hauling children to camps funded by anti-poverty funds is among my earlier memories. All those public funds have dried up and more or less we are on our own with these efforts, finding the necessary dollars here and there.

This tiny camp, the modest try is worth doing. Wandering the streets in the summer heat, I see children everywhere day and late-late night. The small houses and apartments must be furnaces in the humid heat, and being outdoors where the air is still humid and hot is the only relief.

Improvised day camp seems so little, so old an effort that I am surprised when again it happens. Like many old things, it keeps happening because it is tried and true, something rather than nothing. The alternative is letting the project children wander the streets, gather on corners—curiously enough near trash dumpsters. No books, no games, no crafts, nothing even to spark young imaginations almost completely dampened already by everything going on and not going on around them.

That sense of weariness is increased by the notice that these summer programs are far fewer than 20 years ago. Then the war on poverty was new and vigorous and hopeful. Gradually the realization that the needs were more immense and difficult than anyone imagined. A conscious or unconscious decision and policy evolved by which those who have and do and succeed and prosper would just get on with their lives. Interstates were built over these neighborhoods, and just now an interstate below street level so that suburban people can get through the city to the New Jersey seashore resorts without having to see the city or even stop for a traffic light. Out of sight out, of mind.

## *3*

Dave Hagan also has a summer project. Many years now I call it his "chain gang." He begs some dollars here and there and takes on about 12 young teenagers to build or rebuild small parks on empty lots which were glass and old tires, littered and wildly overgrown with weeds. Planters are made with railroad ties, topsoil found somewhere, grass and trees and even flowers sown in the planters and around. A path, a bench or two, and the hope that the new oasis can survive the night or a week or even the whole summer. Winter is hard on this work and the yearly renovation almost total.

Dave pays his workers minimum wage or a little more, and he has to stand over them, at his age now and weight and weariness in the brutal summer sun. Most of these fellows have never had any sense of organized work, and if you leave them just to fetch another shovel or broom at home, you return to find them sitting on the planter bulkhead "waiting."

Years ago I assisted Dave in this summer work, but now I am submerged in the thousand demands of my own place here. Dave is more weary and yet still more patient with all this than ever. During the week or two between school closing and this summer project, he took a few days at the seashore. A few days means two or three. I know him well enough to say that he measures any personal summer luxury by what is available to people around here. He, too, is clumsy, not really very good at getting vigorous work out of his workers. Sometimes he loses patience or energy with the summer heat or some mishap. He calls it a day early and pays the workers for a full day anyhow. He justifies such a liberal gesture by say that if Alexander Haig or whoever can receive $25,000 for one talk and say nothing worthwhile, then Dave Hagan is not going to count dollars too closely for fellows out in the noonday sun.

And he has very modest images of what he is doing: putting a few dollars in pockets which seldom see a dollar. He has no illusions about his summer project beyond that. A man who has learned—not learned well but learned—to live with precious little return for his awesome effort. An important lesson to learn up here. I call Dave tonight to ask how the "chain gang" is going. Or rather he calls before I get around to calling. He says the effort is a minor ordeal he will survive. "It's not them, it's me," he says referring to the years and increasing age and weariness and the extraordinary heat.

# 4

A morning run through the local hospital. Now with the Sister there, I notice I do not get into anything with the patients. Just the sacramental work that only the priest can still do. A sign of my aging self and diminishing energy: one less thing that I have to attend. Save my energy for the world waiting for me back at the church.

Two of the patients have AIDS. A Hispanic fellow in his 30s looking much older and now beginning to catch the diseases and infections which develop. The cheerful little woman is also Hispanic and she was anxious to assure the priest that this illness had nothing to do with drug use or such. She was in for her seizures. Only when I left the room did Sister say I should wash because of AIDS.

Life can be so wretched that even something as lethal as AIDS seems tame. Another fellow named Willie had ugly scar tissue all over his neck and chest. He told me that several years ago, he and some fellows were drinking in an empty building and in a stupor the others poured kerosene on him and ignited the kerosene for mischief.

Now he is in the hospital because of a girlfriend who has a drinking problem and was angry with him for not being more sympathetic when another woman cut her up in a fight. The girlfriend, while drinking, poured Clorox into hot water and scalded a sleeping Willie. He asked to pray for the girlfriend by name so that she would come to the hospital sober today and they could have a sensible conversation about her behavior.

I return through the littered, desolate streets under the cover of a cloudless sky and brilliant summer sun. Today there is even some air moving, warm enough but not so humid so far today.

I do not understand this. Even as I write it my hand hesitates. I do not want to dismiss or minimize his wretched miserable life with piety or devotion.

But I sense this larger truth, only sense it. When I slip into church here or at the Sisters' cloister where the Blessed Sacrament is there circled by that stylized sunburst, I do sense that there is a larger reality in which that man is encircled, else he would not even exist and the love which gave him or me existence is awesomely greater than any clouding of the splendor of the gift by AIDS or tragedy or whatever.

As I sit there in the dark, two forces within me ebb and flow.

Nothing is out there. No one. Never was. The affect I bring to prayer because of my story—the oldest, alone, on my own so early on.

The other is that sense which seems deeper and stronger: love has you here at all, sustains you, draws you to this Mystery. The words of Pascal: "You would not seek Me unless you have already found Me."

That same back and forth many mornings. I awake and the burden of this difficult place and a wounded self are simply there, waiting for me as I put my feet on the floor beside the bed. *Nada*, nothing, nowhere, nobody. Yet framed in the morning window such splendor, such sun and sky and birdsong, even in the worn city, that I am drawn in. Something greater is going on than this melodrama of mine. I must attend to this personal routine, but I should never lose sight of all that the window brings in here and invites me out into simultaneously.

## 5

A visit from a younger priest who is a Maryknoll missioner in Guatemala. Years ago—1975 or '76 he tells me—he spent a summer with me at Most Precious Blood here in North Philadelphia. He was returning from overseas training in the Philippines to finish theology and be ordained a priest and then return to some Third World mission.

His visit stirs the embers: that unfinished love affair with Maryknoll. How during my own seminary years my sense was that local priesthood was not or would not be serious enough. Thus all the reading of Thomas Merton and his severe Trappist life or the stories of Maryknoll missioners off alone in Manchuria or wherever. And there I was in a seminary just a 20-minute walk from my home. Although the isolation and restriction during the school year was almost severe enough to be a Trappist monastery, the life I was preparing for seemed as full of automobiles and seashore vacations as any secular choice I might have made.

And here I am in North Philadelphia 32 years later, still wondering whether my life is serious enough. A tendency in the Church toward ceremonial solemnity without any substance. Certainly this is a difficult society in which to be serious. So many playthings, such distractions. I can find myself going out to lunch or dinner in an expensive restaurant just after turning away a beggar at the door because the emergency food cupboard is empty.

Dave Hagan mentions that pretense when invited to speak on poverty at workshops of his religious order: "I am not poor," he says. "Poor means being like those fellows at my door with empty pockets who must ask me, more or less a stranger, for a dollar. I have never been in that position for one minute of my life—nor do I especially want to be there."

At 58 I must surrender any honest or imaginary yearning for Maryknoll. Perhaps I never made the move for want of courage. Perhaps I would not have found myself more serious in Guatemala. Perhaps, perhaps, perhaps. . . .

At 58 I am who I am and where I am. Enough suffering and need in North Philadelphia for my limited and clumsy self and then some. I stop this writing to go down and open up the meeting room for Alcoholics Anonymous who use the room all weekend, every weekend. The young woman who came early to prepare coffee has her two young children with her. Serious enough reason just to be here and keep the old place going.

# 6

Last night Dave Hagan and I stood on the deserted blocked-off section of the main street through North Philadelphia, watching wreckers smash the south tower of the old church just north of here. The collapse of the north tower earlier in the day was warning that the other tower should also come down.

Dave had the sense that the moment was historic and we were alone watching history. The scene had all the makings of history: the white granite facade was breathtaking in the bright worklights. Where the granite was polished, the shine was almost silver. The church entrance has the recessed pilaster look of Rheims or Chartres. The feeling was the sound and light show of European cathedrals. The wreckers were hoisted high onto the parapets in a steel cage by a long cable at the end of a huge crane. Piece by piece they dislodged blocks of granite into the steel cab with them and were lowered to the street. The cab was emptied, and up again they went. We stayed several hours until the wreckers took their midnight lunch break.

Dave left, saying how we would never see again such buildings or the faith or guilt or brimstone religion which built them. He would have to say faith or guilt. Seeing the religion or lack of real religion around now, he would not want to idealize some unknown time or church and priests then. Yet the whole image of facade and brilliant light turning white granite to silver against the dark of a deserted street too strange and beautiful not to be moving. We both know and Dave keeps saying: "We will never see churches like this again. What does it all mean, the faith and work which made them now coming apart all around us." This lovely old place not even a Catholic place anymore. A monument to the faith of an earlier age neglected and abandoned and falling into the subway.

So. The smashing going on up in that crane truck above the eerie beauty of the illuminated facade speaks loudly to the likes of Hagan and myself. He keeps saying: "What does it all mean?"

# 7

A walk back from the hospital run where I saw about 15 patients for confession and anointing and Holy Communion. I take the long way home to stop by the post office which sits at the head of the most soiled, dreary, littered street anywhere.

Only 11:00 a.m. and already the heat has everybody outdoors in various stages of dress and undress. I nod to women in nightgowns standing at shabby doorways. The musty smell inside has them out trying to catch a breath of outside air, however hot and humid. I nod and say hello as I pass, either "good morning" or *"buenas dias,"* according as the person is African-American or Hispanic. The stale air coming from the open doorways reaches me also and I notice the long-broken multiple mailboxes which show the house has several apartments.

Life here seems so erratic or purposeless compared to the hustle and direction downtown whose steel and glass towers I can see behind me in the haze and over the rooftops of these relentless three-story crumbling homes.

Life here is coping, dealing with this heat without the escape of air conditioning, a trip to the corner store for bread or a small bottle of some tropical fruit punch or potato chips. Life is sitting on the front step until the step loses the morning shade.

I pass under an elevated train track of a commuter line. Ironworkers are installing new steel beams before the whole structure comes falling down into the streets. Must be federal funds. No money around this city for such work. A worker waves down at me. He is curious to see a priest walking these littered streets, and I am pleased to be here and strike his curiosity.

I am pleased to be here. Simply. I used to "hang out" in this neighborhood years ago when a friend ran a Puerto Rican settlement house for Catholic Social Services here and I was an assistant at the Cathedral, wishing I were free of bishops and baccalaureate Masses and could be among the poor.

Well, once Dorothy Day and the Poor Peoples' Marches and the Vietnam resistance surfaced in me, that was the end of the Cathedral days, and these neighborhoods have been my home ever since. The memory of walking these streets so close to downtown, yet so full of the forgotten and abandoned people so dear to Dorothy Day, brought me back here. After six years as curate across town and three away in a West Philadelphia black neighborhood, I asked the now-retired Cardinal whether I might come here because I knew the place. Reminding me of my activist tendencies, he told me that he "did not always have the confidence in me that he might." Yet he did send me here, and I am grateful. His confidence vanished with the news from Chancery or wherever that I was protesting the Vietnam War.

So. As I walk these streets, the obscure but deep sense that I am where I want to be and should be. Yet again the ebb and flow. The chaos and meaningless misery of these streets make it difficult to believe anything at all—to say nothing of some personal sense of being where I should be. If two dimensions exist simultaneously; if on an opaque stage I achieve some understanding, where does that leave the women who stand in these dreary doorways as I pass along? No interior getting it together for them, I suspect; they show no signs of that kind of reflection and their impossible external situation would have them avoid it at all costs.

# 8

Part of Saturday afternoon spent with two Haitians who want to marry. Both are Catholics and have previous civil marriages which require from the Church an informal declaration of nullity to say they are free to marry again. Of course the Church does not process all this without civil divorce papers and baptismal records to show that those seeking this decision are in fact Catholic. And so my sitting at the table in the rectory office up to my ears in legal documents and baptismal papers and questionnaires, and taking testimony from a witness who knows and attests to the Catholic faith of both parties and knows them well enough to say that they never were previously married in the Church and are free to marry one another. A happy fact for their baby, sitting in mother's lap during all this.

Of course Catholics and other people are confused by all this. The legal side of the Church which is substantial and formidable. Some would even say scandalous. I remember my first pastor, the little Italian immigrant, saying to me: "Father, we have made this Church a legal fright which the Pharisees never dreamed of." He was, of course, referring to Jewish legalism about observance.

Somehow all that Canon Law sunk into me during seminary years so that I understand the concepts at work and even respect them. Here the idea is that Catholics are bound to the Catholic form of marriage and if the form of "duly authorized priest and two witnesses" is not observed, then no marriage exists. I even have sympathy for the Church in her effort to own marriage as a sacrament and to discern who is or is not bound by a marriage, using criteria different from the secular where marriage is just another consumer item. Liberals in Ireland were enraged with the late great Sean MacBride for his opposing divorce in the famous Irish referendum. His hope was that the Irish could come upon some solution to unhappy marriage from their own religious tradition and quite apart from whatever is coming at them on British or American television.

So. Here I am with the chronic awareness that conditions just outside the rectory door are a disaster, from the drugs to the unemployment to the housing to the arms race. And I am here going through a legal maze like a divorce lawyer. The one difference is that no money crosses hands here. I cannot ask a Haitian New York City taxi driver who just moved down here and has a common-law wife and child for two times $50 even, the modest Catholic Tribunal fee for this paperwork. I do not want these people to pay because $100 would be a hardship and I do not want them thinking they are paying for some kind of annulment. If necessary, I will pay off the cost myself or have the parish absorb it.

This reticence of mine about money is becoming a real problem. So many stories and excuses about school tuition, so little support for the parish from the parishioners, and I cannot get demanding with them because my sense is that the money is not here.

I also know that a very real limit of mine is my inability to ask money or press money out of poor people. I would rather do the endless begging I do among friends and acquaintances. There I can do it with a blind letter, without knowing clearly who is receiving the letter and who is or is not responding.

As for spending an hour this afternoon going through legal documents when I want vaguely to be reading a book or preparing some great effort to save the whole neighborhood, I recall that saying which the principal at my last parish had on her desk. Something about everything coming down to helping people one-by-one, patiently and attentively.

Besides, Simone Weil says that perfect attention is prayer, and filling out these forms requires real attention.

# 9

Today the summer sun boiled this Sunday afternoon into a steambath. Even now, at 8:00 p.m., the setting sun looks as fierce and hot as the glow at the heart of a smoldering fire.

Lately I have been trying not to need to go anywhere on Sunday, just unwind after the Masses and the many people looking for me after Mass. Just to be here in what seems a scary, lonely quiet after the rush which extends into the afternoon.

At 7:00 p.m., I was sitting in my room where huge windows look down on a grass plot, a cul-de-sac of a street and, unfortunately, the local trash deposit.

Suddenly I hear another large stone crack wall or window of this big old house which connects with the church. I suppose once the front door of this house opened onto this back street, which later became a cul-de-sac with the project-like housing development plan.

I know the sound. Four or five windows and screens on that side of the house have recently been torn or broken. A fierce summer and the project children just across the street have to find new ways to express their conscious or unconscious anger or frustration at being so locked into this torrid block of concrete with no place to go and nothing to do. So the rock-throwing up at the big old building larger than the other houses around and having larger screens and windows to break. Something to do.

Once before I tried to connect with them after a rock throw. They were around the corner and lost in the projects before I finished my sentence.

Today I was moved to give it another try. Suddenly, but trying not to be threatening, I appeared at the door which is now our back door. The youngsters ran far enough to feel safe but not quite out of sight.

I waved them back and cautiously they came. Now one, then another and a third. One fellow held out, the seeming leader. All of them about 10 years old.

Of course, the conversation begins with fierce denials, protestations of innocence and the right to be here. They seem completely ignorant that this house is lived in or this is a church or what a church is even. Hard to get talking about anything more than police and circumstantial evidence and their suspicion of me. And I have been here eight years and walk all over these neighborhoods, including in and out of the projects.

I invite them in to see that this is a "church-house," and that the house is even connected to the church, which they might like to see.

The darkening church stirs their already-wary selves and at first they run back out. From the safety of the door they ask about a water fountain and consider a deeper look.

One fellow, the smallest, who says he is visiting from Florida, asks about the confessional: "The place where you talk through."

I am distracted by trying to keep these little fellows all in one room, knowing that their impulse is to pick up and steal anything moveable which fits in a pocket. I see two of them in the small pulpit pulling at the microphone hard enough to break or remove it. They stop when I protest.

They leave as suspicious as they came, and I feel no less fear for my windows later tonight. Now that the place can be a personal target, something they know, someone they can imagine angered or whatever by their vandalism.

# *10*

Across the casket of his father from me, a 50-year-old priest who returned from the missions a few years ago and has apparently decided not to be a priest any longer. I do not know him well enough to know his reasons. I do know him well enough to attend this funeral, try to be some comfort for the rigid rules of in/out or yes/no, which means he cannot say the Mass and Christian Burial for his father. He seems comfortable with his new lay role. His family is probably having difficulty with it.

I wonder whether he just lost confidence in mission work. Simone Weil said she would never give a penny to people trying to impose some religion on people other than that which surfaces from their culture. Of course the matter is more complex.

The former priest is now working with the homeless. Perhaps he just needs a more simple, direct work without needing to believe or stand for so much theology or whatever.

He is not married, but perhaps he needs to marry. That has to be acceptable. And the objection that people promised or vowed otherwise is not adequate because the tradition bound and sealed them so before the self-knowledge that reveals the need. Most people need to marry.

Then again, as many people married too young or too unaware and still must stay with it for a hundred reasons—mutual responsibility which transcends personal change or whatever. Maybe much of life is staying with hard choices once they have settled in, and loving means doing it with your deepest self, patiently and generously. Living with people who have so little makes words like happiness impenetrable—I almost want to say meaningless—to me.

Whatever. I do know that a Church which uses the biblical term of reconciliation so easily should come down from so ethereal an understanding of the term and flesh it out by making peace with people who can only meet her halfway or whose lives are determined by chance and choice beyond further reversal. When the few former priests attending Sunday Mass here receive Communion, I try to save for them a large portion of the Sacrament broken from my own celebrant's portion. A small gesture pulling them back to the altar or something. I think they get the message. I hope it is reconciliation for them.

# 11

Dave Hagan and I sit in a bar and I fondle my drink without saying much. We are in a shopping mall just away from our neighborhood and across from a theater where we have just seen a film which subdues my garrulous self. The second time Hagan has seen the film this week. He wanted me to see it so that we could talk about it. Perhaps words will come later.

The film is everything from black exploitation to real-life horror show. The film has already caused riots in some cities and has shut theaters down.

The story is the life or nonlife of parentless, roving, bitter, violent gangs of young black men in Los Angeles: their guns and girls and drink and drugs and wars and all the other ingredients of lives that are going nowhere.

Dave wants to see it because the film and story is his own experience right out there on the big screen. The ghettoes of Los Angeles look tame against the impacted rowhouse landscape of Philadelphia. The small western bungalows with small lawns and space between houses almost luxurious after these homes here jammed so close to the sidewalk. Concrete sidewalk and a few front steps only a step or two more back from the curb.

I cannot even say whether everyone should see the film or no one. The raw language and sex and violence and brutal repartee between young men and women so cynical and sarcastic that the audience laughed at matters that were hardly funny, only obscene and so outrageous and vulgar that laughter was a predictable, if inappropriate, response.

As we drove back into our neighborhoods at 10:30 on a sweltering night, everyone was out. People everywhere, drinking and sitting on steps and roving gangs of youth. Noise everywhere. Bedlam almost, for city block after city block. The film replayed back in real life, only worse.

The one thought I could not shake: the frightening sense that this problem of countless young lives being lived without parents or direction or belief is wildly out of control, and the only one I know who lives there, deals with it, is submerged in it over his aging, bald head is Dave Hagan. The problem of homelessness and the rest are nothing compared to the brutality and size of this problem. Society cannot begin to look honestly at it. The churches have to narrow their vision to inhouse tribal concerns because this reality eclipses the tradition of Church as massively as the grim high-rise public housing towers eclipse the old church steeples that stand in their shadows, unless the steeples are falling down from neglect and abandonment by the Church off in the suburbs, taking on more manageable projects like a new dormitory for resident students at a Catholic college. We can deal with that, even raise funds for it, whatever it means. These streets we cannot handle. Never at a church meeting have I heard church-talk about the reality portrayed in this film. Never.

# 12

Haitians meeting in one room after Sunday Mass while a Filipino woman in another rectory room talks to some people about the Philippines. All this hides from me the painful fact that very few parishioners came to Mass this Sunday morning. Summertime and the living is easy. I must not become discouraged. Lots of distance between the immediate needs around here and Sunday Mass attendance. St. Paul had to deal with situations where those rowdy slaves of the Greek Mediterranean cities were coming to church and thinking they were at a party and getting so drunk they did not know whether they were party or sacramental drinking. Just keep at it. Trying to get people jobs or out of jail or free lawyers. And along the way visit their homes or visit them in hospitals and make the Sunday worship as attractive as possible for those who do come.

Today, after the big Catholic Worker wedding yesterday and a house full of wedding guests and the two Sunday Masses this morning, something inside me shut down. I had no energy for the Filipino gathering or the Haitian Baptism and gathering of the Haitian community from around the city for Mass with a young priest visiting from Haiti. Instead I withdrew to my room, closed the door and crashed into bed for an hour. The weariness had the hint of respiratory symptoms, and rest now might fend off a couple of bad days or worse.

A blessing I have Haitian Jean Baptiste around. I went to see him at a prison in South Jersey where he stayed for two years after trying to enter this country illegally.

At first I thought I was the fellow being generous: the many immigration hearings, sessions with lawyers before he won status as a political refugee. Then the federal marshals simply dropping him off at the front door here because I had offered to take him in earlier.

Even after he lived here in the rectory, we still had the court dates and hearings before he was able to bring his family here. Five years altogether. Then the search for a home for him and a mortgage and a job and schools for the special needs of his French and Creole-speaking children. Then a job for his wife and still another mortgage when the first plan failed. Refugees are too high-risk people for money lenders.

Yesterday I was able to retreat to bed knowing that Jean Baptiste will take care of his own Haitians and the Filipino meeting, and he will see the AA people into the rectory meeting rooms, and if I decide to squeeze in an overdue visit to mother and sister for Sunday dinner, I will return to find the building in the secure hands of Jean Baptiste Pierre. One of those times when a generous gesture returns a hundred-fold.

# *13*

The hospital always there just off-stage, even though I need not worry so much about it now that two Sisters do full-time pastoral care.

Today a call from some office of the archdiocese about the care of an AIDS  patient, and I knew I would not get to see the fellow before night.

So. The lonely walk through littered streets and under the superstructure of the commuter train tracks. As desolate and dirty a corner of the world as anywhere. Into the empty lobby of the hospital, with a nod to the security guard, and up on the elevator to the third floor.

I am too tired for this task. Perhaps even too old. The fellow I am seeing is in the solarium, attending a small AA meeting which he quietly leaves to accompany me to his semi-private room.

Homeless, HIV-positive, a drug addict who probably got AIDS from dirty needles, this fellow, about 45, begins to cry. The patient regularly calls his mother in New York City, but she will not accept his collect calls. Family often have to do that with addicts. The mother probably does not know about the HIV-positive.

So besides the big worry, this fellow has the smaller worry of nowhere to go when they discharge him from the hospital. The person from the archdiocese told me that I need not get involved in all that. Just attend his spiritual needs.

For once I am glad for that distinction, however real or unreal. We do talk about the big worry, as the crying man is asking me how his still-young life could come to such a shabby end, and I realize that I am tired from a long day and just not ready to hear and absorb all this.

I try to shift to a lower gear, put aside my weariness, my impatience, my urge to finish this and go home and watch an hour of mindless television before sleep. I try to listen, let his story in.

After listening and absolving and anointing and giving the fellow Holy Communion, I took out my rosary and said: "Here, take this, you do not even need know how to use it. Just move the beads through your fingers, making up brief prayers."

Somehow this small effort seemed to comfort the fellow. The tears gave way to a slight smile. I told him I would be over in the morning for my regular weekly run, and I would look in on him again. Walking home, I thought of that phrase from *The Catholic Worker*: "the primacy of the spiritual." I was glad that circumstances made me attend the fellow in his big worry.

# 8.

## *Simply to Be Here,*
## *Or to Be Here Simply*

# 1

The feast of Saint Alphonsus Liguori who founded the religious congregation which staffs two neighboring Catholic churches. Both these churches were once German-speaking parishes and are now trying to pick up the pieces of the ravaged Hispanic neighborhood just beside us here. Despite efforts to theologize the Catholic Church out of the black neighborhoods because so few blacks are Catholic, no way the Church should be able to excuse her scandalous neglect of these Puerto Rican people who are all Catholic by origins.

One Redemptorist parish sits elegantly just across from a park which is one square city block. Two years ago, neighbors were having night-long candle vigils in the park to chase away the drug dealers.

And about a year ago, on a pleasant fall morning, I drove up there—I should have walked—for a monthly priests' meeting which wanders from church to church in these neighborhoods.

Passing through the devastation of empty lots and abandoned cars and gutted houses and ruined streets, I drove into the schoolyard to the greeting of some beautiful Hispanic children, girls in parochial school uniforms and boys in blue shirts and darker blue ties and gray trousers. They were smiling and courteous and even pleasantly officious: "Park here, Father, use those doors over there. Coffee and pastry upstairs." Others were opening the doors for the arriving Fathers.

I thought: what an island of civility and graciousness in the midst of the ruins all around. I know that the average yearly income here is the same—$8000—as my own neighborhood. And the tuition the parents pay to send children to this shelter in the storm of North Philadelphia is about $800. A considerable sacrifice and expense. Proportionately as much as suburban parents spend to send to private schools, Catholic or otherwise, and even to college. Justice is proportional, and I wish teaching religious were as eager to provide quality instruction here as they are in fancy academies. I fear not. "Money is the blood of the poor," says Leon Bloy.

I noticed all this courtesy of children and the shelter that school provides from the fierce realities of these streets because rumors were around that the school was going under so fast that it might not survive the year. The pastor was a hardy New York fellow familiar with the worry and impossibility of these old buildings and their finances, but he did go under soon with a heart attack and had to step back from it all.

Again this summer I hear that the school is in still deeper crisis: the pullout or threatened pullout of some religious teachers who were being counted on for September and a new school year.

So the feast of Alphonse. I pray at Mass for the impossible: that somehow his Fathers up there can hang on. Against all odds, doing the right thing. I pray that somehow that little island of civility and grace can survive another year.

And I pray for the fellow up there who had to step back with his battered, broken heart. He is the Catholic Church I can identify with: an overweight, aging guy who goes from one combat zone to another in another city. All his adult life has been living in these neighborhoods devoured by their voracious needs, harassed by their vandalism and in charge of impossible situations.

He is not looking for an easier life or looking for any applause. At Mass today I pray for him. I wish him a few more years. Easy to be lost or hidden or dead in these places which are not important by any measure, even that of the worldly Church.

## 2

Not easy this effort at being part of another culture and not very successful. Twice in three days I had to attend two black Baptist funeral services, and the whole experience is so difficult for me that I question whether I should be here trying to do it at all.

The absolutely linear character of things: the unadorned church, no art anywhere, the informal, almost make-it-up-as-you-go-along service where every visiting clergyman or woman has to have a say, and everyone stretches the two minutes into ten minutes—or more. Even the fierce, upbeat music and singing leaves my flinty Celtic heart unaffected.

But we are who we are, and if I do not try to be here and adapt myself, who will? Better me than nobody.

So I continue with a painful sense of my limitations. I am poor at the black Church effort and good at being on the street, friend of the fellows out there who have no one. They do not go near a church, and I sense I connect with them better than most do.

Yesterday a doctoral student interviewed me about the history of effort from the local Catholic Church toward the black community or early civil rights or whatever. I felt keenly my weariness with such ecclesiastical conversation. More recently, I simply experience the Church as a place to be—by geography and identity—so that I can be with and for people here as much as I am able. The Catholic Church gives me a home here so that I can live among the poor, or at least closeby. Not many come to church so that I must content myself with being with them in courtrooms or by getting them jobs. This Ignatian year we are going to try to gather the few who might show some interest in the Ignatian Spiritual Exercises—prayer and meditation— for weekly sessions in the fall, so that we do not neglect altogether the "Primacy of the Spiritual" again, as Catholic Worker tradition calls it.

But nowhere do I see the racial or cultural crossover as very successful. The recent Catholic Worker wedding of people four years now hidden and immersed in the African-American and Hispanic neighborhood here was almost completely white also: friends from here and there and only a very few children from the neighborhood.

Not that all black people are poor or even all my immediate neighbors. At one nearby restaurant I notice many black couples and families and their presence makes it easier for me to be there. Yet the project people are never there.

One of the bewildering realities of this society is the way some of us move in and out of different geographies and how close these landscapes are without much interpenetration. I do not mean to make some big deal out of not being present here in some absolute sense. I just experience my own limitations at adaptation and my inability to do or even enjoy black religious expression. I comfort myself by saying that I do other things better than most. Things like the street. Perhaps that is what we are to do with our limitations, see other areas where we do well. If something is worth doing, it is worth doing poorly.

No way that anybody is going to be in this chaotic, unravelled world of North Philadelphia except clumsily. Everything in my background makes me blame myself. I have to keep reminding myself that the main work here for a long time after my lifetime has nothing to do with churchgoing. The primacy of the spiritual, yes. That this should unfold before me in some obvious sense, no. The primacy of the spiritual means the quality of my attention and intention. How that all plays itself out—if at all—is beyond me.

# 3

Night court. Just like the movies or television, only more seedy and dirty. The husband of our one intact younger family violated a restraining order and was arrested again. I feel very bad for him. I can just imagine what emotions surface as he watches his life coming apart, everything he has been building for 12 years: anger, panic, fear, grief. Eventually the kettle boils over into some frantic effort both futile and destructive.

My pity did not prevent my screaming into the phone when he called from jail at dinner-time, just after Mass. Some post-Communion prayer, that half-hour. And someone here prepared a good dinner for me which I ate alone still upset over my screaming, his predicament and the night ahead of us both. I had counted on a quiet night for some letters, some progress in a book or two which I am reading. End of evening. Poverty of spirit, I hope. Nothing compared to the crowding, lack of privacy, of leisure on every side here. A way of being here, sharing the deprivation.

I use the priest role to get through to night court. My man is not on the 8:30 docket. Probably at midnight. Can someone call me? No, but I can call back at 11:30. I am so distracted I can do little more than watch junk television.

At 11:30, still no sign of his name on the list for a bail hearing. Now the shift has changed and a friendlier clerk or policeman says he will call me. At 1:30, before the 2:30 hearing, his call jars me from an uneasy sleep.

I drive through the deserted city. Not far. Just about 20 city blocks. Police headquarters is full of night people: those under arrest led in handcuffs, their friends in the bleachers awaiting their release. Druggies and prostitutes and even a fellow picked up for a murder back in April.

A gallery with a dirty plastic shield overlooking a room as unkempt as a neglected closet: boxes of computer printout paper in one corner, and old coatrack empty in the summer heat, an antiquated water cooler, littered desks for district attorney and public defender and court clerks who are furiously filling out forms, tearing out old-style carbon sheets and tossing them into disposal baskets.

The arrested are brought in, about 10 of them. Men and women are seated separately on old park benches. The bail commissioner is at a desk of his own up behind the two desks over which attorneys and clerks face one another.

One by one the defendants come before the commissioner, almost buried behind law books and stacks of printouts on his desk. His voice and manner have an intelligence and concern more than this seamy room would suggest. Little talk though, mostly paperwork. The filling out of forms and signatures.

Angry as I am to be there again, I know I was right to come. My friend is released without bail deposit or fine because the commissioner notices me in the bleachers. A friend, a priest, an anchor in respectability despite this surfacing in the rivers of the night.

The ride home is quiet, sullen even. He is still enraged at himself or his spouse or both. I am exasperated by this third foolishness of his: expecting the courts or police to be any help in his domestic troubles. A few furtive efforts at serious conversation from both of us. Too unlikely the hour, too weary the two of us. Sleep will dissolve some of this irritation. He stays overnight in the rectory. We can talk in the morning.

# 4

In and out the little rowhouses of the neighborhood. Someone sick or elderly here and there. The basic duty and privilege here that which I should be doing before all else.

Yet in a sense the most difficult to attend. So much conspires to have me at a meeting, or at a printer this morning preparing the fall appeal letter, or on the phone, or at the desk.

Meanwhile they are out there. Hidden heroic lives. First visit a lovely home where a 50-year-old man is enduring terminal brain cancer. His wife and he tend their little grandchildren every day. The children attend a suburban Catholic academy. The whole feeling here is family care and sustained Catholic faith. The home is such an oasis of everything in this wilderness. They are so grateful for these erratic, brief visits of mine, though the parish Sister visits more often. They attend the Cathedral more than the parish. Although black, they are not comfortable with lively black Gospel music or hand clapping and go to the sung Mass at the Cathedral. Again the thought that I should do a better music program at the parish. One of the many things I should do better.

Next we visit a woman, a young great-grandmother now. She and her unmarried daughter seem to have taken in granddaughter and niece's baby whom we baptized here some months ago. The mother of the baby is still a high school girl and her own mother works.

The daughter unmarried and at home is as lovely and proper and courteous a woman as I have ever met. The dense, battered block where they live is as rough a neighborhood as anything around here. One senses they have been there since earlier, more gentle times and that the neighborhood has come apart around them, leaving them quite isolated up here.

Beautiful and even striking, the daughter arrives at Mass each Sunday with mother and a learning-disabled, middle-aged man whom they bring to Mass each Sunday as faithfully as they bring one another and now the baby.

Occasionally the daughter says something humorous about finding her a man, a husband. I hear her sadly because the sad truth is that in the community there are few able men out there who would suit her, and she knows it. Last Sunday she said she would call me about her mother and an illness that has come up. Cancer, of course. Her mother needs surgery and perhaps radiation and chemotherapy afterwards.

The mother says she is prepared for the worst, wants nothing more from life. She is concerned about this lovely daughter who will be alone after a lifetime in which they so closely had one another.

At both visits I gave the Sacraments of the Sick: Absolution, Anointing and Holy Communion. So wonderful how Catholic worship can transform a casual visit into a gathering of the Church according to the promise: "Where two or three are gathered in my name, I am in their midst." Quietly, yet marvelously, an ordinary visit becomes an invocation of the Communion of Saints and asking that this trouble be taken up into Mystery and Love in which we are always present. And we all know what is happening and are grateful for this faith, this richness which the several of us there all understand without having to say much to one another.

# 5

The late-night writing never works well. The day hours are impossible. Then life *is* interruption. At night I am too exhausted. My only other option is getting up earlier than the 6:30 rising.

Tonight as I write in late-night quiet, a fellow passes the room. One of eight Chicago homeless advocates staying upstairs. They are in town for meetings and someone told them they could find beds here.

The fellow stops by the door, and after asking my year of ordination, he tells me that he too was a priest, ordained in 1965, went off to work in Panama where he married a woman of Panama and they have five children, ages eleven to one.

After his marriage he worked for a while with Jesuits in Panama, but the U.S. invasion there, the destruction and the aftermath of war drove him home to Chicago, where he works with the homeless.

I guess we look across this small room and a whole universe at one another: I could be he and he could be I. The burdens of family probably have him idealize my role here: the lone, faithful priest keeping things going in an area of immense need. My being alone here probably has a romantic image, and the place seems busy enough to be an effective effort. Sometimes these fellows must wonder whether they should have ever left or should have stayed until the panic passed.

And I look across at him and wonder at his strength with family and this desperate work, and recall my own panic those years ago when everyone seemed to be leaving and the only way to prove you could leave if you wanted or should was simply to leave. Otherwise you would never know.

So I stayed and still do not know. All I know is that this fellow has strengths I do not see in myself: five young children and this wearying work.

And he left and does not know whether he should have stayed.

Perhaps these are not the important questions. Perhaps the important matter is that we are who we are and where we are by a maze of reasons unknown even to us. Our work is to make our way through our situation with faith and courage and whatever else it takes. Playing the hand we have been dealt—or even dealt ourselves or something.

In the end we are not only a mystery to one another but even to ourselves. The task is to live the mystery rather than unravel it.

# 6

Two foreign mission Sisters lived here in the neighborhood for about eight years. Their home became a kind of little church to a small gathering of people who were orphaned by the closing of a neighboring Catholic church about seven years ago.

The Sisters came and went, were as often away to their religious community for weekend meetings as they were here for Sunday Mass.

But they did tend people with immense needs. One family has about five members with a degenerative disease apparently inherited from the mother, who had the five in a home for invalids. As the disease was taking down the children, I was glad the Sisters were here and caring for them.

Another woman has two adopted sons who are learning-disabled and more than she can handle. Again the Sisters were a great help to her, as they were to the elderly people whom they transported down here to Sunday Mass when the Sisters were around themselves.

This week I helped the two Sisters load a truck and move to Baltimore where they will do the same work in a similar neighborhood. The Baltimore house already exists and the intention is to enlarge the community and train novices or something.

I think the Sisters felt as bad about their leaving as I did, but they are more accepting of the reality of religious life than I am.

My honest question is: how can you do that? Stay eight years with people who are stuck here, come to depend on you and then move on, leaving them high and dry?

Part of it has to do with not being married. We lack roots, the anchors of children and a relationship and even a mortgage which all keep people together for the best of reasons which, because they are so unromantic and practical, seem like the worst of reasons. But Simone Weil says the real virtues look like their opposites: real love looks like indifference because it tries to acknowledge the full human reality of everyone. The love of God which is indifferent in that he/she makes sunshine and rain fall on just and unjust alike.

Not having to love, to stay, to hang in there, to be stuck, to see it through from necessity, we priests and religious tend to translate ordinary human restlessness into geography, a little here, a little there, a little of this and that. Job changing every couple of years, living in community somewhere, and when my tape plays as far as it goes in my maturity, rather than exploring new frontiers here with the others, I rewind my tape and go somewhere else to play it all over again as far as it goes.

I do not mean to make an absolute out of this business of staying with people or a situation. Obviously change is a human reality and even necessity also.

But the poor are so terribly stuck in their neighborhood or home or dreadful situation or raising their grandchildren because the mother is lost to the streets. French worker-priest Henri Perrin was so sensitive to criticism of the workers that as priest he was not really one of them, was there simply to convert them or worse, write a book about them before he was again gone. When the decision came down that the priests could not continue in the work, he heard this news as fulfillment of the workers' suspicions: he was not one of them. His understanding was that the priest should indeed be one of them, one from them, or he had no reason to be their priest, to lead them in the Eucharist.

I know this ideal can be realized only with great inadequacy. Here I am the white priest to a black community, and I must work at overcoming that difference without affectation.

All I can say is that I can try further not to use any more of those privileges than I do and diminish my need to be away or different from life around here. In any case, I am grateful for my place in the Church which has me see my main community as not fellow priests here and there whose identity comes from some suburban motherhouse, but someone whose office and role makes sense only in terms of the ordinary people around me. The idea is that I am one of them. Simply.

I know all of this is fraught with difficulty and even illusion.

Almost no one at Mass today. Most will not even notice it as the Feast of the Assumption.

# 7

A humid, blazing summer Saturday, and after morning Mass I feel the warnings signs of a summer cold: the aches, the sinus drain, the weariness. Tomorrow Sunday so I had better rest with this so I am able for Sunday morning.

I was to attend a wedding in a Baptist church this afternoon but do not feel up it. I call the housekeeper here who lives just down the street to say that I am not feeling well enough to attend her niece's wedding.

Despite the heat and the bride surely coming late and the long wait in some reception hall for the wedding party off somewhere for pictures, I do like to accept these invitations. Often you are the only white person there and a more visible sense emerges of the importance of being up here. I mean at least the sense that I with my own presence, body even, am trying to heal the awful wound which has black and white, rich and poor, so utterly separate in everything: work and weddings and housing and even church.

I hope that sense not grandiose or something. I do not mean to make a big deal of it or say my presence at the wedding is doing anything. All it might be doing is making visible to me the importance of staying here, doing these frantic, often futile things, being at least one clumsy presence of the other.

All this might sound very romantic, pretentious even. All I mean is that I feel good being there, being accepted by those who invite me and want me there. At least in me or by me the wound is being closed. Usually I do not see it in myself. I see it in Dave Hagan up there in that anonymous house having a Labor Day picnic in his concrete postage stamp of a backyard, while others like him are at the ocean or wherever. Dave is simply *there* with those fellows who have nowhere else to go.

In any case, I did not make the wedding today. These symptoms so heavy on me that all I could do was wander restlessly from room to room, crash down onto the bed for a half-hour every so often. Wake up in such a sweat from the fierce heat and humidity that I check to see whether I have a fever.

No fever. Just the weight of myself. Still another place to be: alone and unable to do anything to ease the aloneness. I steal into church and the weight of self makes prayer leaden. But leaden prayer is still reaching up from a place that is human, if only because I am there now. That is how it feels to pray in such a mood on such a summer day after wandering heavy and lonely around this big old house: it feels smokey, too heavy. But it is still prayer and I can well learn to pray from that mood or part of me as from any other. Who knows.

# 8

A routine meeting brings me uncomfortably close to some of my very real limitations. In this case the subject is money.

On the one hand I am to some a marvel. About $115,000.00 raised from friends outside the parish to keep the operation going here. My sister tells me that my mother recently expressed something that she would never say directly to me: that as a child I would simply refuse to sell chances or do any other kind of begging for the parish school, and now all I do are these begging appeal letters.

The other side of the picture is that I am very poor at generating dollars here within the parish. I hardly talk about money at Mass, and the local people seem to just presume that Father will come up with the dollars to keep this expensive operation going. I further that impression of black people that white people simply have money or know where to get it. Not an altogether inaccurate impression all told.

The meeting yesterday was with a fundraiser from the new archdiocesan effort. We poor parishes must participate, and his unpleasant job is to come around and help me raise money for the archdiocese from within the parish when I can hardly raise money within for the parish itself.

I try to respond rather than react. Years ago, a friend told me that Samurai Spirituality says we should always refrain until we can respond rather than react. Fair enough.

I put aside my complaints about being recently taxed about seven thousand new dollars for diocesan high schools, even though very few of our children can afford tuition now and so do not attend. The old assessment was based on students attending so that we got off easy.

The fundraiser was uneasy, and I tried to make him comfortable by a sense that I was not going to unload my complaints on him. He was obviously relieved.

I told him that I knew local Black Baptist churches made it on the contributions of their members, and that I knew the overall health and stability of this place depended more on self-support and that I must do a better job of bringing that about. "Better job" means still another way among a thousand ways in which I could do a "better job" here—everything from visiting people at home or in hospitals to tending the school better to knowing names better to doing more for youth or whomever.

But I also know that at 58 I am over the hill, and in some respects should do less, not more.

I look at the fall appeal brochure recently prepared and almost ready for bulk mailing. The emphasis is on the school and the fact that we are beginning without a religious Sister for the very first time since 1863. Still ten Sisters in a wreck of a convent and the place needs $100,000 worth of repairs easily.

I look at the appeal brochure and am proud of it. A wonderful color photograph of our school children and a more wonderful letter from a parent saying how our smaller, gentler place was all the difference in the world for her two daughters from the brutal realities of a local public school and their crowded, dilapidated public housing project.

The brochure looks and is expensive in the making, and I suppose some will say: if McNamee is so poor down there, how can he afford to produce this expensive item? My answer to no one but myself at this point is "poor but not cheap."

The brochure also intercepts some comments from policy-making priests at diocesan meetings. Comments about schools like ours, where 180 of 210 students are not Catholic, are an expense hard to justify precisely because we tend so few Catholics. In the brochure I insist that life up here is so often a disaster for everybody that Catholic or not Catholic is not pertinent. I suppose someone at diocesan level could be angry with my public criticism of plans or half-plans or mere suggestions at private meetings. I will take my chances. Someone has to start challenging that "specious theology," as I call it in the brochure.

And the meeting with the fundraiser concludes with the amicable agreement that we shall call a special weekday evening meeting of the Parish Council so that he can present to us our obligation for this diocesan effort. I am very mindful that the fall brochure mentions $7100 as the 1980 median annual income of this neighborhood, 1990 census figures not yet available. The figure will again be low and appalling, and I shall try to measure my energy or success in raising funds within the parish by that statistic. On the other hand, I shall remember the widow's mite story and the neighboring Baptist churches who make it on their own. No school for them, however. That difference makes all the difference.

# 9

August ennui. My head is spinning. I leave the downtown law offices of friends who are helping me for a nearby hospital to see a parishioner who has a brain tumor. At least the lawyers and doctors have some focus and some limits. Their real job is making money to support their families. I feel as unreal as I must look out in the noonday sun in a black suit and high, suffocating collar. A moon man, someone running around trying to comfort people dying of brain tumors or get other people to help people caught in impossible marriages or legal problems.

Do I look as ridiculous as I feel?

My life feels so foolish, pathetic, unreal. Am I in over my head?

Next stop the place where my sister works to fetch the expensive watch she took for repairs. Someone bought me the wristwatch six years ago when I was twenty-five years ordained. They bought it at an expensive place where I would never shop and the watch is probably expensive enough to return there for repair.

For the third time now the repair is unsatisfactory—expensive beyond belief, as well as unsatisfactory. My sister and I in frustration walk around to the elegant shop.

And all this confirms my ennui, panic that the world just does not work. The whole city and society is "out to lunch," including or especially this international jewelry franchise that spends millions creating the illusion of competence and integrity. They probably send the watch to some little repairman and then charge me three times—five times—his fee because of their elegance and reputation.

So. The world does not work, and here I am in completely over my head trying to make it work, or keep people out of jail or pray over a fellow with brain cancer, trying to make my image more honest than the jewelry firm's by praying only that the sick man has the grace of God in his sickness.

One more visit before starting home. A hospital for stroke victims and patients with spinal injuries. A young fellow is paralyzed from diving into a swimming pool. I wait in a corridor filled with people in wheelchairs who can scarcely move a hand or arm. The immense care and personnel these patients need. Life reduced to sipping water through a straw from a plastic bottle strapped onto the chest. Whatever life is about in the mind of the Mystery we call God, from all appearances here it is not about the moving and doing and achieving that we imagine.

My stress and overwhelm such that I decide I had better walk home. Walking is good for stress. Buddhists even have walking prayers or praying walks.

I strip off coat and collar and begin. About 20 blocks and 40 minutes. The sun is boiling and I plow along the littered streets busy with traffic and pedestrians. Halfway up, a call from across the street: "Father Mac." Across he comes and I recognize a friend from days across town at a former parish. The request is not explicit. Only when I ask where he lives now do I discover that he is walking farther downtown than I am uptown because he has no carfare. Three dollars gone.

At a busy crossroads just into the all-black neighborhood, a short, white woman is hitchhiking. I use my collar visible on my arm to ask her problem. Again, no carfare. Purse stolen. Out another three dollars.

No sooner do I step back to the sidewalk than I see coming at me a rectory regular. A fellow with a fierce stutter who arrives at the door day and night or anytime and just stutters on until I give him something.

Seeing me just as he is leaving a blood bank across the street is an unexpected opportunity. They probably would not take his blood because he is returning too soon from the last sell or because he is HIV-positive. Who knows? No way he is going to let me pass without a jab at it. The other two stops took all my single dollars, so I had to deal out a five. Expensive this walk home. I hope it was good for the stress. Kipling says only mad dogs and Englishmen are out in the noonday sun. And this Irishman.

# 10

Dog days. Temperature was almost 100°. New record for the day. And the humidity fierce.

After dinner a much-delayed visit to the high-rise project up the street. Not the one which overshadows the church. One that I drive past a dozen times a week. Only once or twice was I in there. Ten years ago, I went in to fetch a young friend for his arraignment for murder. The elevator ride up was in darkness; the trash drop was belching smoke and his concrete apartment for 16-year-old common-law wife and two children was without furniture, carpet or food in the pantry. While two naked children played, I talked to the teenage mother, while asking myself how anybody could believe in Divine Love when nothing, absolutely nothing is coming at you here. Then I thought: well, priest, that's where you come in. Your little intrusion into their life is the sunlight coming through the stained glass. God help them. God help me.

I know I have told that story before. I tell it at weddings. I say that is what sacrament means in marriage: spouses are the daily sign to one another of still deeper love—in which we live like fish in water. Told it so often that I am tired of hearing it myself. What else can I say. . . .

Tonight the high-rise looked as grim inside as it did 10 years ago. Now entrance security is like a jail: a security guard in a bunkerlike booth and you must describe your destination and purpose to get in.

The windowless corridors have apartments on both sides. Some brighter lighting only exposes more the trash, the graffiti, the house insects scampering about. And children playing in these corridors. Children everywhere looking at me as though I were an extraterrestrial. I am embarrassed that I am such a stranger here only five blocks from the church. Embarrassed that any priest is such an unfamiliar sight in these bunkers of the poor. Embarrassed that I am seen driving up in a seven-year-old car even. Any car must look luxurious to the women and children everywhere outside in this awful heat and humidity.

The elevator opens and out comes the smell of urine. On my visit I bring a refined Hispanic woman who is a schoolteacher. Her mother is our only Hispanic parishioner and something about the mother fascinates me. She seems quietly holy. Like that other little black woman who comes to Communion every Sunday with the hint of tears on her cheeks. I always think of the old grace or prayer state called the gift of tears.

The schoolteacher daughter is with me because over a month ago a Spanish woman came to the door to ask me to baptize her baby. My Spanish is so poor. I reached a stage of words and phrases which enable me to tend the sick at the hospital but nothing more. I keep meaning to get a tape deck in my car and hear those New Testament tapes. The idea is that since I know the story, I could soon pick up Spanish spoken rapidly, even though few opportunities here for that. The Puerto Ricans go to a neighborhood parish and we tend to be a black place.

The fourth-floor apartment door opened cautiously, and the fellow seeing the collar figured he should let me in. The apartment was an island of neatness and civility by contrast with the devastation just outside: some fine new furniture, some carefully-chosen pictures hanging, including religious images, a cloth-covered table neatly set with place mats. Even a very small microwave.

Down toward the floor, the cherubic little girl who needs Baptism. The mother appears. I guess I recognize her. A handsome son about 13 who needs *La Prima Comunion.*

Everybody is dressed down for the heat. The apartment is so high that some air is coming in the open windows and we are treated to the courtesy of iced tea.

The young father has long, full curls flowing back from a thinning scalp. He works at a fancy suburban golf course. A groundskeeper, grass cutter, I guess. I try to disarm him. This visit of priest and talk of Baptism is woman's work, but he is courteous and even curious.

Here they are, a little family trying to live a decent life with everything from drugs to mugging to frantic sex going on just outside the fragile door of their tiny apartment. Against all odds, doing the right thing or trying to do the right thing. This young handsome son will soon try crack in the corridor, and everything will come apart. Or maybe not. Maybe he won't do crack.

Soon another tiny Hispanic woman enters. She has a baby for Baptism also. Both were at the church that day a month ago. One came "priest shopping" to the door. The other waited outside watching their babies. At first I thought the little woman was about 14. Now I realize she might be 24.

Hard for me to help them. No one but the schoolteacher and myself to do Spanish with them. Some instruction for Baptism and First Communion. I cannot begin to turn them over to some program of ours. I shall have to work it out. Somehow. It will not be easy or orderly. That young fellow is not going to want to sit for instructions. These women are going to come sporadically and always late because of babies and distance and crises. Cannot ignore the faith or hope of two little Spanish women timidly knocking at the rectory door looking for Baptism for their children. I cannot even pass them off to another church. They expect to get passed on or refused because they are not properly married or whatever. A month or more since she stopped by and not a word from me until now—this visit and the earlier call.

They even have a date in mind: October 21, when the sponsors will come down from Brooklyn.

Leaving, we are accompanied all the way down and out to the car by the young man, who performs this courtesy with European *elegancia*. Spanish culture seeping into this hellhole from chivalric Spain by way of Puerto Rico. I have not seen manners like this anywhere in years, not even in fancy neighborhoods.

I drove the Hispanic woman home farther up into the barrio. The heat had everybody out:  street corners, front steps, empty lots. Fellows playing dominoes or in groups of three or four along the sidewalk in improvised or old-fashioned beach chairs. Not many air-conditioners in windows of the tiny rowhouses dense upon one another. One rowhouse had a TV satellite dish the size of those at the network station on a roof hardly large enough to contain it.

# *11*

The holiday weekend blows in with heat that would deny this calendar end of summer.

A difference about being here and just working or even living here is visible on holiday weekends. The people here are simply here. Holidays mean perhaps a cookout or a block party. Those who work here or merely live here are gone—off to seashores and mountains.

The difference is obvious but not acknowledged. Only a Charles de Foucauld or a Damien of Molokai or a Dave Hagan is able to pull off being here as the people are here. De Foucauld lived among the Berbers and tried to be one of them. Damien went to Molokai and more than serve lepers became a leper himself. A priest in Brooklyn these 35 years in a tumultuous Hispanic area follows the de Foucauld tradition of the Little Brothers of Jesus and has tried to learn Spanish without the hint of an accent and learned to eat Latin-American foods.

And Dave Hagan. This Labor Day weekend the thought will not occur to Dave to go somewhere cool or green; at best he will have a cookout in his concrete backyard with the fellows who frequent his house and have nowhere to go themselves. And the best part of all this is that it is unconscious; he is just "there." Simply.

Someone told me that Protestant-American Church historian Martin Marty connects all this with celibacy, no less. In *Righteous Empire*, he says how Catholic missioners among the Native Americans entered into that society more pervasively and respectfully. Protestant missioners had family and lived more apart from that society and tended to be more condescending, less respectful of native culture.

All this by way of being content simply around the neighborhood this holiday weekend and resist those invitations to be elsewhere.

A neighbor who looks over things around these streets reminds me that he will be wanting folding chairs and tables from our school hall tomorrow morning for the local cookout. He also reminds me that I will be expected. He and the other fellows regard me somewhat as a drinking buddy, and I guess that is a compliment and incarnational. They will do lots of drinking over the next few days of fried chicken and potato salad alfresco.

# 9.

*There Is No Payoff*

# 1

Back to school time and the local Catholic high school teachers threaten a strike which takes me back almost 25 years. Bittersweet memories of an earlier strike.

I was an assistant at the Cathedral parish, busy about hospitals and baccalaureate Masses and bishops. Church renewal was still new, and even lowly curating at the Cathedral seemed a strategic place to install worship reform or ecumenism or sessions of social justice inspired by Vatican II documents. And the Cathedral rector was sympathetic. More than sympathetic. I was in awe of my own opportunity.

Suddenly a road block. A special delivery letter on a September Sunday, assigning me as temporary teacher at a local Catholic high school. Trembling, I called around to see whether other young priests had similar trouble. No avail. I knew I could not become a strike breaker. I had carefully avoided high school teaching when classmates were assigned there. Some need in me to explore being simply a priest. Not priest as teacher, priest as scholar. Priest as priest. The nearest thing I could imagine to the French worker-priests possible in this American landscape. Even this Cathedral duty was a detour. A seduction of Vatican II: I know this is a bad job but think of all the good I can do.

All afternoon an agony of self-doubt after a diocesan official who lived there at the Cathedral with me told me that my duty was to teach. Simply. The old invocation of ordination promises. My joined hands between the two hands of the ordaining cardinal: *"Promittis mihi et successoribus meis reverentiam et obedientiam?"* My nervous, affirmative response.

But deeper than self-doubt, I knew all day that I could not go. The official said we would talk late at night when he returned from whatever. A long day for me, unable to eat or attend anything else. Even paralyzed by the fear of the consequences of this decision. Religious obedience. The confidence shown in me by having me at the Cathedral. Heavy stuff.

The late night session was difficult. Anger coming at me full force. Something I handle very poorly. I held my ground, was told that I was making a serious mistake. I responded that the mistake was probably not my first and would not be my last. I was told that I seemed confused. I pleaded that the best of our tradition said that one did not have to act with a confused conscience. I returned to my own room with all the solemnity and doom of Thomas More returning to his cell in the Tower of London after holding out against Henry VIII and his minions.

Next day, the Catholic teachers strike ended after 20 minutes of a picket line. Nothing obvious ever came from my refusal, but I knew this meant the end of my Cathedral days. Now 25 years later, I feel good about that decision. Good to know that when the pressure was on, I was once able to take the heat. Do the right thing. Even the official clerical theology, which can cynically make clerical obedience a means of control, recognized that religious obedience is quite limited and not intended to intrude upon conscience or integrity. Nor do I recognize it as something the authorities can use to have me help them break a strike.

Dorothy Day was always most respectful and quite reluctant to criticize Church or cardinals, even when they disappointed her with their support of war. She did express outrage almost when Cardinal Spellman used New York seminary students to break a Catholic cemetery workers' strike.

## 2

The young Hispanic fellow from the high-rise public housing project appears at the weekday evening Mass. He was here on Sunday with his mother, who came for instruction about the Baptism of her younger child. In her apartment we discussed First Communion for the sixth grader about to enter middle school. Here he is back again. Something about the place must attract him. He is dressed quite formally: shirt and tie and dress shoes, even in hot weather.

I just want to scoop him up and take him away from that brutal project where chances are that he will not make it. Drugs and early sex and the lack of privacy and the noise will undermine any school effort.

My mind begins to work, threatening and oppressing me with still another project which I can hardly afford by way of sanity or my nervous system: the father of this boy works at a suburban golf club. I have contacts at several private schools near the golf club. Perhaps a school would take him in free. The Catholic school especially. He could travel back and forth with his father going to work. He could know the Catholic culture which is his Spanish birthright and which poverty and projects have prevented.

He is artistic. After walking through the empty church, he asked for pencil and paper and began to draw some impressions. Somehow he wants to tell me that he feels and knows and hurts, that there is more to him than a public housing poverty case. I sense his effort at communication. He is wary of a priest. He has some of the uncertainty of his father about us fellows. Yet something here draws him. He wants to trust me, find out what I am about being in charge of such an elegant, mysterious place.

Can I take this on? Or can I not take it on? It means the first of many phone calls. My initial contact will understand. He knows how hopeful and simple I can be about these things: that the Sisters or whoever will simply make room for him. Always room for one more or so it should be.

It will become complicated. The principal will not believe that I expect it to happen so easily and free of cost. She will want to see his transcript or whatever elementary school children have. Clothes and uniforms will enter the picture; who will pay for all that? I will or somebody will. Where can I find the time to run him back and forth for these negotiations and interviews? Forget it. You are exhausted already. A nausea setting in. One more thing. That fellow getting out of the projects into the Jesuit college was something that happens once in a lifetime.

The change might not even be good for the youth. He would be in school with children from fancy homes and he going home to the projects. Even if he is bright, he probably is several levels behind his age group, given the reality of his present schools. Forget it. A romantic notion. What good taking this one fellow out of his environment?

But I cannot forget it. I am going to make that phone call, begin the process, even if it leads nowhere. Even if it means a more impossible week in what looks like an impossible week already.

And if the Catholic contact does not work, I will try the other contact. An even fancier school. Why do I suspect that the fancy private school that is not Catholic might be more helpful than the Catholics?

# 3

Today the feast of Peter Claver, who has been with me almost 40 years since I read his biography in early seminary days. I was overwhelmed by the heroism, the almost savage courage and endurance of his life.

Everything about him appealed to me: his leaving aside the Jesuit intellectual and academic track to take care of slaves in the hold of ships. His hanging in there with it all for 40 years. Doing the impossible thing against all odds and with little sign of success. Even his heaviness of spirit attracted me. "A knight of the woeful countenance," indeed, with his quixotic effort against misery that would easily overwhelm the helper as well as the victim. A biography says of him that he seldom smiled and people tell me that I look sad or stern often enough, and this warning that I might be revealing too much of my desperate interior worries me. Besides I do not want to communicate sadness around me. The world is sad enough. People have enough trouble without my reminders.

Of course, Claver did not address the social evil of slavery and he can be criticized for that. Like all of us, he was a child of his times and accepted too much of what should not be accepted. Besides the very humility and inner deprivation or whatever which enabled him to identify with such suffering probably prevented him from any assertive, furious protest against the whole slave trade. He would not have had such "confidence in his own convictions," as they say, apart from Jesuit obedience and all that. If the Jesuits corporately accepted the institution of slavery as they did, Claver would not presume to question it. His own inner struggle would grasp intuitively the suffering of slaves and the response would be visceral, not intellectual.

Anyhow, I think I am right about the fellow from much exploration of him over the years.

Most scary and horrific and mysterious is that during his own later years, when this man who took care of others was himself aged and sick, he was relegated to the "fourth floor rear" of the Jesuit residence and for years so neglected and forgotten and even abused or beaten by a community slave that he had vermin, lice on his body. It recalls a line from the film version of *The Razor's Edge* which says, "there is no pay off."

# 4

Burdened and heavy beyond my burdens, I hear my street friend of 20 years on the phone. He has a test next week for possible heart trouble. Now that he is not drinking, he has from the doctor some medicine for stress, with warning from the doctor that these pills could become addictive.

His former wife is insisting he take in his stepson for two months until a Job Corps berth opens somewhere. His own older son broke up with a girlfriend and is now sleeping and eating again at this one-room, third-floor flat with an improvised kitchen and bathroom where he already hosts his young son and dependent, unemployed brother.

He wants to talk to me about two things: some need to connect with Church again, away from the severity of his childhood Seventh Day Adventist family, and how he can resist the impossible manipulation of his former common-law wife who will respond to his reluctance to accept the stepson by just sending the stepson here from a neighboring state.

All this while trying to put in a day at work, a commercial office where attention and accuracy are required of him, despite all these personal worries. An office he gets to by using three different urban and suburban buses every morning after walking to the addiction clinic for his daily morning treatment.

And here I am heavy and so much less burdened, hardly feeling able for the conversation about Church that he wants. My own heaviness has me so dry that I can scarcely get religious language onto my lips.

I guess I can just suffer my minor worry and discouragement as a way of being here and poor the way my friend is poor. His poverty so more immense and real than mine. He carries it all so much better than I do.

# 5

The tedious meetings. This one I manage to believe in more, say, than the one tomorrow night when the fundraiser from the archdiocese comes to meet the parish council to tell us the details of our participation in the diocesan effort. I know the *participatio* is only right and even appropriate. I need look no further than the local Baptist churches to see how the pastors there are so much more able than myself at getting the widow's mite. The problem is my own difficulty asking money from people who seem to have so little. My fall appeal letter quotes a 1980 census statistic (1990 not yet available) saying that the average household income up here is $7100, and thus parents spent 12% of that sending children to our parish school.

The meeting today, which I do believe in even when it is tedious, is that three-year effort to organize local churches into a coalition which could become another player in the urban scene besides government and business. Our organizer is part of an effort which has had spectacular success in New York City, Baltimore, Los Angeles, Memphis and elsewhere.

Not easy gathering in the churches. Black Baptist churches and pastors seem to operate like Lone Rangers and are spread everywhere onto boards and coalitions so that the serious focus which this serious effort requires is hard to obtain. The Catholic Church did come through with funding from a national source in the Bishops' conference. The need of the archdiocese to control is a problem. Difficult for them to enter a coalition as equal among peers. We are not asking the archdiocese to enter anything, just to allow us to enter as individual parishes and not send down signals that will make pastors wary of something they should not be wary about. Or even if wary, not unwilling to risk and experiment with this new effort.

The organizer had a newspaper article in photocopy. The article had appalling statistics saying that "in 1990 there were 71,824 vacant housing units in Philadelphia, 78% more than in 1980."

Welcome to the neighborhood where I have lived and worked almost 20 years. Most of these vacant houses are up and down these streets, so you can imagine what the neighborhood looks like—a war zone. Up and down these streets burned-out, caved-in, litter-strewn rowhouses. Sometimes an entire block of ruins with trash falling down the front steps and one inhabited house in the whole row. You wonder about the impact of this landscape on the sensibility of the young children who are everywhere. They must absorb this ugly human ruin as normative.

# 6

Late in the afternoon I am waiting for Dave Hagan, who is late stopping by. When he does arrive, I have news that someone called here to tell him that the Catholic church around the corner from his own house is on fire.

Dave arrives and we are quickly off to the fire scene. The crowded streets appear more soiled than ever in the bright afternoon sun. Business as usual. A four-alarm fire only blocks away means nothing along these streets. Calamity and tumult on every corner, no need to look for more action.

Closer by, the scene is, of course, different. Fire trucks and police cars, flashing red lights, the water department, streets blocked off. The static of police radios, crowds of people across the street from the seedy old dowager of a church now full of smoke, with firemen still breaking stained-glass windows and water pouring in through highly-mounted water cannons.

Dave and I hang out too much together not to be processing the same metaphors: in July the collapse of the stone church tower of the long-closed neighboring Catholic church here. Now this fire devouring this old place hidden in the shadows of the projects. As though fire finally devouring old church is dramatic expression of the human destruction or devouring going on in these streets every day.

And is the Church devoured by these brutal realities as is this church building finally after years and decades of decay and collapse under the realities of this neighborhood?

Our cynicism is full: how extensive will this fire be? Will the authorities use it as reason for further withdrawal from these neighborhoods? Next door, a large parish school of 500 students. Almost twice as many as other inner-city Catholic schools, including our own. We recall that the school building is much newer than the burning church because the school is a replacement for a school destroyed by fire about 20 years ago when several firemen perished. Dave recalls how that fire was the beginning of the end for heroic old Monsignor McHale, who was pastor then. Those deaths just the weakness he needed to undo whatever defenses he had against the sense of failure which goes with the pastoral territory here.

Dave often tells a story about old McHale. How Dave moving into the neighborhood and sweated up from carrying furniture into his house needed to shower and went across to the rectory. The Monsignor answered the door to a dishevelled Dave, and only after Dave returned from showering in the Monsignor's old rooms did the Monsignor ask gently: Who are you anyhow?

As we stood in the noisy crowd watching firemen at work, another former pastor of the old church arrived. He had spent many years here and worked hard in every direction: fundraising, school service center. Against all odds doing the impossible. Five years ago his worn self was moved elsewhere. A place not easy, but easier.

Standing beside him I soon saw tears, full tears streaming down his cheeks. Not sobs, but tears. I can imagine the feeling he has for this old place. Good man. Gave much to this place. Years of his life, years off his life, I reckon.

# 7

Yesterday on my hospital run, the Irish Sister friend who does pastoral care had a book for me. A biography of the bishop who founded her Irish missionary order.

The book was given her by an elderly member of her sisterhood whom I know but do not know. Rightly or otherwise, I am in awe of the elderly Sister.

I know her story because she was friend and cofounder with the heroic man who was my pastor in Southwest Philadelphia years ago. Together they founded a nursing home for elderly black people, and her sisters came from Ireland to staff it. But the story of the elderly Sister who stills lives in a suburb here is larger than that, much larger. I see she is even an important source of information for the biography of the bishop who founded her missionary congregation.

Years and years ago, she wanted after high school to go from her native Philadelphia to Africa as a missionary Sister. No American congregation would promise her Africa, so she went all the way to Ireland and a new mission society which then served only in Africa.

Soon enough she found herself back in Philadelphia on the very street where she was raised, making an American foundation for her order. The years were the early 50s and the United States was overflowing with religious vocations and generous Catholics waiting to be asked to help the missions.

I remember those Sisters moving there into my home neighborhood during my own seminary years. I vaguely remember the Sister about the card parties and raffles and teas she needed to found an American house for the novices who were crowding in.

Finally the building of a handsome modern novitiate for 50 or 75 sisters in the area of Villanova University, with the intention no doubt of using Villanova for schooling.

Then one day I was asked to come to the new novitiate to say Mass for a former resident Sister whom I knew somewhat. News had just arrived concerning her death in Africa.

During the Requiem Mass, I could see beyond the Sisters the foyer where box upon box were awaiting removal. The novitiate was to be a victim of the vocation slump that came after Vatican II. The Sisters could no longer use or sustain the expense of this place and had sold their American house to Villanova University for a student residence.

The now elderly Sister was there in the congregation during that Mass perhaps 15 years ago. Then and even until now I wonder what must go on in her. What does she think of her life and work? Going off to Ireland to Africa, back to the United States to organize and build an American foundation being undone even as we commend one of her Sisters to the grave.

Later, even her nursing home was taken away. Catholic Social Services took over and removed her Sisters for other Sisters.

Now I seldom see the elderly Sister whom I notice is often mentioned in this biography, which itself is a tragic enough story of her Sisters and their later alienation from the bishop who founded them. Sister inscribed this copy of the biography I am looking through with a note to the Sister who passed it on to me. She asks the younger Sister to garner from the book some appreciation and love for their "dear founder."

When I do see the elderly Sister, she seems quite at peace. She must be a mystic or something. Unless old age brings a peace of its own quite beyond the troubles of life or the kind of agitation I feel so often about so much.

# 8

A friend is in town, and word from his brother here is that he wants us to go to dinner. The fellow from afar knows me mostly from my begging appeal letters. Especially concerning the school. His own memories of childhood and Catholic school make him want to help keep the parish school going as the very best way the Church can serve impoverished people. Somehow he has a sense of these neighborhoods and knows how bad things are. We connect. A seriousness or urgency about all this which we sense in one another. *Actio in distans,* as in that old philosophy I studied about somewhere or other.

Of course the dinner means to be a treat for the priest struggling in inner city, so the evening will be an expensive and extravagant treat. And I pleased enough for the affection and eager enough for a fancy dinner that I look forward to the evening.

So earlier tonight I head towards Old City and Society Hill. First drinks in a new hotel lobby, then up the street to an expensive seafood restaurant.

Just as I am driving across the street which is bordered more or less between ghetto and downtown, I see a familiar fellow crossing the street or waiting for my car to pass before crossing.

He has a shirt in hand and is bare-chested in the cooling evening. He looks like he has not had a good day wandering these streets, looking for food or drugs or cigarettes or carfare or whatever. Once we had an almost violent exchange in the rectory foyer. He comes on rather strong, insisting on seeing me, and once when they told him I was not home he pushed past the housekeeper to find me in the house.

I was coming down the steps just in time to see his push and I was suddenly in a rage. We pushed at one another so as to frighten housekeeper and visiting couple following me down the stairway. The couple were, I remember, dismayed at how close I live to anger, how easily and dangerously I exploded. They were as appalled at such lack of control in a priest as they were afraid I would push him to something desperate—a knifing or something.

Once an exchange in the same foyer was even worse. A now-recovered addict who then occasionally fell off the wagon had drug dealers at the door looking for their money. He got rid of them by saying the Father at the church had his money. Holding it for him.

The day was Holy Saturday and the place here was wide open. People fixing flowers, people preparing church for the great Easter Vigil. People making dinner. People practicing for their Baptism later that evening. And I was trying to arrange in my head the lengthy and complicated service when I would have to hold everything together.

Suddenly the drug dealers were in the foyer demanding their money. I reacted fiercely to their boldness: get out of here, you junkies.

The larger fellow lunged at me, saying no honkie priest was going to call him a junkie. It took several of the people around doing flowers or whatever to pull us apart. I asked how much was the debt and tried to calm things down with $20 which I had in my pocket.

Drained of all peace and this time appalled myself at my own temper, I soon had to go out into the darkened school yard all dressed in fine Easter vestments and invite the people to the peace and joy of "this most holy night." I felt like a robot mouthing empty words which had no echo within me. Sometimes faith can be like that: going through the motions in the hope of better times.

I drove past the fellow wandering the streets, looking like he had a bad day and not a cent in his pocket. I could stop and treat him to a dollar or five. Big treat coming my way that evening. I did not stop. He did not see me. He still does stop at the house in his wanderings, and he puts my teeth on edge every time I see him at the door. I am in no shape to encourage his visits. Off I go to dinner. Across the street he goes to wherever.

# 9

Somewhere in the Bible a Jewish prophet or somebody is called a man of immense desires or yearning.

I hope that is the stuff in me when I come from a meeting like that the other night when people came in out of the rain for a worship meeting. I hope my yearning to do so much more with Sunday Mass is holy desire and not a pathology in me unable to accept the awful limitations, my own and those around me. Life is limited. Life is mostly limited. I cringe under those limitations. I feel powerlessness here. Eugene needs a house and a fellow out of jail needs a job, and I return from that worship music workshop wanting to make Sunday Mass worthy of the mystery we celebrate. In every case, one must settle for so much less than that imagined and desired.

Another priest returned my call today. He is my age but newer at this than I am. For years he had the full life of organizing high school and college youth eager to come into these neighborhoods to tutor or whatever. Then fate left him off as pastor at a place near here where the landscape is even more fierce. A literal battle zone with shootings every night and his need to learn Spanish in his late 50s.

Across the phones I could hear him hurting. His able young assistant took another job away from the poor, the Spanish and the parish because the new work suits his interests more—inspiring middle-class youth or whatever. Something not very different from what the pastor friend did for years. Sometimes I wish I had that freedom or self-expression or whatever enables people to follow their own needs. Most times I do not. I hold fast to the Simone Weil idea of necessity—playing the hand you have been dealt, doing what comes along regardless of your feelings might be precious because there is less room for self or ego. Less of self in it. Simone Weil kept running off to work in factories or on farms, and the brutal or monotonous physical labor would regularly crush her exacerbated sensibility. Her parents would have to intervene when she had collapsed or was near collapse. After some recuperation, she would return and do the same thing to herself.

My priest neighbor talked over the phone of the stress we work under. Stress in ourselves, those who work with us, those we are trying to help whose lives are one uninterrupted stress or catastrophe so often. I could hear the wonder and worry in him: is this it? Are we here for the duration and going down with the ship? One gradually learns that things are not going to get better, that whatever we are doing here will come undone more quickly than our doing. By any human measure, failure is the predictable outcome down the road. And the precarious reality that the authorities or the new planning office could at any moment close us down, discontinue our school.

The only answer or method is, of course, a kind of mystical attitude. Spooky word meaning that one simply stays here sharing the uncertainty, stress, confusion, instability of the poor as a way of being with them. A severe, lean way of being here. Perhaps not possible for everybody. Many days it seems as impossible for me as anybody else. You have to come to believe in being here more than doing here.

# *10*

The sense of inadequacy continues. Bad enough were it just a sense of personal inadequacy. Still more painful when I fear that I am part of a conspiracy that conceals corporate inadequacy by rhetorical excess.

Of course, I mean the Church. I almost admire the capacity to suppress doubt and mediocrity. All the ills and needs the Church should be tending simply ignored and moral passion and vigor and insight assumed by our horror of abortion.

Or closer to home. Not enough that the parish here maintain a small school as alternative to the larger and more difficult public school. I should not presume that anything more valuable is going on in our school nor should its existence deliver me from concern for the local public schools which most of the neighborhood children must attend.

People tell me that I am far too hard on myself. That as I get older in this exhausting work, I must learn to do less not more. That the conclusion from the anxiety and dissatisfaction I feel is not to try harder or do more.

No doubt what I must do is enter more deeply into some patience with the world or myself. I often envy those who can simply do their job without seeming to question much the value or quality of what they are doing. Image of the Church as some big salvation machine which beyond our sight does its job if only each of us tugs away at his oar.

The paralyzing fear that the whole operation might be obsolete, inadequate or anachronistic. Then all one's blood, sweat, and tears working for the Church might be a waste of time because the institution might be so petrified that the whole thing is irrelevant.

These fears are precisely my fears, anxieties, crippling worries. I do not intend some huge judgment on the theological validity of the Church, nor do I presume to see the whole picture, which of course is larger than anything I can contain or understand.

All that I want to say is that being around here on a Saturday more quiet than usual, when the busy traffic of the workweek is not drowning out doubt, the ghosts come flying out: what am I doing? What am I doing here? What do I believe? And no quick answers are forthcoming. Sometimes I verge on talking this way at Sunday Mass. After Mass in the vestibule or outside, I am embarrassed at my poverty or nakedness. I imagine, say, the young people doing good and generous and even heroic work at the nearby Catholic Worker wondering: what is his problem? He has here the chance and even reality of good work on behalf of others. What more does he want? Why all the doubt? The pathology of a stunted intellectual.

I find helpful expression of this inner darkness in Hopkins and his terrible sonnets.

# *11*

A Sister comes here to Mass on Sunday and I know little about her except that she is a neighborhood activist at a center just a few blocks away from here. A neighborhood of Hispanic and African-Americans in big old rowhouses around a seedy old park or "square," since the park is exactly one city block square.

A note from the Sister invites me to Open House at her center and it is about time that I returned the courtesy of her Sunday visits here. I discover that she was the principal of the local Catholic school on the Square and went off to an assignment in the sunbelt after her tour here. Somehow this neighborhood pulled her back, and still a religious Sister, she lives alone on the second or third floor of her settlement house, a place of the aroma of frying chicken and the colors of mums blooming in the improvised greenhouse beside the ramshackled old house. Children and women come and go. Little girls with their older sisters' babies in tow on their hips. My hostess tells me that the father or brother is in jail doing time on drug charges.

At times the Sister describes her work as though she was reduced to keeping drug dealers off the square and away from the children. Not even having the drug dealers arrested or prosecuted, none of us here interested in sending anybody off to the brutal prisons.

Just keeping the square drug-free by vigils and alternative activities for the children. Around the old house I notice bright-colored, huge plastic disposal drums marked for recycling. The place is full of children's books and peasant art, as they would call it in Latin America.

Sister seems direct, almost simple. Oblivious of the mystery and courage and even heroism of her solitary life. No apparent anguish in her. No weighty philosophical pondering about what this all means or how one can make a life from keeping one city block drug-free.

One of the desert fathers says that the best prayer is when you do not even know you are praying. I come away from the visit thinking that the Sister probably does not know what a marvel she is. She is probably not even interested that much in herself. Content to be there among the poorest of the poor, quite alone with it all apparently. The best presence not even to know how wonderful your presence is. I do not know whether this kind of generous hidden presence is something particularly Catholic because of the freedom and intentionality which religious life allows. Whatever it is, certainly it is the very best part of the Catholic tradition.

# *12*

Monday morning coming down, and among the early phone calls I have across the wires the familiar voice of a woman in her 40s who is black and poor and very overweight and diabetic and so alone that I can feel her aloneness even by telephone.

She said she was thinking of me and just called to say hello. I could hear the television in her little dilapidated house. Her surroundings so bleak. This Monday is dreary and overcast, her loneliness so fierce that I wonder how she got out of bed in this morning, let alone keeps her spirits up.

She asked my prayers. The sense that she is weaker or the struggle is harder than should be. And I am marvelling that she can cope at all. I ask her for particulars: does her difficulty mean that she is drinking again. No, she is not drinking at all. Several times she has gone under with alcohol and has been in institutions.

She says that she reads the Bible. Not great quantities, just enough to hear some story about a fragile person like herself who somehow manages because of divine help, and she realizes that her own survival depends on that help. And my prayers are part of the survival.

Years ago she came in off the street and asked me to instruct her in the Catholic faith. The rather cool, detached business of Catholic parish life has been so much less than what she needs, so now 20 years later, she is back in Baptist churches looking for the emotional experience and Bible teaching that will keep her going. And she regards me as a friend beyond any in or out of the Catholic Church, telling me about her Baptist return as though I can understand that need and have no problem with it.

And here on Monday morning I tried to heed the words of Thomas Keating in *Open Mind, Open Heart* that the growth is contemplative *life* more than contemplative *prayer*. The "letting go" that one does sitting in church or wherever is not just for formal prayer time. The idea is that when the call comes on Monday morning from a lonely person who wants the relief of being in touch and asking prayers and telling me her troubles, I should be able to let go of whatever important letter I am writing or the laundry list of things I have prepared for this Monday morning and be with her over the phone because she is as important as myself, her loneliness as real as my own, her need as real as any.

Sometimes I think the whole reality is not about anything more, that there is no large social problem to be solved so that this woman and others like her will not be poor or alone.

The saying of Christ, "The poor are always with you," might be a hint in that direction. Not some denial of social progress or need and possibility of social change. Just that what is along the way is the important and we shall arrive by tending what is along the way.

Dorothy Day moves that way also by saying that the real work is the soup kitchen and hospitality and not the promulgation of some new social vision less important than the concrete Corporal Works of Mercy which get us there.

And even for ourselves the interior process might be the very same as stopping to listen to the poor, overweight woman so inopportunely on the telephone first thing Monday morning. Important for me as well as her that I let go enough to listen. More than 25 years since I read *Franny and Zooey* by Salinger, in which Franny tells his sister something about shining his shoes for the fat lady.

So then what a windfall being here where there is such clamorous need pulling at me all the time, so immediate and urgent and physical that I have no choice but to be "letting go" all the time.

# *13*

Not much in the morning newspaper even, So little that I can miss the occasional worthwhile piece. A good friend directed me to a piece by a columnist who does write fine pieces. She directed me to his Sunday column on turning 60.

The columnist mentions how during his 50s he ended a 22-year-marriage and suffered two heart attacks and finally open heart surgery. He married again, and the survival of that second marriage and even survival itself became a matter of "admitting—and then doing something about—the anger that I carried around."

Last time I tried this journal, a Trappist monk friend who read it said that I indeed carried a "head of steam" around inside and that I should "cool it." I think he was naming that anger which infects and pervades me as well as the columnist as he and I both approach 60.

I know a good anger exists and probably exists in me. But there is also this other stuff: the anger that life is so limited, so dense and impenetrable that we can do so little to change the awful realities all around us.

The anger must explain some of the, well honestly, depression I feel coming to the overnight stay to discuss and build the serious and important community organizing effort that we have been working at for three years. All of us on board know how important that we build this coalition as a third party in city life, besides government and the business community. City government is in ruins and business fleeing, and all of us involved have seen the work this same community organizing has done in East Brooklyn with housing, in Baltimore and in Los Angeles.

And we arrive at the overnight, and instead of the 25 who should be there, six or eight of us are there, and four are Catholic priests and only one is black.

Inside I must be enraged. I write us priests off as duty-bound from seminary. I am as busy as anybody who should be here, and they are not here, I am certain, because they are going to allow themselves to be carried along.

Other rage comes from my personal limitations. Not being able, say, to pull this place of mine together the way my priest friend across the river pulls his place together: 45 completely-renovated houses developed for poor people for his parish alone. And I cannot find one house for my friend living in a third floor with son and step-son and older son and unemployed brother all devouring him.

I cannot with letter and exhortation and the promise of instrumental accompanists pull off a decent choir rehearsal earlier tonight for the important anniversary Mass and celebration for Dave on Sunday. A fine light rain and everybody stays home. The few who do attend are themselves discouraged by the poor showing.

I could go on and on. The anger with the shortcomings of the Church, exacerbated by the rhetorical excess. The anger with the loneliness of my lifelong choices.

So much. The columnist says, "I am less serious about myself and life now and that pleases me." The small book of theologian Henri de Lubac, S.J., I was reading this morning adds: "He who takes himself too seriously will never dominate his pain. It is his pain that dominates him, even if he seems to have got the better of it. It puts a strain on him, hardens him, withers him" (*Further Paradoxes*).

Dave on the phone tonight. I could notice in him a muted anger or dismay or something about the seeming deadend of his life right now. His house overrun with young fellows who have been around him for 20 years. Only now they are 30 years old and having babies themselves and he feels almost dispossessed of house and eaten out of refrigerator by fathers and children. He would not want it any other way. They have no other place to go and are the reason he is there. But that does not make a chaotic evening of a too-crowded house and crying children easy. And one of the responses is a pervasive anger at them, at self, at society. And the more he feels it, the more anger he feels with himself for not absorbing it better. But maybe I am talking more about myself here than Dave. Projecting on his substantial self the anger I do or would feel, and deep down even harbor further anger with myself for not absorbing it as well as I imagine Dave does.

# *14*

The Dave Hagan day. I knew that numbers of people would show up for his marking 25 years as a priest. Even I did not expect those numbers. The old church was full. Eight hundred people must have come, some from as far as Florida.

Mostly white the crowd. That is just the way it is. Whatever any of us is about up here, appreciation is as dissolved as for any heroic grandmother doing it all over again with grandchildren. They know and Dave knows that there is no payoff. You do it because you are here and the thing needs doing.

Which does not mean that the brothers who are around Dave's house or their mothers and sisters did not arrive with the babies. They came, enough of them, but the gathering of one year in these neighborhoods is scattered by another year, by jail or moving across town with a new girlfriend or lost on the streets to drugs or occasionally off to some distant small college for basketball. Enough neighborhood people were there, given those realities. The numbers present say nothing about the 20 years and the numbers who played basketball with his coaching or had a cemetery groundskeeping job by his effort or stayed out of jail because Dave was in court for him.

Nice to know that people everywhere have good instincts. Dave was overwhelmed by the turnout. People know the real thing when they see it and do respond with gratitude and awe. Many do not take formal Church life so seriously anymore, but childhood and Catholic school and family give us the sense of Gospel behind Church so that they know what is really required of us and cannot but respond when they see it fleshed out now and then, which is to say that there is faith there, hidden, wounded, suspended, disappointed by Church. Still there enough to flare up, stir to a flame being with Dave for his 25th.

The whole gathering was great: the full church, the music, the great touch of black Gospel—just a touch—in the way our black woman reader did the first reading and the visceral "My Tribute," sung after Communion by an awesome black Catholic gentleman whom Dave and I have known for years. Whatever the poverty of this area and the black people here, the Mass reveals how much richer emotionally the faith and life.

You would have to call the Mass overflowing into party in our school hall Catholic or Mediterranean. Maybe Irish. People just out of church with a Scotch or bourbon or beer standing around in groups inside and out—a wonderful day for alfresco, and the hall could not begin to hold everybody. A party which no one wants to leave because the sense unfolds that everything is real: Dave is real, and the reality of his life is worth celebrating, and the easy informal style is extension of his persona. People here feeling good about Dave and enjoying feeling good about Church or another what could have been a dreary invitation and formality. And they come, and even in coming they know because of Dave it will not be formal or dreary. And that feeling so rare and precious that people want to linger in it. A great day.

# 10.

# The Primacy of the Spiritual

# 1

An important feast today. At least important for me. Saint Thérèse of the Child Jesus. The little Victorian French woman who became a Carmelite nun at 15 or 16 and was dead at 24.

One can read her story—her autobiography even—as a disaster or a miracle. Or both. Several years ago a film about her called *Thérèse* won the Cannes film festival, and an eminent secular American newsweekly called it "the film of the year."

I was so curious and pleased and surprised that I went all the way to New York City to see it because I was not sure it would make Philadelphia. It made it for about one week.

The film just puts the whole crazy story out there without much comment. Brief impressionist vignettes from her autobiography, with the filmmaker apparently saying: "Well, here she is; here it is. Maybe holiness, maybe pathology, but here she is as best we can discover."

Pathology because a Carmelite cloister is no place for a 16-year-old girl, especially someone going there because her mother died and three sisters who mothered her had left her for Carmel. Crazy because she was hypersensitive and emotionally needy in a place where the danger was that older Sisters would dote on her and keep her a "little flower" indeed, the eternal child.

Somehow she made it. Locked in that cloister, feeding her the worse *petit bourgeois* pieties, she made it through until she was 24 and died. She did not let her older sisters pamper her. She did not have much direction from an older and wiser head. She did not collapse into sentimentality. She was physically and emotionally incapable of the whole scene, yet somehow made her way through the impossible. At one point before Carmel, she read in the newspapers about a murderer named Mazzini about to be executed and still unrepentant. She took him on as a prayer project, asking some sign through him that her silly little life might have some meaning beyond the petty details. When she read that on the scaffold or guillotine, he grabbed a crucifix from the accompanying priest, she took that as sign of approval.

The seminary routine was hard on me. Looking back, I can see that part of me could not absorb the petty detail as well as Thérèse. I did not know that clearly then, only that something was terribly wrong and that something was probably myself who therefore did not belong there.

Yet I was determined to be a priest, no matter what. Regularly I would expose my insides to some priest on the premise that honesty and transparency were essential here. Sometimes I must have hoped that the listener would ease my anguish by sending me packing home: anybody so uncertain here, so unhappy even must be in the wrong place.

That never happened. As I recall 40 years later, the listeners either did not know what to do with such burdens or dismissed them out of hand as part of the ordeal. Or earlier childhood wounds that I had to discover eventually and deal with there as well as anywhere.

So I stayed. And I discovered Thérèse, her love of priests, her taking them on as brothers, her promise to spend her "heaven doing good upon earth." I understood my own dark—so dark—passage as something like hers. Her utter inability for Carmel as something like my own inability for seminary, which in those days might have been as severe and difficult as Carmel.

Over the years I have not always been attentive to this little sister. As poor at it as we unmarried people can be with relationships. Not hanging tough with a tough thing as married people more often must—or should.

Yet I keep coming back to her.

Simone Weil says somewhere that Thérèse is a poor choice for the Church to be putting forth as saint. Simone would have been put off by the sentimentality. Perhaps that early on Simone only had the contrived image presented by the calculating sisters of Thérèse. Simone Weil and Thérèse had this in common: the surest and most reliable way is the way of suffering. Both were unwavering disciples of that passage as the inevitable one for anyone going anywhere with it all.

And Thérèse saying that she would spend her heaven doing good on earth. An elderly priest friend tells me that in all the tradition of saints no one ever said anything like that, that kind of concern there for what might be going on here.

# 2

A spare hour or at least an hour to attend things waiting on a desk and suddenly a sick call—which is not quite a sick call.

As I return to the house for that spare hour, the secretary is anxious, almost frantic to have me return a phone call, and the voice on the other end has a Spanish accent. His mother died at 8:00 a.m. and the hour is now 11:00 a.m. and would I come and anoint her before the undertaker removes the body? I almost begin explaining how we do not anoint people already dead for three hours. Suddenly I realize that I simply must go there and say some prayers over the woman's body. No explanation. No discourse on sacramental practice. Just go. Gather the family around the bed and say the prayers.

The name means nothing to me. The house is in a ruinous, devastated block where here a house, there a weed-overgrown lot, there an abandoned car, and here and there an empty lot between houses because a row house has fallen down.

The house is unfamiliar. The Puerto Rican people over here who go to Catholic Church at all go to another church nearby. My place is African-American. The other place Hispanic. All this leaves me wondering why I was called.

A familiar face greets me at the door. Familiar, he says, because I anointed his mother last January in the nearby hospital. Again the reason why I was called. Having given the Last Rites to the old woman 10 months ago, I am the designated pastor.

I usher the family members upstairs. Second floor front and a tiny body hardly larger than a child lies carefully veiled in a sheet. The morning sun is still over the back of the house, and we begin our prayers in the shadows. Spanish seems more appropriate than English so I read from my Spanish Ritual, reprimanding myself for not practicing my Spanish more. Apart from the few anointing prayers, I seldom have the opportunity to use Spanish, but it would surely be opportune now. I know my accent will be rough and I will mess up possessive pronouns and adjectives—not handily substituting feminine for masculine.

I am doing well enough so that they understand when to respond to the prayers. I go on with those lovely commendations of the soul to the angels and "the bosom of Abraham."

Unto the end I am trying to free myself from the responsibility for the funeral. Almost—not quite—suggesting or rather presuming that they will go to the Hispanic parish. No way. The husband of the deceased was buried from Saint Malachy, and they will bury her from there right after the weekend. So be it, the funeral will mean a whole day with cemetery, and they will expect a priest at the funeral home on Sunday night. I was already planning how I might be free for an overnight at the seashore after the weekend. Goodbye, plans.

What is my resistance, and why do I resist doing a decent thing even as I am doing it? I will be easy on myself and say exhaustion rather than laziness. Everyone says that I take too much on, and these several days have been so busy, so many people looking for me, so many phone calls and inquiries and deadlines and people in hospitals or gracious people just wanting to tell me how wonderful the celebration for Dave.

You reach a point where you feel panic, sense that if you try to absorb any more, you will collapse or go crazy. And just at the height of the exhaustion, the sick call or whatever it is comes, and what can you do but go there, knowing you're doing the right thing even if whole parts of you are holding back, resisting even.

# *3*

Off to New York City for a funeral. A longtime friend who years ago left the Catholic priesthood and became eventually an Episcopal priest and pastor in New York City. All during his illness, I worried whether he should or might even want to make his peace with the Catholic Church.

And here someone who went the other way. And the modern sensibility and even secularized Catholics would perceive any Christian church and some partial expression of the whole reality and where one winds up with it all having no significance beyond itself. Curiously, even John Henry Newman would support this. His opinion about the primacy of conscience: a toast to the Pope indeed, but to his conscience and then the Pope.

But I worry. I worry whether the reasons for leaving are disappointment or hurt and how we should heal those wounds rather than let them dispose us. No more—that a reality exists out there to which we should conform ourselves and that reality out there is the Catholic Church claiming fullest possession of the Mystery.

I have no problems with people who come the other way: people who leave, say, a Protestant church even for disappointment and disillusionment. But off to New York tomorrow, I will wish my friend had made his peace with Mother Church or something, and his burial in his new faith will leave me with real sadness.

I perceive myself thus as an anachronism, a medieval person trying to use obsolete norms to make my way, and thus isolated from friends who cannot in a hundred years comprehend my sadness or difficulty. They have come to experience life as so dense, so impenetrable that truth or reality out there is simply unavailable.

One does well to hold onto anything, and if some alternative nourishes faith or hope whatever, so be it.

I record all this to tell how incomplete, unable I am. How I stumble and wander through this new world so much more poorly than others do. We all carry baggage, and a large part of mine is the classicist mold that shaped me over the seminary years. At best one of the last Renaissance men. At worst an obsolete curiosity. I can be glad that I have the resources to be here and able so far to do a work that others say they could not begin to do, either by living or working here.

So. If a large part of me is an outworn sensibility, someone with intellectual and moral problems a modern person should not have, well, that is the downside. The upside is that I am living and working in a difficult place and doing better with it than others say they could. And as I walk these ruined streets, I sense beneath the surface discontent with self and world and Church an obscure gratitude that with all the contingency and free-fall of life, I tumble into this corner of the world, not far at all from my childhood neighborhood, not far from the downtown of this city where I have always lived, not far even from the hospital where I was born. I shall have to discover and inhabit more familiarly and comfortably that gratitude so elusive but also abiding. Without much sense or belief in Providence governing the details of our lives, I must be grateful for the free-fall which has me here, more or less on my feet most of the time.

# 4

As the weeks continue, I continue to worry about my friend in that third-floor walkup room with improvised bath and kitchen which serves as apartment for himself and young son and stepson and unemployed brother and now older son who had broken up with a girlfriend.

He calls occasionally to ask whether anything is happening with the house or two which might be available for rent. And in the way life happens around here, I find myself doing what comes next rather than giving any urgency or priority to the items. Sometimes I feel I should—must—make myself less available to the phone. It has such a way of interrupting whatever is happening, however important and more important than the phone call. One reason I take the calls is to avoid callbacks. I know I dread calling back because most often I do not. A recent coping device is not to call back. If the call was important, the caller will call again. This discourtesy infuriates some people, but I do not know what else to do. Life cannot become a series of telephone calls.

What I should do is search out that woman who owns that empty house which is fully furnished and will be vandalized if left long empty. What I should do is call that other woman who has a second home in the neighborhood and see if she would consider a rental after renovations. Perhaps the renovations are completed. Probably not, but I should call anyhow.

Amazing how we are all culturally afflicted. Because my street friend is poor and suffers patiently the intolerable situation of four people in one room, I also do not give him any serious attention. Against all advice of his counselor, I do give him money regularly for his transit pass or new sneakers for school for his young son. Last week he asked whether Saturday I might accompany him to a distant suburb where his young son is playing football. He is very aware that the son has only him for parent right now, and my friend is anxious to do for him what middle-class parents do: watch the son play football on Saturday.

And I have to be in another distant suburb for a wedding which I promised to attend because the father of the bride is worried about the whole affair, and my presence will reassure him. So often when I should simply be in the neighborhood for neighborhood matters, I am away from the neighborhood for this or that. Over the years I should have learned how to be more fully here, more pervasively here, not so caught in other worlds of my origins which require me in less desperate ways than my friend needing a real apartment or a Saturday ride so that his son can play football.

# 5

A day away. The Jersey shore in October. The air and light and monarch butterflies and geese flying south, apparently using the ocean edge for navigational guidance. This morning, early, several of those V formations, three or four separate ones within 15 minutes. I wonder whether they are separate or together in some larger sense.

The dune grass has a golden tassel of ragweed or something and smaller birds dart in and out the dunes. Thousands of them quietly. Impossible to tell whether they are also part of some migratory process.

Over a cleft in the dune the midmorning sea. The slant of light right now licks the shimmering surface so that sea is as bright as or brighter than the cloudless sky.

And the silence so unfamiliar to this city fellow. Uncomfortable, threatening even, summoning my own depths as nervous and dark as the sea just beneath that shimmering. I resist the impulse to play music, make some distracting sound. Learn to be ever more comfortable with my insides, the darkness, the worry, the doubt. Let everything surface. Better to meet the updraft here rather than go home tomorrow and play all this out in distraction and impatience and that chronic weariness which affects everything and my conduit with everyone from friend to coworker to stranger at the door.

Something to be learned from loneliness. Facing it here and becoming unafraid certainly better than those thousand devices seeking comfort and affection at every turn.

Some would wonder why we should endure loneliness when others out there are also lonely, and we can comfort one another. There is some sense in easing the loneliness if we do not devour one another.

Another possibility is to face the human truth that we are all alone. Years ago at a wedding, a Protestant clergyman responded to my almost-apology that I was there alone because I was a Catholic priest and thus unmarried.

He gestured across the room to his striking wife, and avowing that their marriage was as good as any, he added that in a sense we are all alone.

So being alone here in the silence of this seashore place after the summer visitors leave is a way of facing a truth of the human condition. Not the only truth but an important truth.

And facing my loneliness is a way of being poor, as so many around me are poor. I would insist that I am there to share their life more than help them.

How much can I help? A job here, a few dollars there, helping someone obtain admission to a substance abuse program.

I know I am in dangerous terrain here. The taking on of more difficulty than might otherwise have happened in my own life. Simone Weil says that enough affliction will always be around without our having to search out trouble. Affliction makes saints, but most of us are hardly saints, and presumption is an offense, a sin even, against grace.

But it is not so much searching out as accepting the free-fall of my life. When and what I am at 58 because of choice and because of Church. Yet as much from Church as choice. Early on into the priest track and accepting the cultural accoutrements as normative and even normal, so that eventually you are where you are with it all as people are where they are in a marriage or with children "for better or worse," as the marriage vows say.

Some felt need toward closure here. Better to leave this open. Like this day away will be. As life itself is. Not affliction sought out, but necessity embraced. Necessity perhaps more open to grace, say, than choice because there is less ego. Yet even that decision ambiguous. Surrender to necessity can mean lethargy or even cowardice, the fear of deciding or trying something else. Finally we are reduced to an unknowing of self so that we must live with uncertainty. So I shall practice by living with the uncertainty and unfamiliar—or all-too-familiar doubts which surface in this lonely day away by the sea.

## 6

Only an hour from the city. Last night I watched the sunset over the water into the pines of New Jersey.

A few hours ago I sat on a deck outside the bedroom and waited for the sun to come up out of the ocean.

Last evening and this morning were both crisp October. No clouds except a few long, thin tissues last evening which made the sunset even more exotic as they held the orange long after the sun had fallen behind the trees far across the bay. I stood on a dock and stayed long enough to sit down afterwards on a bulkhead. The low tide was flapping on the bed of sand and shells. Lonesome sounds and the smell of low tide. Another sound was the rope lashings against the metal masts of the small craft tied up beside me.

This morning no clouds whatever. Just the fireball coming up from the sea after almost an hour of painting the eastern horizon every shade from port to dark orange to a yellow as bright as the goldenrod on the dunes between me and sea and rising sun.

The beauty of the world. A friend who was a priest and then not a priest and then a priest again once told me that the mystery and splendor makes him believe almost despite himself. I had always thought that if anyone could put belief aside, he could then believe better than most.

Another priest and friend long-ago-married visited me last week. I had thought that Church and ministry had squeezed almost all belief from him those years ago when he left. A vague Unitarianism at best, I surmised.

Either I was wrong or he has come full circle. Healed as this new morning sun heals and commences a new day. Curiously, I sit watching creation at its very best and remember my friend's words last week. He had little feeling for creation theology. More the sense that the world is a desperate, mostly brutal place if we remember the war and famine and suffering going on at any minute. He felt more the need for saving, healing, redemption if you will. I recall how artist friend Bob McGovern said once that the word "salvation" might be better translated as "salvaging."

So my sense of myself as I linger here beside the sea. The late morning sun splashing on every blessed flap the wind raises on the water, making sea as brilliant as sky.

Soon this bruised, weary self must return to the city, the asphalt. The sunrise invites me to believe the beauty of the world. My affect comes mostly from the lifelong sense that no one is out there. Never was to the amount of my need or desperation. But the glow of that rising sun coloring the whole ocean orange for the moments before sun is finally out and up invites me more deeply than affect or feeling or reaction. This happens every blessed morning, whether someone is watching or not, and what happens every morning or evening is never quite repeated. A small bird there now gone, hidden in the dune grass. The Gospel invitation is to believe that even that tiny, utterly unimportant creature is known, cherished in some mysterious sense. The dune grasses too are lilies of the field adorned with goldenrod right now.

How can I believe all this when I know to what cruelties this sun has already awakened starving children in the Sudan? How can I believe this when the emptiness within me is so that I am little more than a huge, hollow vessel for the beauty of the morning? I linger and resist leaving it. Yet even if I stay, the sunrise fades into full day. Apparently we must accept the transience, the elusive Mystery that comes and goes. And in our desolation we must wait patiently. Simone Weil says waiting is our appropriate posture. More: the Gospel says we should be like servants awaiting the return of the master. So I must wait for another opportunity to return here to this quiet, this barrier reef where I can see sun rise and set on the water. Meanwhile I can look for Hopkins' "Brown brink" from my window mornings, even if now the sun rises behind that abandoned factory. At least I can see sunshafts through the broken, empty windows. Sometimes that will have to be enough. Simone Weil wrote to that fellow in jail, telling him that she would feel sorry for him walled in unless she knew that from the prison yard he could at night see the sky.

# 7

Dave Hagan and I stand in early evening beside the schoolyard. Over his head I can see the new downtown glass towers. The hour is dusk, and Dave is leaving after dinner. He continues to need conversation about his celebration, to sort out the surprise and pleasure and confusion and worry about it all.

Surprise and elation because so many people know and admire the hidden, demanding, discouraging daily effort required. Worried because perhaps they believe too much, imagine him something he is not, that he is doing the work better than he does, that his wary self has the stamina for another 20 years and they will hold him to that. Not that he has any plans, but one feels so fragile, exhausted often. It could all collapse tomorrow or next week or next year. Rather he could collapse. Everything else around here has already collapsed.

So we look within and without. Back over our shoulders to the complex which is Saint Malachy, and Dave ponders what it means to know that in 30 years all this will be gone. Not so much Saint Malachy physically but the Church as we know it.

Including ourselves. Whatever Dave's life means to those hundreds who to his astonishment came here for him that Sunday, we know that the cause and circumstance and meaning that got him here is priesthood and Church. And the undergirding for all that people admire in him is vanishing from their lives or at least from the minds and hearts of their children.

Again and again Dave notices and mentions how young people as old as 30 are simply not so attached to these realities as their parents before them.

I presented Dave's life and service that Sunday as living out of Eucharist. His own words: "Unless I am willing to pour out my blood, break my body. . . ."

But Dave insists that Eucharist does not mean much to younger people, and less and less will it mean anything.

And with Eucharist gone, what will move people to do these things that Dave does? Neither of us have any confidence in secular inspiration or concern to nourish the long haul or help people to be sacrificial as this need requires. All this is a long distance from the correct political agenda or whatever.

All this in Dave is not arrogant or judgmental. Well, not altogether so. Anyhow. His own moral transparency makes him want people to know and see him for what he is. He does not want to appear different or other than what he is, and the fear that people discon-

nected from Eucharist might not understand him as he wants to be
understood.

The other worry is what will happen. What will become of these
lovely old places? The few generous, holy lives hidden here in service when the Church as we know it leaves or is no more or whatever.

Will all real connection with these abandoned people cease,
apart from political posturing and diminishing social services and
scholarly studies?

Finally Dave drives from the schoolyard, leaving me with those
heavy thoughts and questions I handle more poorly than he does. I
enter the rectory and go into the church for night prayer with my breviary. Against the dusk or a street light I can obscurely see the Agony
in the Garden window. Whatever reality is coming down on this
brave new world with Dave and me in it, I shall see it as part of the
cup the angel ministers to the sweating, worrying Jesus kneeling there
alone with the Apostles sleeping: "Father, if possible let this cup pass
from me." However brutal, impenetrable the whole cup is, love all
that is or happens or comes about in the wake of that orange sunrise.
And the meaning of all that unfolds is love; the beauty means to tell
us that.

# 8

Even here among the poor, I notice in myself a stubborn sense of the
daily tasks as burdens. Even Saint Paul could see his "worry for all
the churches" as the burden it was. For me the hospital runs and
courtroom visits and funerals and telephone calls and rectory traffic
become obstacles preventing me from the really important—like
peacemaking or poetry, *la vie intellectuelle* or whatever. All those
unread books which I continue to buy.

Yesterday I drove across town to bring my house guest Ivan
Ilich to his weekly seminar at the University. I saw students waiting
for him with books of Teresa of Avila and Ignatius of Loyola in their
satchels. I know he is working on the knowing and union that is an
affair of the heart as well as the head. Bernard of Clairvaux . . . Hugh
of St. Victor or someone.

I so wanted to stay and enjoy the class and all the morning matters close to my heart. Matters that interest and delight me.

Yet after two days away, lingering there is a luxury I do not allow myself: back to the tasks of the parish. My real life of rectory traffic and financial worry and seeing whether the school principal needs me. The letters which need answering, even though the pile never seems to diminish. The details of parking and security for the benefit Irish concert at the very beginning of next month.

The intellectual pull so strong that at times I imagine I should have been a Jesuit, or at least followed some academic track which would have me a teacher and able to regard *la vie intellectuelle* as my work rather than some luxury I must squeeze into my own time, whatever that means. When you live where you work, life becomes simply doing what is the next thing waiting for you.

I comfort myself with the possibility that my prosaic tasks and duties keep me from some dilettantism. Years ago the wonderful old Benedictine monk, Damasus Winzen, described the Rule of Saint Benedict as a marvel of balance: the three elements of prayer, study and work and the balance lost when any are telescoped, as when monks become teachers or professors and work and study become one. He said this to explain why he built Mount Savior out in the hills, requiring the tasks of heavy farming.

Simone Weil too was unable to avail herself of the privilege of education and degrees and needed instead to be a farmworker or a factory worker. Regularly her taut spirit would collapse under the burden. Her parents would come and take her off for recuperation, and she would get well and go off and do it all over again.

They say Dorothy Day also was impatient with Catholic Worker people who would sit down in the middle of a day with a book. The day hours were for the soupline and the housekeeping necessary to keep the place clean and civil. Study and even prayer were for one's own hours and the space of early morning or the leisure of evening.

So perhaps my instincts about all this are not so bad, although Simone Weil is hardly someone to follow for moderation. Still I cannot but admire her heroic self almost more than anyone.

Friends tell me that my situation is in fact a precious opportunity to make poems out of a geography and work few have. Hopkins had his "thrice-removed self" to plow into poems, the dark insides he explored in the terrible sonnets as few have explored that terrain. "Poems like nothing else in English poetry since the metaphysical poets," says a reviewer, quoting from a new biography of Hopkins.

The suggestion is that my brutal and dreary tasks are a lode where I might mine gemlike poems. Of course they do not mean that anything like the talent of Hopkins is at work here. The friends do insist more ability here than anything I notice in myself. Often enough my own insides feel hardly better than the desolate Hopkins of Dublin days. That must be so since I go to those sonnets often enough to express my own desolation. Or is it just ordinary everyday depression. . . .

# 9

Enough *Catholic Worker* images around the house to tell me my origins, why I might be here. An icon of Dorothy Day here, a photograph of Peter Maurin there, a framed quote of the great woman over the fireplace in my room. And of course the books, coming and going. A recent copy of *The National Catholic Reporter* says that the Paulist priest who made the film "Romero" plans a film around the life of Dorothy Day.

I remember fairly well my first visit to the Bowery and *The Catholic Worker*. The year must have been 1952 or 1953 at Christmas. A seminary classmate was different from the rest of us because his father was a labor activist in the railroad union and an inactive and disaffected Catholic. His seminary son had plenty of the old man in him, and I recall the classmate standing with us around an ashtray, no less, in the seminary poolroom in fierce conversation about some nonsense just told us in class.

From the classmate we learned obscurely that there was another Catholic Church out there besides the dogma-making, ceremony-loving reality being fed to us. Dorothy Day must have come up more than once around that ashtray, as did the French worker-priests and Monsignor John Ryan and Charles Owen Rice and others. Real Catholic liberals in social matters. "Rare birds indeed, likened to the black swan," as Horace (or Ovid) called chaste Roman women of his time.

One of those animated conversations must have led to plans to visit New York City and the Catholic Worker house in the Bowery over our Christmas vacation of 10 days home from the quite monastic lockup there. Monastic since we were quite isolated from newspaper, radio and those beginnings of home television.

I recall someone driving the several of us through New York City down into the lower East Side, Little Italy, Chinatown; traffic lights where derelict men ran out to wipe the windshield with a rag which made the glass still more dirty. Afterwards their hand would race toward the closed car window for a quarter or half-dollar.

We in the car were about 19 or 20 years old and New York was still overwhelming us, not to mention this derelict sea that was—and still is—the Bowery.

And finally Dorothy Day. A calm, severe-looking woman sitting completely self-possessed in the midst of what I remember as chaos and bedlam.

People preparing food and little old bag ladies off in the corner, already dribbling from the mouth the food just eaten. Over there a man talking or chanting foreign phrases. When I asked Dorothy Day who he was or what he was saying, she said he was an Eastern Rite Catholic priest.

Here I am 19 years old, preparing for the glory of the priesthood, and there is a derelict, drunk, homeless and crazy. A priest!

Across the table where this immense soup or stew was being prepared, Ammon Hennessey, the anarchist who somehow became a Catholic also. To this day a mystery to me what brought these people into the Catholic Church. Peter Maurin I can understand. A born Catholic and for a while a Christian Brother. He would be like the rest of us, trying to stretch and pull the tradition into something that made sense to his social vision and concern. But nothing seems further from Dorothy and Ammon Hennessey than the Catholic Church of Cardinal Spellman and company.

Indeed, across the table Hennessey was giving off about Spellman, how he would be saved by ignorance, go to that corner of heaven reserved for "Bingo priests." Dorothy Day was trying either to quiet Hennessey or draw us away without letting Hennessey or ourselves know what she was doing. The exquisite courtesy of the *habitus caritatis,* as we would have called it in those days. She was concerned that the tough old anarchist would scandalize us young seminarians, distract us from our vocations even. Difficult enough that we should see the derelict priest. Eager she would have been that young men on their way to the priesthood share the Catholic Worker vision. Respectful also for the terrible truth which Hennessey embodied and spoke, she would want both to shelter us and to expose us to all that.

The visit stayed with me—permanently, I surmise. Back to the seminary and eager for *The Catholic Worker* arriving every month in the library reading room. And the monthly column of Dorothy Day in those pages would send you off to the library shelves or other periodicals looking for Emmanuel Mounier or Dostoyevski or studies on worker-priests or liturgical renewal in French and German monasteries. Seeds sown in me then suggesting that the moral theology of sexual ethics and Lenten fasting laws was inadequate for the new world of nuclear weapons.

So all that led me here by indirection and detour and short circuitry from earlier illusions that the task was mainly an intellectual one. I am as much among the poor as I found Dorothy Day that Christmas visit to New York, yet I am not here as deeply and awesomely as I found Dorothy Day there.

# *10*

A bank holiday, as the saying goes. My friend who is still in the one-room apartment with son and stepson and younger brother has a small request: he wants me to help get his television set to a repair place. And since he worked at a bank, he could get the errand in between holiday food shopping and two hours in the laundromat.

The difficult life of the poor. No car to take the television to a repair shop. No washer or dryer and so the expense of the laundromat. And in the neighborhood here any services like television repair are lacking. Besides, a black fellow walking down the street with a television set in his arms would easily be stopped by police suspecting him of burglary. And how do you prove the second-hand television is yours?

Confusing to be reduced to being available for such petty chores. Part of me winces at it: here I am spending a good hour on such a modest task when I should be about the larger task of getting him a decent house or building a coalition to demand low-cost housing for the poor or attacking the military budget so that funds for such housing are available. Whatever. Threatening even having myself the sterile leisure right now, not unlike that of the fellows crowding every corner this pleasant October afternoon.

Another part of me is comforted by the personal dimension of the request and errand. It is real. It tells me that my being here, my relationship with these fellows is real enough that they ask me the things they ask one another: a ride here or there, some dollars, the daily stuff.

And finally that is how I want to be here. Sharing the every day as well as I am able. Loading the television into the car trunk, I was embarrassed by the fine car I am driving these days. Only four years old, wine-colored and an Oldsmobile. Without a trace of envy, my friend asked about it. I covered the privilege of being a priest and having generous friends give me outright the car.

# *11*

". . . Let none mislead you by showing you any other road than that of prayer." Words of Saint Teresa of Avila to her Carmelite sisters—and presumably the rest of us. Today her feast.

Teresa and prayer and Margaret Mary tomorrow, another cloistered nun and my attraction and affection for them. All this makes me feel like an anachronism, a museum piece, a curiosity, someone stuck in an outworn medieval mind set.

I do seem stuck with the sense that I should go from work or play to prayer, to being alone in dark churches, to "wasting time" with the Mystery that we call God, as a friend put it years ago.

I fear that psychiatry would have a field day with my dualism or whatever it is. That this need says I am too fragile, not so strong, say, as the senators who have been on television these days, questioning the moral character of a Supreme Court nominee or the woman who says he harassed her sexually years ago. Many of those senators have been questioned for their ethics. The shadows over their own lives do not hinder them. They seem energized by the politics, the media exposure, the combat of all this. They derive energy from the world and all the mess.

And I derive little energy from the world. The mess, my own as well as parish and neighborhood and world, exhausts me. And I run to dark churches for light and strength and life. In doing that I am heeding the big Teresa and her emphasis on prayer. Or the little Thérèse who, child and childlike, made her way through an impossible situation of doting sisters and crazy cloister by cultivating her insides. Or Simone Weil who said that the world would exhaust us of any natural personal goodness, just as the criminal justice system has by contact with the mess long since become emptied of any virtue and only corrupts everybody associated with it. She required some inner contact with inexhaustible Goodness and can only have meant prayer.

Last week Ivan Ilich seemed to be questioning my conclusion. Driving him to his university lecture, I must have been giving off on this, and he suggested that most people have some inner yearning or searching which can be called prayer. Students waiting for him in the School of Architecture would support his sense. They carried books on Teresa of Avila and were ready to discuss with Ilich seeing and knowing with the heart as well as the mind. That would be prayer in some implicit sense as would be architecture itself and the cultivation of beauty.

All that not enough for me. I derive little energy from the world and am constrained to search within. Not very healthily or effectively, I fear. And the effort is often all too muscular. The Mystery we call God will not be bent to our pathology.

# 12

Last night I was pleased at the prospect of a more or less quiet night at the desk. Often a meeting here or something elsewhere five or six nights running. The AA group would be using the meeting room, but they take care of themselves. The inevitable phone calls. One hopes they do not wipe out the entire evening.

An afternoon phone call. A university professor asking that I see his graduate student and his foreign fiancée. They want to marry within a week. Of course, can I see them right now.

No I cannot see them right now and probably cannot help them without minimal cooperation from the diocesan officials. I can hear myself trying to get out of this. Tired of all this.

A return call. The diocesan official says that he will provide the necessary support if I can gather some documents. So I shall see them in the early evening after all. Here goes that one night this week without a meeting or whatever.

The couple will try to gather the documents, and if unsuccessful, they will just have a civil marriage. The fellow a religious studies doctoral candidate. So much for the Church.

After the session they have one more need: to call a taxi. Easier for me to drive them downtown. Since no taxi will come up here or we will wait longer than my driving them a mile or two.

Along the way they tell me of their plans: to teach, bring people together, their semester in Germany with Hans Küng. I can hear my own disaffection from all that academic enthusiasm. I comment about the northern European thing—that all this can be accomplished by headwork and how I am not all that sure that is enough or even the most important ingredient. I hear myself as they must hear me: exhausted ghetto priest cynical about theology and studies. I almost apologize, saying how after 20 years up here, one has to learn to live with diminished expectations. The T.S. Eliot business about living without hope because hope would be hope for the wrong thing. The faith and the love and the hope are all in the waiting. And whatever I am waiting for, it is not a new book on world ecumenism.

Back home, alone and tired enough for bed without any of the desk tasks I intended. Often enough the case.

No sooner am I in the house and trying to say Vespers in the dark church than the sound of the phone.

Of course the call is from the prisoner I met last week at the hospital. He is about to be released now at 10:30 p.m. and has nowhere to go, his scalded leg bandaged and he still walking with a crutch.

Again the coping reflexes begin as they did with the university couple: can he shift for tonight and perhaps tomorrow. . . .

Mercifully for me, guards come and he has to hang up. Out on the street he will not even have a dime to call me, so I am off the hook until tomorrow at least. Tomorrow could be difficult. These fellows can be a full-time job.

Neither junk television nor sleep can deliver me. I am bothered by my coping and evasion. This fellow needs help more than the university students. Why am I so resistant but finally courteous to the students and so unwilling here? My only comfort is that what I have done is done, and despite my negligence no possibility of putting it all back together tonight. I presume the fellow is out on the night streets with his bandaged leg and cane but I do not know where to find him.

Just into sleep I hear both phone and door. The door: the Alcoholics Anonymous people telling that they are leaving the meeting room. Of course, the phone is a collect call. The prisoner now on the street: can I fetch him at Front and Allegheny, about two or three miles away?

I dress, remember to take my wallet, and am off across the war zone between me and his corner. The night world of the bombed-out Latino neighborhood north of here. Just outside our schoolyard, a police emergency medical wagon at the public housing high-rise. Almost at the other end of my journey another emergency vehicle flashing red lights and double-parked, facing the wrong way on a one-way street.

Night people in noisy old sportscars running redlights and stop signs. Bars flashing arrows inviting you to see their go-go girls. *Chicas* and macho guys on every corner either giving or inviting the sexual harassment endlessly on television these days with the Senate hearing and vote tonight about the Supreme Court candidate. I do not even know how the vote went nor does anyone up here care. Sexual harassment is the name of the night game up here. What poor people do, at least the younger ones.

My man is surely enough waiting for me at the appointed corner. When I tell him that we are returning to the rectory and he is staying there tonight, I can tell immediately that he has other plans. Phrases, deferential and courteous, about needing to return to the prison tomorrow for his clothes and a few dollars on account. Here he knows a house where he can stay just down this completely dark street here, and staying here means he will be closer to the prison for the morning.

A thin black woman comes out of the dark house. The street is so dark I can barely see her. Michael introduces us, and she says how Michael, whom I met only once, has told her all about me. Michael could not have told her anything except by way of a collect phone call while waiting for me. He probably told her that I would arrive with a few dollars, and those dollars would be hers.

So dark I could scarcely see my money. I gave Michael the $15 in my wallet, warning him not to call tomorrow night in the same fix. If he had to call, please, please call during the day when I could find some place for him.

For a few blocks I had no idea where I was going. I saw a black fellow crossing a street carrying a stuffed panda literally as large or larger than himself. Michael will probably call tomorrow night in the same predicament. Yet some relief in driving back alone without the trouble of having to settle Michael into the rectory. Apparently that was no more attractive to Michael than to me.

What kind of a society or world is this where prison guards turn a fellow out at 10:00 p.m. without a dime for a phone call and with his leg swathed in bandages and walking with a cane?

# 13

The feast of Ignatius of Antioch summons such memories of seminary years. His seven letters written while being taken to Rome for martyrdom are important evidence for very early Church life and teaching.

I notice how the Mass text quotes or refers to his own words in those letters: ". . . he offered himself to you as the wheat of Christ formed into pure bread by his death. . . ." Ignatius had said that he would be chewed by lions in the Roman Colosseum and like wheat ground on stone becomes bread, he would become Christ whom we become by the Bread of the Eucharist.

Living in this uninspiring Church, I shall have to toss my lot with Ignatius rather than the university professor who is Catholic and stays within the Church to reform it.

All too practical for me. But then the professor is German and I am Irish. His reasons and methods more rational and purposeful than mine. I would not have the confidence to think I could even help reform the Church. Here I am living on the margins having, to the best of my knowledge, no influence. They dismiss me easily as someone out there disaffected, doing his thing.

I do not even know whether I believe or hope the lethargic inept Church will ever be much better than it is. Not much reason in history to hope for that outcome. Or perhaps in the long haul, the evolution of history or something. We seem to be some distance from the horror that Simone Weil thought an early medieval papacy was. Again the picture is mixed. Some popes were quite enlightened leaders delivering Europe, as a friend said, "from a Gothic nightmare."

My own view of being in the Church would borrow more from the mysticism and martyrdom of Ignatius of Antioch. The passage through pain and darkness and even death in the hope of coming out the other end somehow. And not another end here necessarily. I have that hope for Church as well as self.

Meanwhile, I want to stay with it, not because I think I can help reform it. Rather because the Church is part of my story, like my family and origins. Something given that I must work through as I would work through the human factors of a marriage or parenthood. Something to be worked through as the Apostles had to work their relationship through the disgrace and blood and catastrophe of the Cross. So. I have to see whatever priesthood or celibacy or the accoutrements of clerical life or the lackluster Church cost me as the personal story I have to work through with delicacy and faithfulness on my way wherever.

I do not even mean that my fidelity is the same as that of someone else. I no longer need to look at the choices of others as better or worse than mine. All I know is that right now I need to try to understand my aging and my cul-de-sacs and even greater disappointment with the Church around me as some kind of dying, not unlike the mystery which Ignatius of Antioch sensed for himself on the way to Rome to be chewed up by lions.

A year ago or more, I mentioned Ignatius at Mass on this his feast with some younger religious. I went on about how important his witness of early Church life. While I was speaking, I had the sense that my listeners did not distinguish Ignatius of Antioch in the second century from Ignatius of Loyola in the sixteenth century. Nor did they care. I hope I am wrong about that. Perhaps even pretentious of me to think that. Yet not far from the general disappointment I feel with the Church overall.

# 14

A distant wedding. Earlier rehearsal and Nuptial Mass today threw me into the world of my own kind for a while. The bride and her bridesmaids all attended the Jesuit college quite near my childhood home. Both diocesan seminary and Jesuit college are in that neighborhood and some truth in saying that I owe my vocation to gravity as much as anything else.

That small Irish world with Italian neighbors was all I knew, and unless I went to the nearby seminary I would have gotten no farther than the Jesuit school also on City Line Avenue. My grandfather had a flair more than others in the family, and during high school he talked about sending me to Notre Dame. Seminary decided all that. Yet I am sure that the others would have prevailed: Notre Dame would have been ostentatious or something. The local Jesuit college was the neighborhood track.

Seminary in those days was severe. We were never out except to see a dentist in an emergency or home for holidays and summer. Regulations required that we stay 50 feet or so from that fence along City Line Avenue, but of course we could sometimes see fellows our own age coming and going to the Jesuit college—with dates and cars and freedom of movement so different from our lockup.

For me an attractive part of the lockup was the freedom from so many distractions: freedom for books and study, for prayer and a kind of solitude I confusedly desired. Much of the seminary regime was hard on my taut self, but instead of seeing the outside world as some relief or alternative, I sensed that going ever more alone or deeply within would resolve that trouble.

I notice that the wedding today with young people from that Jesuit college surfaces in me questions not very different from those 40 years ago when we walked the seminary fence watching fellows our own age off to a beer party or a basketball game. Not without humor we seminarians said to one another: they are not happy. We are happy.

I notice within real regret or sorrow at early choices around that kind of love or intimacy. A world quite distant and unknown really. The only dimension I really bring to the sexual is moral, and surely that is not enough. Reason enough for others to be wary of us celibates when we give off on the subject. Most of my years as a priest I have avoided any involvement with marriage preparation or counseling, beyond that inevitably coming my way. Marriage and all intimacy would seem very much a matter of nuance and that nuance foreign to me.

Somehow I survived the emotional deprivation of the seminary by cultivating the life of the mind: the library, books. I remember going to the seminary and choosing the Latin text of some medieval work rather than an English translation because Latin—and Greek and French and even Hebrew—were languages I should know.

And prayer. The going within that the seminary ordeal impelled in me. *Solus cum Solo.* To be a priest meant being alone as married people were not alone. As I am and that young woman is not, eagerly awaiting her young husband arriving late at the rehearsal dinner.

Learning to be alone meant learning to be *solus cum Solo.* Alone with the Alone. Alone in the early evening hours in your cubicle room when in October, say, you could see the lights go on at dusk in the warm homes beyond the seminary fence. Alone in the chapel, hurting so much during the long weeks of Lent. Often enough that I had to make my prayer some identification with Christ in his Agony in the Garden when he was so alone with the apostles sleeping nearby.

Whatever the cost in distance from the embrace of the young bridesmaid running to embrace the week-away husband arriving from the airport, I would not want to be without that living within, that search for God or whatever it is that has cost me so much of all that is wonderful in this world and precious in life.

Once, years ago, I was across a table or desk from a friend who had many younger friends in seminaries and religious life. She had just hung up the telephone from a long distance call in which someone very close to her gave the news that he had met a woman, and after months of indecision and even agony, he was leaving the seminary to marry.

My friend seemed accepting but quiet with the news. I knew the caller was so much younger than herself that something must be going on more than personal regrets. When I asked what that might be, she simply said that over the years her experience was that some of us were such that we should belong not to some one person but to everyone. And her experience was that marriage meant this belonging to everybody could no longer be true. Marriage meant in a profound sense that now this young fellow would belong to some one person and that gave her some regret, even though she could rejoice with his having found love and close company and all the wonderful things which marriage can sometimes be.

No argument intended here for celibacy or religious vows. No reason to think that ordination makes one into the kind of person able or available for everybody.

# 15

The Puerto Rican family arrived on time for the Baptism. Three months ago, the little mother timidly rang the doorbell and asked me without a word of English whether I would baptize Ashley Nicole, no less!

Again the impulse to pass the responsibility elsewhere. I cannot take on the Latino people around here. Their living conditions are so desperate. I do tend them at the hospital: tuberculosis, liver disease, AIDS. . . . If I take on the Latinos as well as the African-Americans who are the parish, I will be more overwhelmed than I am already. In over my head in all directions.

In the end, how do I say no to a little woman with a modest request? She had her plans and yesterday was the day she wanted three months ago. The *padrinos* were coming down from New York City.

Little Ashley Nicole was dressed in full, frilly white dress with bonnets and frills down to the lace trim on her socks. She seemed to enjoy the sound of her new leather soles clapping the slab marble floor of the sacristy where we have daily Mass. We would sit around the Mass table and I would baptize Ashley Nicole with water from the cut-glass punch bowl which I fetch from alongside the Limoges china in our fancy dining room. Remnants of the fancy days when the pastor of this parish was a bishop. The glory that was Rome, as I tell guests, half apologizing for the pretense of the place. Using the cut-glass punch bowl to baptize Ashley Nicole is putting the remnants to a better use than any they have had before.

We sat around the table. The father seemed scarcely aware of what we were about. He might be a Puerto Rican hardly instructed in the basics of faith. The neglect of these poor wandering people here and in New York and the beanfields stretching from New Jersey south to Florida and across to Puerto Rico has been appalling. Poor and therefore neglected by Church as well as state. Poor and therefore unimportant.

Also in the small circle the godparents: an older, married daughter of the mother and the young sixth-grade son whom we are trying to have attend free a fancy suburban private Catholic school.

I begin by apologizing for my Spanish. Presumptuous of me even to try, but I cannot neglect this effort. They speak so little English. I shall depend for reassurance on our one Spanish parishioner who prepared the family and came this Saturday morning for the Baptism. Along the way she will nod to tell me how I am doing. So little opportunity here to use Spanish beyond the hospital and prayers for the Anointing or Holy Communion. And this even though the Latinos, thousands of them, are nearby. Just where the neighborhood falls apart into what can only be called ruins.

Often enough I do not understand my own faith: faith in what or whom, belief mostly or mostly unbelief sustained by almost desperate hope that someone, something is out there. Is my faith in the Mystery we call God, the Christ, the Church all the same thing or are they separate?

Across the table, the little mother still intense from pulling all this together: husband, myself, *padrinos* from New York, Ashley dressed like a little princess from a children's book. I would look up and across at the mother to see how my Spanish was doing. I saw more. I saw a little woman who knew what we were about here by some deep awareness. Often her faith is dismissed as superstition, attachment to some vague, primitive magic. I saw something different; she knew what we were about better than I. That we were giving Ashley Nicole the new life of grace, incorporation into Christ, a birth so important to the mother that she has been anxious for this, planning for this two years almost from the day of natural birth. You will say that I am imagining or projecting here, that even the magical sense of the sacrament could give the mother this quiet, this pleasant intensity. I can only say that I had the sense of something else, something deeper. The reality of Baptism taking in her more deeply than it takes in me, for all my theology and such.

# 11.

# *Emotional Exhaustion*

# 1

Fall ending now. These weeks of autumn have been wonderful. These past few mornings we are waking up to a thick, yet gossamer fog. I suppose at this time of year the night air is much cooler than the other so that the fog forms.

And the fog prevents my seeing the rising sun which I have come to await, sitting in a chair in my bedroom where an eastward window frames the morning as it appears on the horizon this last week. No dawn, no sun until later when the haze burns off.

One morning, without the sun, I placed a small red votive candle on the windowsill. The flame something to hold my attention since attention is a part of this watching which I hope is prayer. Simone Weil says unmixed attention is prayer.

Gazing at the flame, I suddenly realize that I am missing the tree for the woods, as it were. Beyond candle and window flaming out through the fog, a flaming maple tree 200 yards away so afire with color that the flame nearer at hand seems nothing at all.

So. I extinguish the flame and remove the small ruby votive lamp. The fiery maple piercing the haze is flame enough. The same Providence which so tends a dying tree will not be less caring of me as I make my way through this new day.

I dread seeing it all begin again. Everything so impossible around here. Unable I am even to find Eugene decent housing. This last hour of quiet before everything starts so precious. Must be my exhaustion talking. I hope that morning time looking out the window at the flaming maple or the rising sun helps bring me more and more to the truth deeper than the ordeal or exhaustion. Life is a wonderful gift, every breath and hour of it. Like the maple, we are in good hands no matter what.

# 2

On my night table still the roses waiting for me the other night when I came home exhausted. It was almost midnight, and I was out all day running frantically from burial to railroad station to luncheon meeting to a birthday party even.

I came in exhausted and lonely, and there on the night table with tiny out-of-season roses, rosebuds actually, with the note: "Roses . . . discovered in your garden."

The lovely calligraphy reveals the roses as thought and deed of a Sister who works here and knows my constant looking for some sign of care from little Thérèse of Lisieux, who said that after her death she would let fall from heaven a shower of roses.

That the calligraphic Sister left the roses for me might mean that I cannot count them as sign and need reassurance from Thérèse. The Sister here knows how I yearn for the occasional sign, and the gesture might be from her more than Thérèse, whom I took on as a sister 40 years ago because she promised to be a special friend of priests, and I did not think I could get through the seminary without her. Her story revealed her as someone as strung out as I was during most of those seminary years.

I shall regard those flowers as love letter from her as well. Across the infinite distance, how can she communicate with me except through an intermediary?

One could say the relief, yes, joy, my exhausted self felt even at midnight seeing those tiny roses shows how lonely I am, how going to bed I yearn for the comfort and company intended—it is not good for man (or woman) to be alone. The interpretation becomes that my religious expression of that need is sublimation of that human need and sexual desire.

Perhaps. Simone Weil has another slant. Just the opposite, of course. Religious desire is not the sublimation of the real thing of human longing. Human longing is fragmentary expression of the larger, more real longing for God innate in us all.

Only an age like ours could choose the reductionist, vulgarizing interpretation, says Simone.

## 3

Bothered enough by the inadequate housing situation of my friend to make the rounds for him, I gather in a Catholic Worker friend on the hope that he has some ideas on resources I do not.

Really I probably feel so alone with this need and worry that I want my Catholic Worker friend to share it. Come along for the ride, as it were. He already has enough worries at the Catholic Worker. He and his new wife are living in a space as small as that of Eugene and children and brother because they share the little row house with a homeless family. Their own living space a single room with improvised kitchen and bath, not unlike the quarters of Eugene.

Perhaps I want the Catholic Worker friend along to test the waters, measure whether my boil over this situation is appropriate or an excess. Hard to know when you are near boil all the time. Always wanting to relieve impossible situations up here. So alone with them because for others like myself, priests and regular folk, they are out of sight and out of mind.

Even getting started is an ordeal. The doorbell does not work for Eugene. I shout up from street to third floor. Finally we get in and find Eugene and son and brother getting it together for the day. Here in October, Eugene having the final week of his vacation from the bank.

Young son out of school today because of a heavy cold. Besides his ankle is wrapped from a Saturday football injury. Brother of Eugene has hemorrhoids so bad he cannot walk and no medical card for hospital emergency room. We will have to drop him at the city health center up here where they treat homeless people. Then onto a storefront doctor's office where young son can be treated by way of the health coverage Eugene has with his job.

So all this maneuvering instead of the housing agencies I plan to visit for them. Unless I came alone with a ride they would walk these errands, even the brother with hemorrhoids which prevent his walking.

Finally we leave them at the two separate medical places up here. A bright November morning. Corners everywhere filled with people with nowhere to go and nothing to do. The light is so wonderful that even the old empty houses are pastel in their fading, falling ruin.

Doing the house search without the needy party is no different from doing it with them: no vacancy anywhere. I know two empty houses, and I would be willing to find help with whatever rent is beyond the resources of my friend. Neither owner seems to want to rent to someone she does not know personally. Afraid that someone will tear her place up. The poor are as tough on one another as anybody else.

# 4

Waiting for the elevator at a huge downtown hospital, I meet a fellow I just left yesterday. He called me Sunday morning at six o'clock with a dolorous story of disaster and emergency: wife left him, took all his money and medical cards, a car even. He was just discharged from the hospital. Nowhere to go. No money. Out in the morning cold, etc., etc., etc.

Even as I am screaming at him on the phone that hospitals do not discharge people at 5:00 a.m., I know I cannot fetch him, wherever he is. I cannot put a face with the familiar name, but he indeed knows me. Offended even that I do not remember him, that I once was trying to find him employment at a downtown apartment house where a friend and former priest is manager.

I know that I cannot fetch him even as I am screaming that today is Sunday, and I have the whole Sunday morning church matter. I cannot fetch him because even as I scream, my head is playing another tape: the parable of the Good Samaritan who helps the wounded fellow when priest and Levite did not because they were on their way to Temple duty.

So in Sunday morning darkness off to the appointed corner and, of course, taking the fellow to his appointed destination, a house back in the neighborhood where my $20 bill gains him access. From him along the way horror tales of betrayal and robbery and abandonment by his wife and children.

And today there he is in bright hospital lights, waiting for the elevator and smiling with a smile that knows he has been discovered. He just needed that ride and those dollars. The story was the necessary excuse.

"God will bless both you and me, Father Mac," he says as I leave him. "Yes, Franklin," says I, "me for being hustled and you for hustling."

# 5

Re-entry is awful. As though the weekend was not enough after some days away. Monday morning coming down or whatever. A day after a day away is near panic.

Today began with a call about no heat on the upper floors of the 100-year-old school, and all day I never got far from the boiler room. My pathetic effort to help the plumber, to learn how to set or unset new sophisticated computer thermostats when dialing a telephone is my limit.

I know what the problem is: an impatience, a fierce resistance even, to these chores. As though I should be free to glide through the day and be off in late afternoon to a local college and dinner with a visiting Irish scholar. A rather pretentious self coming through. . . .

Down in the boiler room with the plumber and reading the thermostat manual, I try to bring all of me there to these mundane and petty domestic chores which occupy most lives. Who do I think I am anyhow? Simone Weil says that any attention can be prayer.

# 6

A parishioner has the funeral of her father in a funeral home, and again I am reminded painfully how limited my talents for this work. The Baptist or whatever service is so emotional, so full of feeling that all I feel is disconnected and alienated.

At least Simone Weil in New York City could go in and out of Baptist churches in Harlem, marveling at religious faith overflowing into emotion and even dance.

For me faith is at best the nurturing of a lean, frail sense that something exists deeper than my fragile holding on. Life mostly seems senseless, episodic, without beginning, middle, end or any coherent meaning. I nurse all that I can from the beauty of the world: the strange colors of autumn, the different surprise that every dawn is even the heavy clouds that sometimes block out dawn altogether. I sit and look and wait and draw from the mysterious beauty of the world, the sense that the full story is more than the sum of the parts.

The same sense of the tradition, the Scriptures and a mystery like the Eucharist. The story is so beautiful, so strange, such an overlay of symbol upon symbol that the beauty pulls me in. I begin to swim there, like a fish in water.

Today I was riding home, exhausted by a frustrating day of waiting and waiting for the service to begin at the funeral home. Then when the service does begin, I am completely unable to be part of it in any comfortable sense. Later I was waiting again. This time in a waiting room full of poor people at the Public Defenders' Office. I went there with a friend in big trouble, and because I know lawyers there, the friend will be better received and helped if I take him there and wait with him.

Sitting there I think of the thousand things I could be doing, should be doing at home—people in hospitals calling for me, the housing application for still another friend who needs out of the one-room apartment where he lives with brother and two sons and now daughter and her children these few weeks. Today or yesterday I did not even have the half-hour to take that application to a woman who can help him. I did not have a simple half-hour to sit and be courteous and ask her to help us. And so the applicaion which he went out of his way to leave off at great inconvenience on his way to work yesterday sits somewhere in the chaotic mess that gathers on my desk in one day.

Riding home anxious with this overload, frustrated with a day spent mostly waiting and wondering whether I shall be on time for the daily evening Mass, I try to calm myself by putting a tape into the car tape deck. Gregorian Chant, Easter antiphons, mostly alleluias. First time ever I have had a car with a tape deck.

# 7

Driving across the neighborhood, I pass the house of perhaps my closest friend up here. I do not see her often. Her life is so torn and chaotic, I probably avoid that reality and the powerlessness I feel about helping her in any effective sense.

No one tried harder to stay afloat in those destroying streets. Single parent, she tried to be both mother and father in the absence of her husband who had long since disappeared into the bars and clubs and womanizing and whatever. She even tried to be a neighborhood presence, a kind of social worker at the parish there doing emergency food and clothes. The court appearances and job searches and detox interventions which I still do 20 years later.

She might even have been better at her brand of social work than she was running a family. She seemed to have as little patience with the tumult of teenagers as I suspect I would. Almost unable to run a quiet house or get children to do homework or come in off the streets at a reasonable hour. The exchange with her several children often enough a screaming match or pathetic attempts at punishment.

Now her oldest son is in jail doing life. Her several daughters are all regularly having babies. Years ago she took in two young fellows, brothers without a home or family, and I see they are still with her, going nowhere, neither of them. As much victims of these neighborhoods as the others.

She would never ask me for a dollar, yet often enough she is without a dollar. The daughters with their babies gobble up her dollars like Halloween candy.

Right now is a very difficult time for her. A pregnant daughter was just arrested for shoplifting; still another daughter is due any minute. All of this facing her every day. Every minute. Again I wonder how she can get up in the morning without collapsing back into bed.

Today I saw her as I drove past the house. She is an attractive woman, and her face took on her lovely smile when she saw me. Behind her, I noticed the Thanksgiving decorations on the window of her rowhouse and I marveled at her wanting to mark the season in the midst of such a tumultous life when someone might wonder what she has to be thankful about, what difference a crepe paper turkey in the window will mean.

# 8

Saturday. My friend living in one room with young son and older son and stepson and brother now has stepdaughter and baby for a few days or weeks. I lecture him on taking on more than he can handle or he and I together can afford. So presumptious or righteous or something of me. So in over my head. Easier to dignify that excess when you have the resources I do. His doing it just looks raw and crazy.

He calls to say that today is his birthday, and I am mean enough to accuse him of looking for a "hit." Birthday an opportunity for dollars from me that I can hardly refuse. He does not wait for my offer. He asks me outright. Says he wants to treat himself to dinner. A birthday treat for himself.

Within a half-hour he is over to see me. He wants to talk about the former wife who still calls him from down South. Something about her coming up here and bringing the children back down South. All I see is dollar signs, my dollars. My uneven rule has been that we will never try to have a serious conversation when he needs dollars because the money gets in the way for me. I find myself thinking that the conversation is just a pretext and the dollars the real issue, which is of course true. Life so down and out is so much a matter of coping that enough dollars for the present crisis is as far as one can see. Serious talk waits upon a leisure which never quite happens.

So my rule of not trying to have serious talk when we are doing money means we seldom have that serious conversation; the relationship revolves around money.

Tonight he was soft and wanted to talk. He is thoughtful and another birthday would, I know, have him pondering his impossible life and futile dreams. Here he is 40 years old, wanting nothing more than the companionship and warmth of home and family which eluded him as a child because his father left, because his decent mother drank, because there were too many of the children in the tiny row house, because, because, because.

His birthday has him thoughtful, and he wants to mention his curious vulnerability to the woman who walked out on him and keeps sending children back to him in his one-room apartment. That kind of vulnerability and attachment is part of many human lives. Painful stuff. I should be willing and able to hear him out, tell him I understand, warn him that any effort to have that with Denise is probably a mistake, something that will only cause more pain down the road.

Instead I refuse him that warmth, that intimacy. I am distracted by a hundred things, the Saturday chores I am doing, the visit of a bishop and Confirmation coming up tomorrow, the other people around the house here waiting for me or looking for me. So I hand him the money, say something almost mean about my not being able to afford Denise, even if he wants her again.

I miss the opportunity for real friendship—that delicate balance in which neither giver is enhanced in superiority nor receiver humiliated.

My only hope is that leaving he keeps saying: "I'll call you Monday." He knows me well enough to know a mood. Our friendship is deeper than my mood. Thank God he knows that, is willing to accept the abuse from me as well as the dollars. At the end of a day, I am saved not by my kindness but by his kind tolerance and patience with me.

Again the realization that my presence up here has little to do with the ordinary images of social work or even priesting. I guess I want to share his life, be his friend. Hard to give it a name or even understand it myself. I want to share his hard life in the hope that my friendship will help him. I want to share these lives because the courage and strength under the gun is a grasp of reality that I need. Friendships that help me to live, to understand life. Relationships that deliver me from middle-class fantasies and distractions and pretense. Friendships I suspect more helpful to me than I am to anyone here. Despite my generous dollars, I failed tonight with my friend on this his birthday. What saves the friendship is not my generous gesture, but his. His ability to overlook my mean mood and say: "I'll call you Monday." His recognizing something between us more lasting than my mood.

# 9

Confirmation today. The need to bring some order out of a kind of chaos.

Order because the Catholic culture visiting today in the person of a bishop is complete order. Same ritual, straight lines, well-rehearsed children, the ballet-like precision of Catholic worship, even though Annie Dillard could call the Catholic Mass near her hermitage a high-school play full of miscues.

Chaos because chaos is how the spontaneous local expression seems up against the Catholic scene. People arriving when they arrive, never certainty about everybody even showing up, children coming to instruction every other week rather than weekly—or coming now and then when they get here.

The task presents itself as cleaning up our act enough so that the visiting bishop does not suspect how chaotic things are around here and tell the archbishop—or call the cops.

Today the Confirmation Mass was fine. Friends even called later in the day to say how lovely everything was. The bishop was gentle with the children. That soft side of Catholicism so exasperating when it seems the only thing there.

The bishop talked to the children as though he were a child himself, as though the children were the only ones in church. Not childish either but childlike.

And the church still decorated for this autumn season, together with the red and white of Confirmation bows on the pews and a crepe paper dove hanging from the loft. The music, especially the lovely responsory: "Lord, send out your Spirit and renew the face of the earth," the fragrance of the Holy Chrism with balsam, the red second-hand Confirmation gowns from our suburban sister parish telling the children that they are once again clothed in Christ in the images of Saint Paul.

Sitting there all dressed in red Mass vestments myself, as the Bishop instructs the children, I am touched by the soft childlike beauty of everything: the sun pouring in the great stained-glass windows, the magnificence of this old church, and I acknowledge to no one but myself that these efforts are worthwhile. These children will be helped by this moment in their lives. I look down at two little girls being confirmed. I know the dreadful, unspeakable conditions of their apartment and their entire public housing project just down the street. The loveliness of all this has to touch them. I think of Simone Weil saying that the poor need poetry more than they need bread. I think of Kenneth Clark in his *Civilization* long ago saying how feminine Catholicism is. He meant that as a compliment. Alone among religions of the Book, Catholicism nurtures art and aesthetics.

Again beneath all my exasperation with the Church, including that softness which enables the bishop to speak to the children without a hint of condescension, I do sense my great attachment to the tradition.

# 10

The mysterious flight or whatever yesterday hardly lasted, Gregorian chant not withstanding.

Maybe it was the dog bite earlier in the day when I went to fetch the family for the Public Defender's Office. One of those toy dogs that seem all bark. When I walked across the room, he jumped at my calf and through the trousers punctured the skin. I was more mindful of a bigger family dog also barking furiously from some shed where he was locked back behind the kitchen.

Dogs and cats in city rowhouses are a complete mystery to me. Of course, the poor have them for protection. Even that toy creature would let you know that some stranger was entering the house or, if the house were empty, the barking would scare off the intruder.

So even the wait in the Defenders' Office was distracted by my worrying whether I needed a tetanus booster. I kept trying to call a doctor friend at the medical center across from the Public Defender, all the while trying to hide my worry from the family. They would be so embarrassed that the bite was real and also so solicitous. Bad enough the trouble that had us there without my hypochondria.

After dinner I fell asleep and was only awakened by the doctor getting back to me. By then sheer weariness had displaced my worry about a small skin puncture from a toy dog.

After the phone the doorbell. Going downstairs, I just knew the caller was going to mean trouble.

A fellow with bags and a story at 8:30 p.m. on the dark step. Something about needing a bed and having been an altar boy here and even baptized and confirmed here.

When he said that he had just been evicted from a house halfway across the city and came across town because he had been an altar boy here, I lost whatever patience or control I was sustaining all day.

So screaming was I that two women from the parish going home from weekly rosary stood at the end of the path the entire time the fellow and I went at it on the doorstep.

What pushed me over the edge was the "jive," as we call it. The body language, the unfinished sentences, the absence of any straight answers to me screaming at him, asking why he waits until 8:30 p.m. when nobody is here but me and all the city services are closed: "You have nothing to do all day; why the hell do you wait until darkness and now to lay this jive on me?" I scream.

Of course the purpose is money. He knows I am not going to be Good Samaritan enough to take him in. He knows that the guilt will come around to dollars. Of course, after my torrent he is correct. More abuse and guilt than he expected and $10 is relief and out for me.

Of course, the whole thing could have been handled with calm and courtesy even if ten dollars was the outcome anyhow.

I return to my room discouraged by losing my calm after a long, hard day when I managed to hold it together rather well. Several times recently, people have said they don't know how I do it, day after day, year after year in such an impossible landscape.

Well, this is how I do it—poorly. I falter; I fail; I scream. I upset myself so that sleep will be uneasy. What else to do except to try not to lose it so next time. Also hope the poor fellow, hustler or whatever, is not too harmed by my verbal abuse. For myself, accept the fact that I am going to perform poorly often enough. No other way a human being can be here when the endless stream of hungry people and addicts and hustlers are going to be at the door evenings as well as afternoons. All hours the same to them.

# 11

We must be doing something right if sheer activity means something. One could, however, make a case that activity is often a cover for irrelevance. In any case, the weekend around here was busy.

Saturday morning, the few folks who come for morning Mass were having their usual coffee when the door and phone started. People looking for their promised Thanksgiving turkey baskets which were soon arriving at the back door as fast as they were going out the front door. The need for courtesy at both doors: the suburban church people bringing these baskets and poor local people having to cart them home without a car or a sturdy man to assist.

Meanwhile the friend arrives to begin coaching the acting and dancing which will become a Christmas pageant for the parish school. She needs access to the school, the alarm turned off and the heat on. The pageant is basically a tale narrating the Christmas story between modern and classical and black Gospel music. An immense effort to have the children at least hear the stories in a world where they well might not hear them anymore.

Again in the rectory the three basketball giants arrive to meet a friend who is tutoring them for their SAT tests after Christmas. After the crushing disappointment of Hank Gathers' dying on the court, the tutor is Dave's brother, and this is the third week he has come from the far suburbs.

Soon the Alcoholics Anonymous group is wanting to use the room just left by the SAT class. Saturday the AA groups have two meetings back-to-back and continue into dark this time of year.

On Sunday we have our own two Masses, and there is some confusion after the first because some children arrive for the Sunday religious instruction hour between the two Masses, but most do not. I suspect a holiday was given after the huge effort for Confirmation last Sunday, and these children who arrived are the casuals who come when convenient, not knowing when class is or is not.

An improvisation to accommodate them since their teachers are not here. I quickly search out a videotape. Afterwards a teacher who was here tells me how attentive the children were to the 15-minute Farmworkers' tape on pesticides. "They need to know that the world is bigger than this neighorbood," she commented. Amen.

Just before the second Mass, our Haitian parishioners reminded me that the Haitian community was gathering here this afternoon for a Creole and French Mass with a priest who occasionally comes from New York.

Later as I was going out the door to see a sick friend in the suburbs, I heard the Creole hymns coming from the church. I hope the priest does not mind that I am not here. A chance today to visit the friend, someone whom I neglect because of distance. Besides, I sent a thank-you note for a recent donation, and his wife called to tell me about his cancer surgery a month ago. If I do not get there with the leisure of late Sunday afternoon, I will be mindful of that obligation all week.

More than myself, friends and others notice the demand that kind of activity makes on my life. Not easy living where you work, even if I do manage to keep some space to myself by way of my two rooms. The doorbell has to ring in my room also because sometimes I am the only one there.

I think of the heroic priest whom I know in Brooklyn who has been pastor and before that assistant in the same church for 40 years. His neighborhood is a tumultous mix of Puerto Ricans, Central Americans, Hasidic Jews. Once the bishop came for Confirmation, and after a parish dinner for everybody, the bishop suggested they return to the pastor's room for quieter conversation. The pastor had to tell him there was no pastor's room. He slept in what was in fact a dormitory since he hosted about 25 to 40 illegals at any given time.

I am not there. Yet I do more and more make a conscious effort to let go—let go of privacy, of time, of money, of order even.

On Saturday morning when the dancing teacher needed access to the school, I quietly took the key, went into the schoolyard, opened the several locks, turned off the alarm, put on the lights, checked to see that the heat was on and the lavatories open.

I tried to do it the way Thich Nhat Hanh says you teach a Buddhist monk to pray or meditate. First you teach him how to open a door or eat an orange.

# *12*

Not proud of this but doing it anyhow. This day after Thanksgiving a holiday and no one home or here except myself.

About 8:30 in the morning, the doorbell starts. The now daily, endless stream of people looking for food. The canned goods we have from the diocesan nutritional services who keep us well enough stocked at Thanksgiving, all this is supplemented by the holiday baskets coming from a suburban parish quite generous to us. A sister parish, we call it.

Those at the door are project women with carts. The older men whom I see all day loitering around that seamy bar about three blocks away also arrive. That particular block between bar and post office at the other end is a ruinous and down-at-the-heel stretch as anywhere—here or some Third World country. Abandoned houses with vacant lots between where the rowhouses have collapsed and the lots strewn with the wreckage of collapse and more recent litter of food packaging, empty liquor bottles, the old wood the men gather to feed the fire going all day and well into the night these colder days. The old men gather around the rusty old drums and warm themselves at the fire, wondering how they can hustle a dollar or two for the bottle of wine that will warm their insides as well.

Part of the hustle is coming here. Obscurely we know that the food going out here is currency for a culture of exchange: a can of food for a cigarette or the bag of canned food from here for a joint or a bag or the price of a bottle.

Impossible to figure out who is hungry or needs food for children back in the projects. A woman with a supermarket cart seems respectable enough. Yet as many women as men out there hustling these days. The feminization of poverty, as they call it.

Not much we can do in the end but follow the Gospel: "Give to everyone who asks from you." Something in that passage also about giving shirt as well as coat, going two miles or farther than the request. I am a long way from that generous impulse today, after the second or third early caller. I knew word was out on the street that we were open for business. No sooner would two fellows disappear down the walk with their bag of canned goods than two more would be turning into the walkway heading for the front door here.

I had—or felt the need—to protect myself today, give myself a break after the hectic days before Thanksgiving with the baskets going out the front door as quickly as they were coming in the side entrance. So today I have mostly just let the doorbell ring. Perhaps 20 times so far and the hour is still early afternoon. Some fellows must have read that Gospel passage about wearing out the fellow in bed with the knocking so that he, "caring for neither God nor man," responds just to stop the noise.

Not easy to be fixing something to eat for yourself from a full refrigerator and pantry and ignore the doorbell ringing of fellows who wandered up from the wood fire in the rusty old drum. I probably even miss a woman really needing food for her children or grandchildren.

My retired priest friend at the church down the street would probably not do this. If he is home, he simply answers. Whether he has food or not, the caller is given the courtesy of a conversation and some explanation. Today I am not up to that, at least not ready for the assault on the front door that my response would bring, even more than is happening right now. I hope I am not really wrong with this, trying to maintain some uneasy limits by way of reason, by way of my own resources, by way of. . . .

# 12.

## This Dark Night . . . A Grace

# 1

When I collapse into Sunday afternoon after the morning Masses, my mood is failure or futility or how I could or should have done it all better.

But I should blame large pieces of that feeling on the small piece of reality to which I no doubt attach such immense meaning—Eucharist and First Sunday of Advent and all that. After all, the great homily is given to a few faithful who come for the Mass and probably would come and do go elsewhere too out of their own devotion, apart from what I or some other might say or not say.

So. The collapse I feel or failure is probably the sense that try as I might, the whole morning is just not that important. Nobody here in any real numbers, and the decent, believing people who are here because today is Sunday are hardly here to listen to me.

Today I tried to talk about a new Advent or new Church year or the diocesan renewal beginning today as efforts to bless time which needs blessing because time works against us by wearing us down. The tendency to pull back, stay cool, go easy on yourself.

I suggest that we are all too easy on ourselves in some ways. The need rather to enter more deeply into the suffering of the world, not slacken from age or tiredness or disappointment that I am not more effective. Like the retired pastor down the street, Frank McDermott, who answers every blessed doorbell on the holiday after Thanksgiving when I just let it ring.

I guess my fear is that the personal urge or homiletic call to greater intensity or not to slacken seems much ado about nothing. My greater intensity is not going to change much here. I could say Mass standing on my head and those who come would still come. And those who do not would still not come.

Later in the afternoon, I continue my reading the remarkable John Henry Newman biography by Sean O'Faolain. Newman is described as "quietly bent on cutting the whole world away."

Part of me tries to do that without the elegance of Newman. I try to live in that other world, that other wavelength. I even try not to feel that I have to be out, socialize, go places, do things, rather the effort to spend more time *solus cum Solo*. Alone with the Alone, prayer, study.

Yet the fear that this is indeed much ado about nothing, that inhabiting that world within is to live nowhere and cultivate nothing. So strong this sense sometimes that I come away from that Sunday self-revelation as though I had exposed myself as eccentric, a curiosity, someone locked into an obsolete framework who attaches reality and meaning to things no longer important.

While Sunday Mass is going on, a friend is tutoring basketball giants in the dining room. A fairly-practicing Catholic, the tutor. I wonder whether he skipped Mass back home today, thinking that the tutoring was something more practical, more important even, all things considered.

# 2

Of course my street friend so anxious to talk out his troubles on Saturday never appears on Sunday for his meeting with the young law student from the Alcoholics Anonymous group which meets here all weekend. Of course the law student appears. She comes an hour early for her own meeting to listen to him.

Of course, he does not show—meaning that his not coming is absolutely predictable. Many reasons for this: fear these fellows have of strong women, embarrassment at being so "untogether" before someone who has been undone and has woven her life back together somewhat.

Fear also that someone will insist he start attending the meetings when the idea of exposing himself to a room full of strangers is so threatening. These fellows play it very close to the vest: few friends, a self-reliance always failing them and making them turn to me, the enabler, as AA would call me.

The various problems so verge always on physical need that the mentality becomes the immediate need for a few dollars that will relieve this imminent crisis: food or carfare or bail or the utility bill.

And here looms a meeting with a woman who will tell him that problems and attitudes inside him cause these financial crises. Bad enough the immediate problem without a roadmap of his insides revealing to him problems that he cannot easily or quickly solve. Bad enough the fragile ego of always being in trouble, without the deeper devastation of learning that the whole mess is deeper than the difficulty which will go away with $10 from the priest.

On and on it goes. A cultural thing, this not showing up also. How many times over the years I have heard the mysterious excuse: I thought you would not be there, or I had to get my clothes from the cleaners.

From the house, I put the AA leader on the phone with him and make my way back to the kitchen. I notice from the phone light that they talk a good while. Afterwards she says that she will run out for something to eat now that she has time before the meeting.

She is not so disappointed in his no-show as I am. Something about our not being able to help him unless he wants to take charge of his own life. She says he promises to call me tomorrow about meeting here with her. This tomorrow comes and so far no call from him. I will hear from him again. He will put that call off until he needs money for a transit pass for himself or his son. Again and again and again.

## 3

Leaving the film, "Blackrobe," I stop by the men's room so that Hagan is already on the street lighting a cigarette and voicing his response, "Don't mess with them." Only he uses a more colloquial word than "mess" and adds about the Iroquois torture which costs Father LaForgue a finger, "Head pain is worse than physical pain. The Jesuit was fairly consistent in his head."

Dave sees the film as confirmation that he should not change his manner of being with the fellows in and out of his house. He makes no effort to change their religious or family or social habits. He knows that being poor and black in this society is such a liability that he is content with helping someone find a job or give him a temporary place so that the fellow can begin to put his own life together.

So the fictional Jesuit on the big screen spinoff of the North American martyrs does not speak to Dave because the Jesuit seems so intent upon undoing Indian superstition and providing Christian faith.

Anyhow. My own notice is that we all come at it differently.

Dave is only interested in the religion implicit in life. At best, the fellows around him should get some sense of Gospel from Dave's own life. And not so self-conscious all this. Something will happen if something worthwhile is going on. One never really knows. Just do it.

I know an elderly Sister who was a close friend of Dorothy Day. The Sister is a marvel, still working and teaching at a prison in her 90s. When she speaks, I hear someone like John Henry Newman for whom this world is not real. Not the trouble, not the injustice, not the suffering of the poor so much as Church and sacraments and the eternal life to which we are called. She is not insensitive to suffering, just sees it as an entrance, access to a life for greater opportunity, much as Simone Weil might.

The Sister would be surprised that I see her different from her friend, Dorothy Day, for whom war and the poor and the fierce Bowery are overwhelmingly real. For Dorothy, faith and Church and sacrament were more Divine life and nourishment where she would immerse herself to sustain her "harsh and dreadful love." All that was as real and essential to her as the poor themselves and would help her serve them ever more generously.

And then come the rest of us: fellows like me and the shaky Jesuit of the film whose faith is undone every day by the experience of tumultuous life.

And so many others who seem to survive very well without the faith of Hagan or Day or any faith at all.

# 4

Last evening, an hour walk on the deserted beach. Choosing that hour just before sunset because here at the seashore the afterglow is often a luminous orange filling the whole southern sky. The orange lingers and lingers and deepens to a scarlet or purple before full darkness.

Last night, alas, no sunset. A winter sun which came and went all day disappeared into a full cloud cover. Especially over the bay and horizon the clouds were dense. Over the ocean thin enough that the last light was playing off the dark thunderheads. A warm day, warm enough for the thunderheads rare in winter around here.

I walk for an hour. No sound, no other person, nothing but the gulls and sandpipers strangely still, especially those tiny sandpipers usually so frantic along the water's edge, digging whatever with their long, thin bills.  They manage the small water ribbon where surf begins so that they are never quite into the ocean.  Amazing.  I have no idea why the flocks were all sitting facing southeast except that maybe they enjoy the warm air coming up that way as much as humans might.

At first I was going to say the Joyful Mysteries while walking, the usual Monday meditations and timely for Advent.  But I had just prayed those mysteries of Annunciation and Visitation and Christmas in the car driving down the previous night, so that something in me wanted just silence.  No beads, no words, no images even other than the calm surf breaking into white caps no larger than a pencil line.  Farther out larger breakers but nothing very large at low tide.  I walked in the wet sand where the tide was draining from small depressions which still held the water.

The intent is simply to see water and wet and breakers as the love in which we live, constant and intrusive into us, into me, breaking into my life by crevices everywhere:  good things and apparently bad things, joys and sorrows, troubles and tasks.  The sense which Simone Weil had that the whole cosmos and ocean and history and human contingency and everything is a conspiracy of love meant to gather us in, bring us to our knees as she was brought to her knees at Assisi.  The beauty of the world. . . .

And the ocean an apt image for all that.  It stretches out, goes on beyond our view or understanding.  Something we can see but not comprehend.

# 5

Breakfast plans with a fine young Catholic Worker neighbor become complicated because I stopped to take a telephone call just as I was going out the door last night to give an Advent talk at another parish.

The call was from Marcel, who has been on the streets for 10 years.  He is 35, and last month called me from a hospital because he needed sneakers for the physical therapy required from a gunshot wound that left his leg paralyzed.

Today he has to appear in Bench Warrant Court, give himself up for ignoring a bench warrant or subpoena connected with the shooting.

No. On the way to City Hall, he corrects me from the back of the car where he is spread out with bad leg and crutches alongside. This bench warrant is further business from an attempted rape charge from the woman with whom he stayed last night and with whom he has two children besides the five with his common-law wife. He and the other woman are back on. I fetched him for court at the home of his mother, where he cannot stay because of his drug problems and because 14 people inhabit that two-story rowhouse. Five of those are his children whom I saw going off to school. I was surprised how grown some of them are and recall that I have not seen them in years. Their mother calls me regularly to tell me that she is getting her act together after some years on the street also. I doubt whether she will be together enough or financially able to take these, her children, before they are grown or start having babies themselves.

Years ago, when Marcel and wife were together with two children and living in a public housing high-rise, Marcel killed another fellow in one of those incidents which just happen in summer heat and late night on street corners doing drugs and drink.

His mother put the house where 14 live up for bail, and during the year before trial we found Marcel a job. When trial time, arrived, Marcel accepted a plea bargain for some charge less than murder and again a delay before sentencing.

During those weeks or months, employer and I wrote letters to the judge saying how Marcel had this young family, how a long prison stay would destroy that family, how the incident was "one of those things," and Marcel was not a criminal, how he had been a good and responsible worker all these months.

The judge gave Marcel a commuted sentence. We were overjoyed. One of those small victories which mean so much up here where you always expect to lose.

Marcel took his new, unexpected freedom immediately downhill. Long ago now, but I remember that he hardly worked another week and was soon out on the streets where he has been ever since.

Even now, climbing to the improvised, imitation paneled crawl space which City Hall calls the eighth floor, I would maintain that Marcel is not a criminal. These charges, the obstacles and troubles which inevitably happen on the street, much as traffic tickets and tax cheating are white-collar troubles.

# 6

After the usual medical and surgical floors of the nearby hospital, the Sister chaplain takes me to the old tower building. Up we go to the addiction units to see a young Hispanic fellow with AIDS. He was HIV-positive but says that he senses full-blown AIDS is coming on because he does not "feel right." We talk about his wife and children in Puerto Rico, his panic and anger with himself for becoming ill. Also his hurt over rejection and shame coming from brothers and sisters and parents here.

After drugs and drink, a two-year abstinence before going under again while in Florida and working double shifts at a fast-food restaurant.

When he learned he was HIV-positive, he went berserk, and his wife had to return to Puerto Rico for some distance from him.

Here I meet him in a counselor's office before we go to talk in his own room. Worry and panic rise and fall in him. A roller coaster ride: he knows he should stay and finish the program. Panic wants him to run off to Puerto Rico for the company and comfort he wants and needs from his wife. He is so alone with this.

I am moved by his occasional words about finding peace in a nearby Catholic church open all day because a shrine containing the body of a saint is there. The sick fellow talks about life having a purpose and we all have to shoulder our own cross, just as Jesus shouldered his. And coming to this desperation is, he says, "a purification."

Then he falls into panic again, says how he is going to call his wife and scold her. He comes back.

This visit is more than I expected, almost more than I can handle, coming here as I do now for the sacramental necessities that the Sisters cannot handle. Today is Friday and I have a dozen projects awaiting me back at the church. "Let go," I say to myself while he is talking and I am trying to be fully here, fully attentive. Let go of everything back there. Just be here for the frightened, isolated patient. All this so much more important than any of that. Again that book on prayer by Thomas Keating, *Open Mind, Open Heart*, says that the task of contemplative prayer is contemplative living, and the method is letting go—letting go of my own agenda, letting go of my own impatience and simply being here and patient and attentive for him. Later in the day, letting go might mean foregoing that second look at a beautiful woman on the street when I am downtown on an errand. Part of the letting go that maintains the celibate life.

Here and now, letting go means listening to him and forgetting myself and the hundred Christmas projects which intrude and distract me from this task which is clearly my only responsibility right now.

Take all this a further step: extend the conversation about his being alone with all this, with his family at odds here and his wife in Puerto Rico. Tell him that we are all alone finally; tell him about the window back in church: Christ in the garden drinking the cup of suffering and the three apostles whom he needed for company and comfort sleeping in the bottom panel of the window. The patient brought up the passion of Christ. Speak to his image. You might really help him. What else can a priest do or say?

I venture further: the risk of his returning to and wanting his wife. Important that he not infect her, that she stay alive and stay well for the children, especially since he very well might not survive for them.

The risk that she would fear being intimate and he would need and want it and read her reluctance or refusal as rejection.

# 7

Saturday morning and around the sacristy table for Mass with five or six, I am mindful that today is the feast of St. John of the Cross.

But only when I read to them parts from a wonderful biographical note by Robert Graves do I notice that today is not only the feast but the very fourth centenary of the death of "the Father of Spanish lyric poetry."

Years and years ago, I was in Spain with two priest friends. In Segovia I noticed a lovely old church removed and small enough to seem unimportant.

Yet lovely enough to explore. And just inside, an ornate sarcophagus dissonant with the Romanesque simplicity. But on the monument that wonderful inscription in Latin:

Here lie the remains
of
JOHN OF THE CROSS
the Father of
Spanish Lyric Poetry

So wonderful. Not Doctor of the Church. Not Great Mystic, but "Father of Spanish Lyric Poetry." This spoke to something inside me that wants to knit those threads together: that spiritual yearning that life and poems and love and real work need not be so separate. That devotion is not some small side act which I nourish to help real living, which other people do and which they nourish with other things like money or even family.

And John of the Cross seemed to do that. His poems are as erotic as any, and until you read the saint's own commentaries, you have to take the words of Robert Graves and others that they are *a lo Divino*. The edition of poems by John Frederick Nims with the Graves comments are even from Grove Press, home of people like D.H. Lawrence and Nabokov.

According to Graves, life was all of a piece for John. He could hear street love songs and turn them *a lo Divino*. No need for Freud here with divine love some sublimation of the human need. Nor some Platonic descent either where human love some vestige of the higher and better. John moves in and out. Despite his detachment and dark nights, those love poems tell me John knew human beauty when he saw it; even if for other reasons, he continually chose that larger mysterious Beauty available only in "the beauty of the world," as Simone Weil says—or in poetry. For John, one was not more real than the other. Each pointed to the other: an intimation or conversely an incarnation.

And real life for John substantial and dangerous even around matters that seem trivial now. Much as the adventure of Columbus seems trivial in the age of the Concorde.

John was hunted by the Inquisition and persecuted for advocating such Carmelite reforms as secret ballots, which would help friars to vote reform more freely.

He was then for a more egalitarian Church. Today he would oppose secret negotiations in Rome which send conservative bishops across the chessboard to install a restoration agenda. He would oppose that intrigue and want bishops to surface in a community as natural leaders organically connected with the local Church they lead. He would trust the spirit and not need the reactionary maneuvering.

Yet all around I notice John of the Cross summoned by conservatives as *laudator temporis acti.* The reactionaries just presume that the Doctor of the Dark Night, the celibate, the religious in a traditional habit, the reformer is on their side. In the 60s, this was called co-opting.

## 8

My sense of isolation comes from the fear that most people are in fact able for their small lives better than I am. A friend reading this journal has that response. He has children and can almost say about his children in paraphrase of Descartes: they are; therefore, I am.

Yet the isolation follows me into the celibate world. Most seem able to survive, make sense of their lives, live with the nonsense of the Church without that nonsense seeping inside and undoing them the way it seems to undo me.

Or perhaps they see more meaning than I do, not seeing the woods for the trees.

Or perhaps we are all isolated and alone, and the others do suffer the same doubt, and the real isolation that will be healed only by heaven is our inability to reach one another alone with his doubt or her loss of meaning.

Yet some do seem able to believe very much about their religious community: we are; therefore, I am.

## 9

Life so fragile. Gliding into the Christmas traffic around here more calmly than usual, and suddenly the unwelcome news that a friend is facing surgery for a malignancy.

And not just a friend. A heroine really. Someone 25 years almost alone in a poor neighborhood, doing a community center against all odds. And infinitely weary and aging and the place requiring more and more of her, despite her increasing years and exhaustion.

As if all that were not trial and ordeal enough without this—illness.

Three years ago I was almost undone by my own worry of chest pain and heart trouble. Nothing significant followed. For the few uncertain days, the worry and realization that this whole life is precarious and balanced on health as crucial to continue; all other worries and troubles, however burdensome, became quite unimportant: I may be sick. What will I do if I am sick and cannot continue?

The Sister friend has, in the Gospel image of the vineyards, "borne the heat of the day and the burden" enough with her lonely and impossible work. She does not need this. She should not have this affliction.

I guess there is no payoff. No promise that the trouble will be measured except by some mysterious measure which fits the burden to our backs in the mystery of grace. Sister and I both know and admire a local black woman about 50 whose life is an unbearable mess of troubled children, dependent grandchildren, babies making babies. Nothing in the house works, and no money is available to keep the rain out or make the toilet work. Here all these years, why should our lives be more intact than hers?

Yet sickness is something more. Simone Weil talking about workers not fully initiated until they are injured or "christened" by the tools of the trade. The ultimate assault is on our body.

So the anger, outrage even, that my friend has to be afflicted so. Yet more deeply the sense that she is being taken further along. The "costing not less than everything," which Eliot says is the Gospel Pearl of Great Price.

Or G.M. Hopkins and the terrible suffering of those his last years when terrible tears distilled into the terrible Dublin sonnets.

One needs to enter into Mystery and faith to hear that. My Sister friend lives there, and that will sustain her more deeply than any of our sympathy and assurance.

# *10*

Wild, just wild around here. Christmas hysteria: food and toys from suburbs coming in one door and going out the other.

And the great giveaway does not bring out the best in people. The poor are like everybody else in this, climbing over one another for the bags. Simone Weil says somewhere about the human condition that we would hardly wait a minute for some worthy cause or reason, yet would stand in line for hours for a free egg. Of course she was noticing hard times in World War II Europe when food was becoming very scarce in France.

I am confused by the whole thing and do not try to figure it out. Whatever problems people have around here will hardly be solved by a free turkey.

But it is cold in winter, and some fragile gesture of concern from those distant suburbs at the other end of the expressway is welcome, so I will not dismiss it.

A priest, a younger and newer pastor in these neighborhoods, was here for a meeting I was too busy to attend. Afterwards, he climbed around the large disposal bags arriving and sitting in the hallway downstairs and up to my rooms. "How do you deal with all this craziness?" he said. I told him he would not be so admiring if he had seen me at the door just an hour ago. The inevitable shivering, wan fellow with a tale about being broke and having to get to Pittsburgh and needing $40 for busfare. I blew him out the door, accusing him of using the season to work on our giveaway, and by the time I was finishing, I was already feeling so bad about my performance that I was reaching for $25 toward the cause.

Our social work sister caught him leaving $25 richer and thoroughly humiliated. She noticed his shivering and lack of a winter coat and hat—I had not even noticed. She brought him back in for a used coat and coffee and even another $10 toward the busfare if indeed he were going to Pittsburgh. Coat and hat suggested gloves and when I asked, he said he would be grateful for my extra gloves as well. His shivering got to Sister Catherine. She asked me to take the phone while she drove him to the bus terminal. Perhaps he will go to Pittsburgh whether that was his intention or not.

# *11*

A process begins which will study and evaluate Catholic parish life in this vast poor neighborhood. Some parishes serve the African-American community, and some serve the Latino people. The consensus seems to be that we have too many churches and schools up here for the number of Catholics. Of course even this study complicated by the fact that few African-Americans are Catholic, and most Hispanics are Catholic.

Hard to summon the enthusiasm and interest for the endless meetings, the endless opinions and process. I have been down this road before all to no avail, despite the assurance that this process will bring concrete results. I just have little energy for these night meetings or the all-day Saturday workshops or the delineation of goals and objectives.

Perhaps I hide my own disorganization and ineptness in the chaos all around here. I reach for excuses and reasons for failure in that I am reaching out to people far beyond any Church statistics here: the dysfunctional, those who cannot pay tuition in our school or hold a job or pay their rent or a telephone bill. The food line at the door is endless and the calls from street friends who need my help getting into residential detox are endless also.

By statistics of people around here coming to church or children coming to Sunday School or financial support from the immediate community, I am very vulnerable.

Simone Weil would say not to hide your limitations from yourself by parading out other accomplishments; learn to live with your own painful truth without comfort.

Yet that other beside or beyond the traditional Catholic or parochial measure is important. I am beside a public housing project which is perhaps the most brutal neighborhood in the city. Areas just on the other side are full of vagrants and people who in this cold weather just huddle around a scrap wood fire blazing in an old oil drum on an empty lot and during the day wander over here for a handout. Important that the Church stay here close to all that need. Important for me, despite my exhaustion, to speak that reality. That presence and service here cannot be measured only in traditional, parochial values.

# *12*

Awaking, I congratulate myself on getting through Christmas and Midnight Mass without the trauma of last year when friends were robbed at gunpoint leaving us in the wee hours of Christmas morning.

My self-congratulation came too soon because I woke up yesterday morning to news that the cyclone fence gate on the schooyard was down again for the third time since the summer.

And this time my car was gone. At first I thought it must be a car of the several which the Sisters park there, living as they do in the parish convent. I thought: not mine. Shattered glass here where a car is missing. No need to shatter my car windows since I leave the car open so that intruders or whoever do not leave me with an expensive glass replacement job!

Well, it was my car after all. Finest car I have ever had. Only four years old and a luxury interior with a tape deck allowing me to ride around in ecstasy listening to Gregorian chant. So much for ecstasy.

Two days later, the police call to say the car is located about three miles away, but I will need a tow truck for recovery. In the end no recovery. In darkness I waited in a desolated lot behind a supermarket scaring off vagrants hovering over the car like vultures at a carcass. As I arrived, one street fellow was detaching a brake light and saying that he had nothing to do with the theft but that the light would suit his car. Long time or never since the poor fellow had a car. One of those fellows you see huddled in the cold with a bottle in a brown bag. He wanted the brake light just to peddle it on the street somewhere for the dollar or less that would purchase a bottle of cheap wine.

The verdict at the body shop was beyond repair. "Totaled," as they say in the trade.

Humorous in that the car only came to me three months ago because I stopped by a home in an old junker I was driving, and two days later the friends called to say they were buying a new car and this fine automobile was already signed over to me. And last night I was teasing a Sister friend annoyed that her car needed repairs when she needed the car for holiday visits and errands. I made up quotes about detachment and the unimportance of automobiles, attributing the quotes to Mother Foundress! Paying for my sins or at least for the tease.

Two nights later, the Sisters' cars were damaged out on the street where the Sisters had removed them for fear that the enclosed schoolyard was targeted again in the wee hours. The Sisters heard the shatter of glass and could see out the window vandals going at the cars. The police were called again, begging the police please to come quickly before the fellows started on still another car.

Sometimes we wonder whether the police or patrol delay response to these radio calls until the shouting or mayhem is over. Why risk life or limb on these streets? That might be more surmise than accurate observation.

Anyhow. Insurance will replace the car. Nothing so fancy or luxurious as what I have lost. Again the reminder of cultural difference, even though I am up here these 20 years. I do have insurance. Many neighbors have simply lost all: they cannot afford insurance, have no insurance and often cannot even obtain insurance in these high-risk areas.

A fantasy of mine over the years has been to function without a car. Once I read that the Superior General of Maryknoll refused the car attached to his office. Always I stop for traffic lights and see in the cold people waiting for public transit, and I wonder whether really being here in spirit might mean managing without a car.

As things go, a friend off to a California convention leaves her car with me for 10 days; that never happens to a neighbor here in an entire lifetime. I am a man well provided-for indeed.

One final thought: the reason or unreason of the assault on the schoolyard. Just the sight of six or eight fine automobiles in the parish compound might excite anger and resentment in the neighborhood. The schoolyard is in the literal shadow of a high-rise public housing project where people have nothing or less than nothing. Where people are desperate, the appearance might be that these Church people are living well on the backs of the poor: fancy cars that accompany their social services jobs. Or perhaps all this is still more crazy: random violence more mindless than the above.

Unlike my neighbors when vandals strike, I do have a support team: my sister anxious to run in here with one of her family cars to keep me operational. So distant this from the fellows at the door even today who are so down and out that they must come and hustle me who am more or less a stranger for a can of soup or a dollar.

It even seems that I have a support team of friends and family who keep me afloat here. What a luxury. (I will not even mention one Christmas gift!)

## *13*

A funeral within the embrace of Christmas. Sad for people. Putting away a parent with holiday spirit all around heightens the grief by contrast. And hereafter Christmas always associated with the anniversary of death.

I try to turn the sorrow around somewhat, saying how Christmas is as good a time as any to go because Christmas is deliberately set at the deepest dark and heart of winter to say that the Word coming among us living our life and dying our death is Light on that darkness.

All this with a sense of futility, though. No one in the family comes to church. I did not even know the deceased was a Catholic, even though I would see him at the home when we bring his invalid wife Communion. He was always friendly enough, and the formal obituary read at black funerals says he "converted to the Roman Catholic faith in 1967." And the young daughter who graduated from Catholic high school never comes to Mass nor has she even had her child baptized. If she continues to live with her now-widowed mother, she probably will want to send the child to the parish school someday and the matter of Baptism will surface then.

Even as I am looking out on them in church and are comfortable that I am saying good things worthy of the elegance of the Catholic Mass and the beauty of this lovely old place, I have a sense of futility. None of this will take. They will be grateful for the comfort and beauty of all this off those desolate streets and winter. And perhaps they will even return next Sunday and the Sunday after. But whatever we offer here or Catholic faith can bring to their little lives will not take hold.

That story can be repeated again and again up and down these small streets. People come for a funeral or a Baptism, for Christmas or Easter and then disappear back into their houses and jobs and relationships.

And all that is a great mystery and difficulty for me. I read how making his way to full Catholic faith through his study of the fourth-century Arian dispute was so important and costly to John Henry Newman, and how his whole life was woven around that struggle and search for understanding and a faith that seems so irrelevant and unimportant here.

I know that Newman was an intellectual, a scholar and a priest, and his whole time and place so different from these cities and this chaos. Yet all that only compounds my problem. As I stand there before them, I am so aware that Catholic faith and beauty would enrich their lives. I say this even with my own shaky hold on faith and whatever.

What comes through in me even as I am saying Mass with them is the futility. I guess we are just to do it. Center self more deeply than that affect. Who says that this tradition and elegance and beauty is to nourish this family by bringing them into familiar patterns or practices? Grace works by ways mysterious and even incomprehensible to us. Why else would we be given that Gospel story about the Apostles fishing all night and catching nothing and again lowering the nets when told? We are just to do it as best we can in season and out of season. Even Gandhi, far from the tradition yet close, says we must be detached from results. More than detached. Indifferent. One could make a case that even the Christ was a failure, and his three years with the Apostles did not take since they all abandoned him in hard times.

# 14

*Sic finitur liber sed non* . . . not a hint whether this year in the life of . . . worthwhile or just a lengthy whine. When I left the older journal for reading by a friend, he later told me that I had a head of steam brewing which needed cooling. He was referring to that chronic anger or disappointment with life and self and others. A gray or blue or some dull or angry colored paper on which every entry was written.

So. The hope that this journal written a year later, after an unrecorded year, shows some growth in me, some mellowing so that I better absorb the world and life as they are rather than anything I need them to be because of childhood or hurt or ego or whatever.

And even the Mystery that we call God. I would want so much more sense of that Abiding Presence with me rather than that constant strain to believe anything at all, teetering all the time on that sense that nothing is out there. So threatened even by friends and so many others in these secular times who have no need to believe anything. Work and love and family and this life meaning enough without having to reach into Mystery.

For me these 20 or 30 years in these neighborhoods, the life all around me seems so incomplete, so deprived and painful. Deep within and almost despite my determination to accept "things as they are," the hope or yearning that some coming together exists somewhere.

And let me be honest about myself: my own insides as desolate and deprived as these forlorn streets. At 58 the interior landscape as unfinished and as rough as anything without. Not unlikely that has something to do with my being here: the urban desert all around a familiar if uncomfortable mirror of my insides. A most incomplete man.

My hope is that this Dark Night or whatever is by irony a grace. When one experiences faith as so illusive, so fragile, one might have to cling more surely, and the fragile hold keeps one close and humble. The Mystery is present by absence in that as Pascal has the Mystery or the Christ say: "You would not seek me unless you had already found me." Holding on so desperately at least makes me hold on, makes me aware that we have here no lasting place, gives me a healthy sense of my own need.

So. I close the book on this year with no sense of anything finished or even ongoing. It looks like still another year is given me, and I have little light, except that I should continue to be where I am and do what I am doing, only do it more generously and patiently.